含MP3光盘

大学英语六级710分预测卷

（含200612—200906真题）

编 著⊙龚 嵘 封宗颖

华东理工大学出版社
EAST CHINA UNIVERSITY OF SCIENCE AND TECHNOLOGY PRESS

图书在版编目（CIP）数据

大学英语六级710分预测卷（含200612－200906真题）（含MP3光盘）/龚嵘,封宗颖编著.
—上海：华东理工大学出版社,2008.3（2009.9重印）
ISBN 978－7－5628－2261－5

Ⅰ.大…　Ⅱ.①龚…②封…　Ⅲ.英语—高等学校—水平考试—习题　Ⅳ.H319.6

中国版本图书馆CIP数据核字（2008）第023929号

大学英语六级710分预测卷（含200612－200906真题）（含MP3光盘）

编　　著／龚　嵘　封宗颖
策划编辑／陈　勤
责任编辑／信　艳
责任校对／张　波
封面设计／戚亮轩
出版发行／华东理工大学出版社
　　　　地　　址：上海市梅陇路130号,200237
　　　　电　　话：(021)64250306(营销部)
　　　　　　　　　(021)64252717(编辑室)
　　　　传　　真：(021)64252707
　　　　网　　址：www.hdlgpress.com.cn
印　　刷／上海展强印刷有限公司
开　　本／787mm×1092mm　1/16
印　　张／15.5
字　　数／472千字
版　　次／2008年3月第1版
印　　次／2009年9月第4次
印　　数／16091－17590册
书　　号／ISBN 978－7－5628－2261－5/H·692
定　　价／29.00元(含MP3光盘)

（本书如有印装质量问题,请到出版社营销部调换。）

前　言

改革后的大学英语六级考试于 2006 年 12 月在一定范围内试点举行,2007 年 6 月已在全国范围内展开。与以往的六级考试相比,改革后的六级考试主要有以下四个方面的变化:

* 听力理解比重由原来的 20% 增加到 35%,命题形式包括短对话理解多选题、长对话理解多选题、短文理解多选题以及复合式听写。
* 阅读测试方式多样化,包括快速阅读、篇章词汇选择以及多选题形式的仔细阅读。
* 主观题量加大,在原来 15 分作文的基础上新增 5 分的汉译英。
* 考试程序有了全新调整。

　　Part Ⅰ：考试开始后,考生首先在答题卡(一)上完成作文部分。

　　Part Ⅱ：考试进行到第 31 分钟时,监考人员发试题卷,考生完成快速阅读(15 分钟)。15 分钟之后,即考试进行到第 45 分钟之后,监考人员收答题卡(一)。

　　Part Ⅲ：发答题卡(二),考生完成听力部分(35 分钟)。

　　Part Ⅳ：进行仔细阅读部分(25 分钟)的测试。

　　Part Ⅴ：进行完型填空或改错部分(15 分钟,二者选其一)的测试。

　　Part Ⅵ：进行翻译部分(5 分钟)的测试。

　　测试题型的变化必然导致应考者学习方式的变化,原来大家熟悉的套路与应试技巧可能不一定适用了。这里特别提请考生注意:新六级不再考"词汇选择"题,但这并不意味着不用背单词了。恰恰相反,由于快速阅读 900－1,200 字的大容量语篇,所测试的词汇广度大大增加。考生要更加卖力地背单词,尤其是要扩大识别性词汇量。由于听力比重加大,考生的听力词汇量也必须增长,平时还应扩大泛听量。关于如何应对写作、翻译、快速阅读等方面的新挑战,本书的上篇"应试技巧 & 捷径训练"部分,为大家提供了简洁有效的最优学习计划、参考书目以及各种题型的针对性解题诀窍。

　　本书下篇推出了根据新题型真卷精心设计的 8 套预测卷,助考生实战演练,步步为"赢"!

　　本书在编写过程中得到华东理工大学顾建华、史晓慧、赵蔚、朱晓琴、华静、董慧敏、秦颖、朱文辉、张慧芳等多位老师的帮助与支持,在此表示感谢。

　　囿于作者的学识与水平,书中错漏之处在所难免,恳请广大读者批评指正。

编著者

2009 年 6 月

目　录

(听力部分录音文稿见所附光盘)

2009 年 06 月 20 日大学英语六级考试试题

Part I Writing (30 minutes)

Directions: *For this part, you are allowed 30 minutes to write a short essay entitled **On the Importance of a Name**. You should write at least 150 words following the outline given below.*

1. 有人说名字或名称很重要
2. 也有人觉得名字或名称无关紧要
3. 我认为

On the Importance of a Name

Part II Reading Comprehension (Skimming and Scanning) (15 minutes)

Directions: *In this part, you will have 15 minutes to go over the passage quickly and answer the questions on **Answer Sheet 1**. For questions 1-7, choose the best answer from the four choices marked A), B), C) and D). For questions 8-10, complete the sentences with the information given in the passage.*

Helicopter Moms vs. Free-Range Kids

Would you let your fourth-grader ride public transportation without an adult? Probably not. Still, when Lenore Skenazy, a columnist for the *New York Sun*, wrote about letting her son take the subway alone to get back to her Manhattan home from a department store on the Upper East Side, she didn't expect to get hit with a wave of criticism from readers.

"Long story short: My son got home, overjoyed with independence," Skenazy wrote on April 4 in the *New York Sun*. "Long story longer: Half the people I've told this episode to now want to turn me in for child abuse. As if keeping kids under lock and key and cell phone and careful watch is the right way to rear kids. It's not. It's debilitating (使虚弱)—for us and for them."

Online message boards were soon full of people both applauding and condemning Skenazy's decision to let her son go it alone. She wound up defending herself on CNN (accompanied by her son) and on popular blogs like the *Buffington Post*, where her follow-up piece was ironically headlined "More From America's Worst Mom."

The episode has ignited another one of those debates that divides parents into vocal opposing camps. Are modern parents needlessly overprotective, or is the world a more complicated and dangerous place than it was when previous generations were allowed to wander about unsupervised?

From the "she's an irresponsible mother" camp came: "Shame on you for being so careless about his safety," in comments on the *Buffington Post*. And there was this from a mother of four: "How would you have felt if he didn't come home?" But Skenazy got a lot of support, too, with women and men writing in with stories about how they were allowed to take trips all by themselves at seven or eight. She also got heaps of praise for bucking the "helicopter parent" trend: "Good for this Mom," one commenter wrote on the *Buffington Post*. "This is a much-needed reality check."

Last week, encouraged by all the attention, Skenazy started her own blog — Free Range, Kids — promoting the idea that modern children need some of the same independence that her generation had. In the good old days nine-year-old baby boomers rode their bikes to school,

walked to the store, took buses — and even subways — all by themselves. Her blog, she says, is dedicated to sensible parenting. "At Free Range Kids, we believe in safe kids. We believe in car seats and safety belts. We do NOT believe that every time school-age children go outside, they need a security guard."

So why are some parents so nervous about letting their children out of their sight? Are cities and towns less safe and kids more vulnerable to crimes like child kidnap and sexual abuse than they were in previous generations?

Not exactly, New York City, for instance, is safer than it's ever been; it's ranked 36th in crime among all American cities. Nationwide, stranger kidnaps are extremely rare; there's a one-in-a-million chance a child will be taken by a stranger, according to the Justice Department. And 90 percent of sexual abuse cases are committed by someone the child knows. Mortality rates from all causes, including disease and accidents, for American children are lower now than they were 25 years ago. According to Child Trends, a nonprofit research group, between 1980 and 2003 death rates dropped by 44 percent for children aged 5 to 14 and 32 percent for teens aged 15 to 19.

Then there's the whole question of whether modern parents are more watchful and nervous about safety than previous generations. Yes, some are. Part of the problem is that with wall-to-wall Internet and cable news, every missing child case gets so much airtime that it's not surprising even normal parental anxiety can be amplified. And many middle-class parents have gotten used to managing their children's time and shuttling them to various enriching activities, so the idea of letting them out on their own can seem like a risk. Back in 1972, when many of today's parents were kids, 87 percent of children who lived within a mile of school walked or biked every day. But today, the Centers for Disease Control report that only 13 percent of children bike, walk or otherwise t themselves to school.

The extra supervision is both a city and a suburb phenomenon. Parents are worried about crime, and they are worried about kids getting caught in traffic in a city that's not used to pedestrians. On the other hand, there are still plenty of kids whose parents give them a lot of independence, by choice or by necessity. The After School Alliance finds that more than 14 million kids aged 5 to 17 are responsible for taking care of themselves after school. Only 6.5 million kids participate in organized programs. "Many children who have working parents have to take the subway or bus to get to school. Many do this by themselves because they have no other way to get to the schools," says Dr. Richard Gallagher, director of the Parenting Institute at the New York University Child Study Center.

For those parents who wonder how and when they should start allowing their kids more freedom, there's no clear-cut answer. Child experts discourage a one-size-fits-all approach to parenting. What's right for Skenazy's nine-year-old could be inappropriate for another one. It all depends on developmental issues, maturity, and the psychological and emotional makeup of that child. Several factors must be taken into account, says Gallagher. "The ability to follow parent guidelines, the child's level of comfort in handling such situations, and a child's general judgment should be weighed."

Gallagher agrees with Skenazy that many nine-year-olds are ready for independence like taking public transportation alone. "At certain times of the day, on certain routes, the subways are generally safe for these children, especially if they have grown up in the city and have been taught how to be safe, how to obtain help if they are concerned for their safety, and how to avoid unsafe situations by being watchful and on their toes."

But even with more traffic and fewer sidewalks, modern parents do have one advantage their parents didn't: the cell phone. Being able to check in with a child anytime goes a long way toward relieving parental anxiety and may help parents loosen their control a little sooner. Skenazy got a lot of criticism because she didn't give her kid her cell phone because she thought he'd lose it and wanted him to learn to go it alone without depending on mom — a major principle of free-range parenting. But most parents are more than happy to use cell phones to keep track of their kids.

And for those who like the idea of free-range kids but still struggle with their inner helicopter parent, there may be a middle way. A new generation of GPS cell phones with tracking software make it easier than ever to follow a child's every movement via the Internet — without seeming to interfere or hover. Of course, when they go to college, they might start objecting to being monitored as they're on parole（假释）.

1. When Lenore Skenazy's son was allowed to take the subway alone, he _____.
   A) was afraid that he might get lost
   B) enjoyed having the independence
   C) was only too pleased to take the risk
   D) thought he was an exceptional child
2. Lenore Skenazy believes that keeping kids under careful watch _____.
   A) hinders their healthy growth
   B) adds too much to parents' expenses
   C) shows traditional parental caution
   D) bucks the latest parenting trend
3. Skenazy's decision to let her son take the subway alone has met with _____.
   A) opposition from her own family
   B) official charges of child abuse
   C) approval from psychologist
   D) somewhat mixed responses
4. Skenazy started her own blog to _____.
   A) promote sensible parenting
   B) share parenting experience
   C) fight against child abuse
   D) protect children's rights
5. According to the author, New York City _____.
   A) ranks high in road accidents
   B) is much safe than before
   C) ranks low in child mortality rates
   D) is less dangerous than small cities
6. Parents today are more nervous about their kids' safety than previous generations because _____.
   A) there are now fewer children in the family
   B) the number of traffic accidents has been increasing
   C) their fear is amplified by media exposure of crime
   D) crime rates have been on the rise over the years
7. According to child experts, how and when kids may be allowed more freedom depends on _____.
   A) the traditions and customs of the community
   B) the safety conditions of their neighborhood
   C) their parents' psychological makeup
   D) their maturity and personal qualities
8. According to Gallagher and Skenazy, children who are watchful will be better able to stay away from _____.
9. Being able to find out where a child is anytime helps lessen parents' _____.

10. Nowadays with the help of GPS cell phones, parents can, from a distance, track their children's _____.

Part III Listening Comprehension (35 minutes)

Section A

Directions: *In this section, you will hear 8 short conversations and 2 long conversations. At the end of each conversation, one or more questions will be asked about what was said. Both the conversation and the questions will be spoken only once. After each question there will be a pause. During the pause, you must read the four choices marked A) B) C) and D), and decide which is the best answer. Then mark the corresponding letter on **Answer Sheet 2** with a single line through the centre.*

11. A) Fred forgot to call him last night about the camping trip.
    B) He is not going to lend his sleeping bag to Fred.
    C) He has not seen Fred at the gym for some time.
    D) Fred may have borrowed a sleeping bag from someone else.

12. A) Summer has become hotter in recent years.
    B) It will cool down a bit over the weekend.
    C) Swimming in a pool has a relaxing effect.
    D) He hopes the weather forecast is accurate.

13. A) Taking a picture of Prof. Brown.
    B) Commenting on an oil-painting.
    C) Hosting a TV program.
    D) Staging a performance.

14. A) She can help the man take care of the plants.
    B) Most plants grow better in direct sunlight.
    C) The plants need to be watered frequently.
    D) The plants should be placed in a shady spot.

15. A) Change to a more exciting channel.
    •B) See the movie some other time.
    C) Go to bed early.
    D) Stay up till eleven.

16. A) Both of them are laymen of modern art.
    B) She has learned to appreciate modem sculptures.
    C) Italian artists' works are difficult to understand.
    D) Modern artists are generally considered weird.

17. A) They seem satisfied with what they have done.
    B) They have called all club members to contribute.
    C) They think the day can be called a memorable one.
    D) They find it hard to raise money for the hospital.

18. A) The man shouldn't hesitate to take the course.
    B) The man should talk with the professor first.
    C) The course isn't open to undergraduates.
    D) The course will require a lot of reading.

Questions 19 to 21 are based on the conversation you have just heard.

19. A) Current trends in economic development.
    B) Domestic issues of general social concern.
    C) Stories about Britain's relations with other nations.

D) Conflicts and compromises among political parties.
20. A) Based on the polls of public opinions.
   B) By interviewing people who file complaints.
   C) By analyzing the domestic and international situation.
   D) Based on public expectations and editors' judgment.
21. A) Underlying rules of editing.
   B) Practical experience.
   C) Audience's feedback.
   D) Professional qualifications.

Questions 22 to 25 are based on the conversation you have just heard.

22. A) The average life span was less than 50 years.
   B) It was very common for them to have 12 children.
   C) They retired from work much earlier than today.
   D) They were quite optimistic about their future.
23. A) Get ready for ecological changes.
   B) Adapt to the new environment.
   C) Learn to use new technology.
   D) Explore ways to stay young.
24. A) When all women go out to work.
   B) When family planning is enforced.
   C) When a world government is set up.
   D) When all people become wealthier.
25. A) Eliminate poverty and injustice.
   B) Migrate to other planets.
   C) Control the environment.
   D) Find inexhaustible resources.

Section B
Directions: *In this section, you will hear 3 short passages. At the end of each passage, you will hear some questions. Both the passage and the questions will be spoken only once. After you hear a question, you must choose the best answer from the four choices marked A), B), C) and D). Then mark the corresponding letter on **Answer Sheet 2** with a single line through the centre.*

Passage One
Questions 26 to 28 are based on the passage you have just heard.

26. A) To help young people improve their driving skills.
   B) To alert teenagers to the dangers of reckless driving.
   C) To teach young people road manners through videotapes.
   D) To show teens the penalties imposed on careless drivers.
27. A) Road accidents.   B) Street violence.
   C) Drug abuse.   D) Lung cancer.
28. A) It has changed teens' way of life.
   B) It has made teens feel like adults.
   C) It has accomplished its objective.
   D) It has been supported by parents.

Passage Two

Questions 29 to 31 are based on the passage you have just heard.

29. A) Customers may get addicted to the smells.
    B) Customers may be misled by the smells.
    C) It hides the defects of certain goods.
    D) It gives rise to unfair competition.

30. A) Flexible.   B) Critical.
    C) Supportive.   D) Cautious.

31. A) The flower scent stimulated people's desire to buy.
    B) Stronger smells had greater effects on consumers.
    C) Most shoppers hated the small shoe store.
    D) 84% of the customers were unaware of the smells.

Passage Three

Questions 32 to 35 are based on the passage you have just heard.

32. A) A goods train hit a bus carrying many passengers.
    B) Two passenger trains crashed into each other.
    C) A passenger train collided with a goods train.
    D) An express train was derailed when hit by a bomb.

33. A) The rescue operations have not been very effective.
    B) More than 300 injured passengers were hospitalized.
    C) The cause of the tragic accident remains unknown.
    D) The exact casualty figures are not yet available.

34. A) There was a bomb scare.
    B) There was a terrorist attack.
    C) A fire alarm was set off by mistake.
    D) 50 pounds of explosives were found.

35. A) Follow policemen's directions.
    B) Keep an eye on the weather.
    C) Avoid snow-covered roads.
    D) Drive with special care.

Section C

Directions: *In this section, you will hear a passage three times. When the passage is read for the first time, you should listen carefully for its general idea. When the passage is read for the second time, you are required to fill in the blanks numbered from 36 to 43 with the exact words you have just heard. For blanks numbered from 44 to 46 you are required to fill in the missing information. For these blanks, you can either use the exact words you have just heard or write down the main points in your own words. Finally, when the passage is read for the third time, you should check what you have written.*

English is the leading international language. In different countries around the globe, English is acquired as the mother (36) _____, in others it's used as a second language. Some nations use English as their (37) _____ language, performing the function of (38) _____; in others it's used as an international language for business, (39) _____ and industry.

What factors and forces have led to the (40) _____ of English? Why is English now considered to be so prestigious that, across the globe, individuals and societies feel (41) _____ if they do not have (42) _____ in this language? How has English changed through 1,500 years? These are some of the questions that you (43) _____ when you study English.

You also examine the immense variability of English and (44) _____ _____. You develop in-depth knowledge of the intricate structure of the language. Why do some non-native speakers of English claim that it's a difficult language to learn, while (45) _____ ? At the University of Sussex, you are introduced to the nature and grammar of English in all aspects. This involves the study of sound structures, the formation of words, the sequencing words and the construction of meaning, as well as examination of the theories explaining these aspects of English usage. (46) _____ _____, which are raised by studying how speakers and writers employ English for a wide variety of purposes.

Part IV   Reading Comprehension (Reading in Depth) (25 minutes)

Section A

Directions: *In this section, there is a short passage with 5 questions or incomplete statements. Read the passage carefully. Then answer the questions or complete statements in the fewest possible words. Please write your answers on* **Answer Sheet 2.**

Questions 47 to 51 are based on the following passage.

There is nothing new about TV and fashion magazines giving girls unhealthy ideas about how thin they need to be in order to be considered beautiful. What is surprising is the method psychologists at the University of Texas have come up with to keep girls from developing eating disorders. Their main weapon against superskinny (role) models: a brand of civil disobedience dubbed "body activism."

Since 2001, more than 1,000 high school and college students in the U.S. have participated in the Body Project, which works by getting girls to understand how they have been buying into the notion that you have to be thin to be happy or successful. After critiquing (评论) the so-called thin ideal by writing essays and role-playing with their peers, participants are directed to come up with and execute small, nonviolent acts. They include slipping notes saying "Love your body the way it is" into dieting books at stores like Borders and writing letters to Mattel, makers of the impossibly proportioned Barbie doll.

According to a study in the latest issue of the *Journal of Consulting and Clinical Psychology*, the risk of developing eating disorders was reduced 61% among Body Project participants. And they continued to exhibit positive body-image attitudes as long as three years after completing the program, which consists, of four one-hour sessions. Such lasting effects may be due to girls' realizing not only how they were being influenced but also who was benefiting from the societal pressure to be thin. "These people who promote the perfect body really don't care about you at all," says Kelsey Hertel, a high school junior and Body Project veteran in Eugene, Oregon. "They purposefully make you feel like less of a person so you'll buy their stuff and they'll make money."

47. Where do girls get the notion that they need to be thin in order to be considered beautiful?
_____ _____.

48. By promoting "body activism," University of Texas psychologists aim to prevent girls from _____.

49. According to the author, Mattel's Barbie dolls are _____.

50. The positive effects of the Body Project may last up to _____.

51. One Body Project participant says that the real motive of those who promote the perfect body is to _____.

Section B

Directions: *There are 2 passages in this section. Each passage is followed by some questions or unfinished statements. For each of them there are four choices marked A), B), C), and D). You should decide on the best choice and mark the corresponding letter on **Answer Sheet 2** with a single line through the centre.*

Passage One

Questions 52 to 56 are based on the following passage.

For hundreds of millions of years, turtles (海龟) have struggled out of the sea to lay their eggs on sandy beaches, long before there were nature documentaries to celebrate them, or GPS satellites and marine biologists to track them, or volunteers to hand-carry the hatchlings (幼龟) down to the water's edge lest they become disoriented by headlights and crawl towards a motel parking lot instead. A formidable wall of bureaucracy has been erected to protect their prime nesting sites on the Atlantic coastlines. With all that attention paid to them, you'd think these creatures would at least have the gratitude not to go extinct.

But Nature is indifferent to human notions of fairness, and a report by the Fish and Wildlife Service showed a worrisome drop in the populations of several species of North Atlantic sea turtles, notably loggerheads, which can grow to as much as 400 pounds. The South Florida nesting population, the largest, has declined by 50% in the last decade, according to Elizabeth Griffin, a marine biologist with the environmental group Oceana. The figures prompted Oceana to petition the government to upgrade the level of protection for the North Atlantic loggerheads from "threatened" to "endangered" — meaning they are in danger of disappearing without additional help.

Which raises the obvious question: what else do these turtles want from us, anyway? It turns out, according to Griffin, that while we have done a good job of protecting the turtles for the weeks they spend on land (as egg-laying females, as eggs and as hatchlings), we have neglected the years spend in the ocean. "The threat is from commercial fishing," says Griffin. Trawlers (which drag large nets through the water and along the ocean floor) and longline fishers (which can deploy thousands of hooks on lines that can stretch for miles) take a heavy toll on turtles.

Of course, like every other environmental issue today, this is playing out against the background of global warming and human interference with natural ecosystems. The narrow strips of beach on which the turtles lay their eggs are being squeezed on one side by development and on the other by the threat of rising sea levels as the oceans warm. Ultimately we must get a handle on those issues as well, or a creature that outlived the dinosaurs (恐龙) will meet its end at the hands of humans, leaving our descendants to wonder how creature so ugly could have won so much affection.

52. We can learn from the first paragraph that _____.
   A) human activities have changed the way turtles survive
   B) efforts have been made to protect turtles from dying out
   C) government bureaucracy has contributed to turtles' extinction
   D) marine biologists are looking for the secret of turtles' reproduction

53. What does the author mean by "Nature is indifferent to human notions of fairness" (Line 1, Para. 2)?
   A) Nature is quite fair regarding the survival of turtles.
   B) Turtles are by nature indifferent to human activities.
   C) The course of nature will not be changed by human interference.

D) The turtle population has decreased in spite of human protection.

54. What constitutes a major threat to the survival of turtles according to Elizabeth Griffin?
   A) Their inadequate food supply.
   B) Unregulated commercial fishing.
   C) Their lower reproductively ability.
   D) Contamination of sea water.

55. How does global warming affect the survival of turtles?
   A) It threatens the sandy beaches on which they lay eggs.
   B) The changing climate makes it difficult for their eggs to hatch.
   C) The rising sea levels make it harder for their hatchlings to grow.
   D) It takes them longer to adapt to the high beach temperature.

56. The last sentence of the passage is meant to _____.
   A) persuade human beings to show more affection for turtles
   B) stress that even the most ugly species should be protected
   C) call for effective measures to ensure sea turtles' survival
   D) warn our descendants about the extinction of species

Passage Two
Questions 57 to 61 are based on the following passage.

There are few more sobering online activities than entering data into college-tuition calculators and gasping as the Web spits back a six-figure sum. But economists say families about to go into debt to fund four years of partying, as well as studying, can console themselves with the knowledge that college is an investment that, unlike many bank stocks, should yield huge dividends.

A 2008 study by two Harvard economists notes that the "labor-market premium to skill" — or the amount college graduates earned that's greater than what high-school graduate earned— decreased for much of the 20th century, but has come back with a vengeance (报复性地) since the 1980s. In 2005, The typical full-time year-round U. S. worker with a four-year college degree earned $ 50,900, 62% more than the $ 31,500 earned by a worker with only a high-school diploma.

There's no question that going to college is a smart economic choice. But a look at the strange variations in tuition reveals that the choice about which college to attend doesn't come down merely to dollars and cents. Does going to Columbia University (tuition, room and board $ 49,260 in 2007-08) yield a 40% greater return than attending the University of Colorado at Boulder as an out-of-state student ($ 35,542)? Probably not. Does being an out-of-state student at the University of Colorado at Boulder yield twice the amount of income as being an in-state student ($ 17,380) there? Not likely.

No, in this consumerist age, most buyers aren't evaluating college as an investment, but rather as a consumer product — like a car or clothes or a house. And with such purchases, price is only one of many crucial factors to consider.

As with automobiles, consumers in today's college marketplace have vast choices, and people search for the one that gives them the most comfort and satisfaction in line with their budgets. This accounts for the willingness of people to pay more for different types of experiences (such as attending a private liberal-arts college or going to an out-of-state public school that has a great marine-biology program). And just as two auto purchasers might spend an equal amount of money on very different cars, college students (or, more accurately, their parents) often show a willingness to pay essentially the same price for vastly different products. So which is it? Is college an investment product like a stock or a consumer product like a car? In keeping with the automotive world's hottest consumer trend, maybe it's best to characterize it

as a hybrid（混合动力汽车）; an expensive consumer product that, over time, will pay rich dividends.

57. What's the opinion of economists about going to college?
   A) Huge amounts of money is being wasted on campus socializing.
   B) It doesn't pay to run into debt to receive a college education.
   C) College education is rewarding in spite of the startling costs.
   D) Going to college doesn't necessarily bring the expected returns.

58. The two Harvard economists note in their study that, for much of the 20th century _____.
   A) enrollment kept decreasing in virtually all American colleges and universities
   B) the labor market preferred high-school to college graduates
   C) competition for university admissions was far more fierce than today
   D) the gap between the earnings of college and high-school graduates narrowed

59. Students who attend an in-state college or university can _____.
   A) save more on tuition
   B) receive a better education
   C) take more liberal-arts courses
   D) avoid traveling long distances

60. In this consumerist age, most parents _____.
   A) regard college education as a wise investment
   B) place a premium on the prestige of the college
   C) think it crucial to send their children to college
   D) consider college education a consumer product

61. What is the chief consideration when students choose a college today?
   A) Their employment prospects after graduation.
   B) A satisfying experience within their budgets.
   C) Its facilities and learning environment.
   D) Its ranking among similar institutions.

Part V Cloze (15 minutes)

Directions: *There are 20 blanks in the following passage. For each blank there are four choices marked A), B), C) and D) on the right side of the paper. You should choose the ONE that best fits into the passage. Then mark the corresponding letter on **Answer Sheet 2** with a single line through the centre.*

Some historians say that the most important contribution of Dwight Eisenhower's presidency （总统任期） in the 1950s was the U. S. interstate highway system. It was a __62__ project, easily surpassing the scale of such previous human __63__ as the Panama Canal. Eisenhower's

interstate highways __64__ the nation together in

new ways and __65__ major economic growth by

making commerce less __66__. Today, an information superhighway has been built — an

62. A) concise   B) radical
    C) massive   D) trivial
63. A) behaviors   B) endeavors
    C) inventions   D) elements
64. A) packed   B) stuck
    C) suppressed   D) bound
65. A) facilitated B) modified
    C) mobilized   D) terminated
66. A) competitive B) comparative
    C) exclusive   D) expensive

electronic network that ___67___ libraries,

corporations, government agencies and ___68___. This electronic superhighway is called the Internet, ___69___ it is the backbone (主干) of the World Wide Web.

The Internet had its ___70___ in a 1969 U.S. Defense Department computer network called ARPAnet, which ___71___ Advanced Research Projects Agency Network. The Pentagon built the network for military contractors and universities doing military research to ___72___ information. In 1983 the National Science Foundation (NSF), ___73___ mission is to promote science, took over.

This new NSF network ___74___ more and

more institutional users, many of ___75___ had their own internal networks. For example, most universities that ___76___ the NSF network had intracampus computer networks. The NSF network ___77___ became a connector for

thousands of other networks. ___78___ a backbone system that interconnects networks, internet was a name that fit. So we can see that the Internet is the wired infrastructure (基础设施) on which web ___79___ move. It began as a military communication system, which expanded into a government-funded ___80___ research network.

Today, the Internet is a user-financed system tying institutions of many sorts together ___81___ an "information superhighway."

67. A) merges   B) connects
    C) relays   D) unifies
68. A) figures   B) personalities
    C) individuals   D) humans
69. A) and   C) or
    C) or   D) while
70. A) samples   B) sources
    C) origins   D) precedents
71. A) stood by   B) stood for
    C) stood against   D) stood over
72. A) exchange   B) bypass
    C) switch   D) interact
73. A) their   B) that
    C) when   D) whose
74. A) expanded   B) contracted
    C) attracted   D) extended
75. A) what   B) which
    C) these   D) them
76. A) joined   B) attached
    C) participated   D) involved
77. A) moreover   B) however
    C) likewise   D) then
78. A) With   C) In
    C) In   D) As
79. A) contexts   B) signs
    C) messages   D) leaflets
80. A) citizen   B) civilian
    C) amateur   D) resident
81. A) into   B) amid
    C) over   D) toward

Part VI   Translation (5 minutes)

Directions: *Complete the sentences by translating into English the Chinese given in brackets. Please write your translation on.*

82. With the oil prices ever rising, she tried to talk _____. (说服他不买车).

83. _____ (保持幽默有助于) reduce stress and promote creative thinking in today's competitive society.

84. When confronted with the evidence, _____ (他不得不坦白自己的罪行).

85. When people say, "I can feel my ears burning," it means they think _____ (一定有人在说他们坏话).

86. She has decided to go on a diet, but finds _____ (很难抵制冰淇淋的诱惑).

2009 年 6 月 20 日大学英语六级试题答案与解析

Sample Writing

On the Importance of a Name

A name identifies a person, and the first thing you learn about a person is his or her name. What do our names mean to us? Different people have different opinions on the importance of names.

Many people think names play an important role in work and life. For them, names carry subtle, yet substantial psychological weight, not only affecting their personality but also their fortune. Some parents spare no effort to pick out a good name for their child, which they think will bring both wealth and health.

However, many others just laugh at those superstitious ideas about a name. They think a name is just a name, a label that helps to distinguish one from another. And that's all. True success depends on one's hard-work and a right attitude toward setbacks.

Personally, I don't think that we should not go so far as to associate our name with our personal fortune. It is simply ridiculous to attribute one's failures to the so-called unlucky name. But it is not to say a name is not important. I admit a pleasant-sounding or meaningful name does leave a good first impression, since it is often the first information we get to know about a person. Besides, our name is the first gift from our parents, a gift that carries parents' affection and hopes for us, and will accompany us to the end of our life. In that sense, a name means a lot to me.

Part II　Reading Comprehension（Skimming and Scanning）

1. ［B］第 1 段提到，莉诺·斯基奈齐让自己儿子独自乘地铁回家，第 2 段第 1 句提到儿子坐地铁的感受"My son got home, overjoyed with independence(为独立行动而格外高兴)"，故选 B。

2. ［A］参见第 2 段最后三句"As if keeping kids under lock and key and cell phone and careful watch is the right way to rear kids. It's not. It's debilitating—for us and for them.（用钥匙、锁、手机限制儿童行动范围，密切关注其一举一动，似乎是养育孩子的正确方式。其实不然，这样做只能使我们、使孩子变得软弱无能。）"故选 A，莉诺认为对孩子的过度关注有碍其健康成长。

3. ［D］参见第 3 段第 1 句"Online message boards were soon full of people both applauding and condemning Skenazy's decision to let her son go it alone.（在线信息栏很快挤满了人们的留言，对于斯基奈齐让儿子独立回家的决定，有人称赞有人指责。）"故选 D，斯基奈齐让儿子独立乘地铁的决定遭遇公众不同的回应。

4. ［A］参见第 6 段第 1 句"... Skenazy started her own blog—Free Range Kids—promoting the idea that modern children need some of the same independence that her generation had. 斯基奈齐开了自己的博客——散养儿童，宣传当代儿童也需要她那一代人拥有的同样的独立。）"与第 3 句"Her blog ... is dedicated to sensible parenting(明智的父母行为)"。故选 A，斯基奈齐开博客的目的是宣传理性的父母行为。

5. ［B］参见第 8 段第 1 句"New York City, for instance, is safer than it's ever been"，故选 B，纽约比以前安全多了。

6. ［C］参见第 9 段第 3 句"Part of the problem is that with wall-to-wall Internet and cable news, every missing child case gets so much airtime that it's not surprising even normal parental anxiety can be amplified.（部分问题在于随着互联网与有线新闻的普及，每一宗儿童失踪案都得到大量报道，难怪就连父母正常的焦虑也会被放大。）"故选 C，父母的恐惧由于犯罪的媒体曝光而增强。

7. ［D］参见第 11 段第 2 — 4 句"Child experts discourage a one-size-fits-all approach to

parenting ... It all <u>depends on</u> developmental issues, <u>maturity</u>, and the <u>psychological and emotional makeup</u> of that child.（儿童专家并不鼓励大家都以同样一种方式去做父母……一切都取决于具体的成长问题，取决于孩子的成熟状态及其生理与情感素质。）"故选 D，儿童专家认为，何时、如何给予儿童更多的行动自由取决于他们的成熟程度与个体素质。

8. **unsafe situations**　参见第 12 段最后一句"... the subways are generally safe for these children, especially if they have grown up in the city and have been taught how to be safe, how to obtain help if they are concerned for their safety, and how to avoid <u>unsafe situations</u> by being watchful and on their toes（学会如何通过小心谨慎避免危险情形）"。

9. **anxiety and control**　参见倒数第 2 段第 2 句"Being able to check in with a child anytime goes a long way toward <u>relieving parental anxiety</u> and may help parents <u>loosen their control</u> a little sooner.（能够随时核查孩子的状况，可大大缓解父母的焦虑，帮助他们早点放松对孩子的控制。）"

10. **every moment**　参见最后一段第 2 句"A new generation of <u>GPS cell phones</u> with tracking software make it easier than ever to follow a child's <u>every movement</u> via the Internet ...（新一代的 GPS 手机带有跟踪软件，更容易通过互联网跟踪孩子的一举一动……）"

Part III Listening Comprehension

11. D　12. B　13. C　14. D　15. C　16. B　17. A　18. A　19. B　20. D

21. D　22. A　23. C　24. D　25. C　26. B　27. A　28. C　29. B　30. B

31. A　32. C　33. D　34. A　35. D

36. tongue　37. official　　38. administration　39. commerce

40. spread　41. disadvantaged　42. confidence　　43. Investigate

44. come to understand how it is used as a symbol of both individual identity and social connection

45. infants born into English-speaking communities acquire their language before they learn to use folks and knives

46. You are encourage to develop your own individual responses to various practical and theoretical issues

Part IV　Reading Comprehension（Reading in Depth）

Section A

47. **TV and fashion magazines**　参见第 1 段第 1 句"There is nothing new about <u>TV and fashion magazines</u> giving girls unhealthy ideas about how thin they need to be in order to be considered beautiful.（报纸与时尚杂志总是给女孩子灌输不健康的想法，告诉她们需要多瘦才能被认为是美丽的。）"故女孩子是通过报纸时尚杂志获得以瘦为美的审美观。

48. **developing eating disorders**　参见第 1 段第 2、3 句"What is surprising is the method <u>psychologists at the University of Texas</u> have come up with to <u>keep girls from</u> developing <u>eating disorders</u>. Their main weapon against superskinny（role）models：a brand of civil disobedience dubbed "<u>body activism.</u>（令人惊讶的是，得克萨斯大学心理学家为防止女孩患上饮食综合征而采取的办法。他们反对超瘦模特的主要武器是被冠以"身体活动"的一种文明抵制运动。）"

49. **impossibly proportioned**　参见第 2 段最后一句"writing letters to Mattel, makers of the <u>impossibly proportioned</u> Barbie doll（写信给马特尔公司——身材比例完全失真的芭比娃娃制造商）"，故作者认为马特尔的芭比娃娃三围比例是完全不可能的。

50. **three years**　参见第 3 段第 2 句"And they（指 Body Project participants）continued to exhibit positive body-image attitudes as long as three years after completing the program.（身体工程的参与者在项目完成后，仍保持积极的体形态度长达三年之久。）"故 Body Project 的积极效果可持续三年之久。

51. **make money**　参见全文最后一句"They purposefully make you fccl like less of a person so

you'll buy their stuff and they'll <u>make money</u>.（他们故意使你自觉没有"人样"，于是就去买他们的产品去减肥，这样他们就可赚钱了。）"

Section B

52. ［B］推断题。第1段提到，当今有自然纪录片拍摄海龟（nature documentaries to celebrate them），GPS卫星与海洋专家跟踪海龟、志愿者亲手将幼龟转移到海边（hand-carry the hatchlings down to the water's edge）以免他们因车灯而迷失回到大海的方向等多种海龟保护行动。本段最后一句再次提到"With all that attention paid to them, you'd think these creatures would at least have the gratitude <u>not to go extinct</u>.（海龟得到如此多的关注，你一定认为它们至少表示感恩，不会从地球消失。）"由此可推知，人们曾作出大量努力防止海龟灭绝。

53. ［D］推断题。参见第2段第1句"But Nature is <u>indifferent to human notions of fairness</u>, and a report by the Fish and Wildlife Service showed <u>a worrisome drop in the populations of</u> several species of North Atlantic turtles ...（但是大自然似乎对人类公正的概念不理不睬，鱼类野生动物服务机构的一份报告显示，好几个海龟品种的数量都大幅降低，令人担忧。）"故选D，尽管有着人类的保护，海龟数量还是在减少。

54. ［B］细节理解题。第3段提到，"... we have neglected the years spend in the ocean. 'The threat is from <u>commercial fishing</u>,' says Griffin. Trawlers and longline fishers take a heavy toll on turtles."人们忽略了海龟在海洋中的生存环境，威胁来自商业捕鱼。大网与长线捕捞的渔船对海龟是致命的。故选B，吉芬认为，缺乏管理的商业捕鱼对海龟生存构成威胁。

55. ［A］细节理解题。参见最后一段第2句"The narrow strips of beach on which the turtles lay their eggs are being squeezed on one side by development and on the other by the threat of <u>rising sea levels as the oceans warm</u>.（海龟下蛋的狭长沙滩越来越小，一方面遭到经济发展的侵占，一方面又受到海水变暖海平面上升的威胁。）"故选A，全球变暖威胁着海龟产蛋的沙滩。

56. ［C］推断题。最后一句的字面意思是，最终我们还要对这些问题（human interference, global warming）有所掌控（get a handle on these issues），否则这些活过恐龙的海龟会葬送在我们这一代人手上，我们的后人以后永远也弄明白怎么这么丑的生灵曾经得到如此多的关注。此句言下之意是，呼吁采取有效措施确保海龟生存。

57. ［C］推断题。第1段提到，有一项网络活动可以让你立刻严肃清醒起来（sobering online activities）——上网将数据输入大学学费计算器，看见弹出六位数的计算结果，不禁倒吸一口凉气（gasping）。但经济学家说，那些即将为投资四年大学娱乐与学习生活（funding four years of partying, as well as studying）而陷入债务的家庭，也有自我安慰的看法，把大学看成不同于银行股票的高回报投资（yield huge dividends）。由此可推论，经学家认为，大学教育尽管昂贵惊人（startling costs），但回报不错（rewarding），故选C。

58. D。细节推断题。第2段第1句提到，哈佛大学两位经济学家的2008年研究指出，大学毕业生收入高于中学毕业生收入的那部分差额在20世纪呈减少趋势（the amount college graduates earned that's greater than what high-school graduate earned—decreased for much of the 20th century），由此可推断，在20世纪大学毕业生与中学毕业生收入差距减小了，故选D。干扰项B，20世纪的劳务市场更偏爱高中毕业生胜过大学毕业生，显然是过度推断，因为高中生收入其实并没超过大学生，只是差距小了。

59. ［A］推断题。第3段讨论考虑学费因素的明智选择，对比了2007至2008学年就读三种大学的不同开支：一是哥伦比亚大学等名校的费用49,260美元；二是去科罗拉多大学跨州就读（as an out-of-state student），费用是35,542美元；三是就读本州的大学（being an in-state student），只需17,380美元，可见就读州立大学最省钱。（背景知识：父母在本州纳税故学费较便宜。）故选A。

60. ［D］细节理解题。参见第4段第1句"in this consumerist age（消费者时代），most buyers aren't evaluating college as an investment, but rather as <u>a consumer product</u>"，故选D，在消费者时代，多数父母把大学教育看成一种消费产品。

61. [A] 细节理解题。参见最后一段第1句"consumers in today's college marketplace have vast choices, and people search for the one that gives them the most comfort and satisfaction in line with their budgets.（当今大学市场上的消费者可选范围很大，人们总是根据自己预算寻找提供最大舒适满意度的选择。）"故选A，如今学生选择大学的首要考虑因素是，预算许可范围内的满意经历。

Part V　Cloze

62. [C] It was a massive project, easily surpassing the scale of such previous human endeavors as the Panama Canal. 州际高速公路是庞大的工程，轻松跨越（很大的范围）诸如巴拿马运河这样前人的工程建筑。massive 庞大的；concise 简洁的；radical 激进的；trivial 琐碎的。

63. [B] 见62题。invention 发明创造；endeavor 努力，本文指前人努力建设的工程。

64. [D] Eisenhower's interstate highways bound the nation together in new ways...艾森豪威尔州际公路以全新的方式把国家连接起来。bound 是 bind 的过去式，表"捆绑"；pack 打包；suppress 压制，压抑；stick（过去式 stuck）粘贴。

65. [A] and facilitated major economic growth by making commerce less exclusive 州际高速公路使商业不再局限于特定的范围（即四通八达交通的流通运输更方便了），因而促进了经济发展。facilitate 使便利，推动；mobilize 动员；modify 改良，修改；terminate 终结。

66. [C] 见65题。exclusive 专用的，独家的，排他的；comparative 比较的；expensive 昂贵的；competitive 更富有竞争力的。

67. [B] an information superhighway has been built—an electronic network that connects libraries, corporations, government agencies and individuals. 已建成信息高速公路，即连接图书馆、公司、政府机构与个人的电子网络。merge 合并；relay 转播，传递；unify 联合成一体，团结，统一；connect（=link）连接。

68. [C] 见67题。figure 人物；personality 个性；　individual 个人，个体。

69. [A] This electronic superhighway is called the Internet, and it is the backbone of the World Wide Web. 该电子高速公路被称作英特网，而且是万维网的主干部分。

70. [C] The Internet had its precedents in a 1969 U.S. Defense Department computer network called ARPAnet, which stood for Advanced Research Projects Agency Network. 英特网的前身是1969年美国国防部的计算机网络，称作为 ARPA 网，代表……origin 起源（时间、地点比较久远的），如：the origin of civilization 文明起源；source 来源，如 the source of information 消息来源；sample 样本；precedent 前辈，前身。

71. [B] 见70题。stand for 代表；stand by 支持。

72. [A] exchange information 交换信息；switch [+to] 转换；　bypass 绕过；interact [+with] 互动。

73. [D] whose mission is to ...其使命是……（定语从句）

74. [C] This new NSF network attracted more and more institutional users, many of which had their own internal networks. 这个新的 NSF 网吸引了越来越多的机构用户，其中很多用户有自己的内部网络。extend（长度）延伸；expand 拓展（业务等范围），（体积）膨胀；contract 收缩。

75. [B] 见74题。定语从句关系代词 which 指代前文的"institutional users"。

76. [A] most universities that joined the NSF network 加入了 NSF 网的多数大学。participate [+in] 参加（活动）；join 加入（成为一员）；attach...to 连接；be involved in 牵连，涉及，参见（某活动）。

77. [D] The NSF network then became a connector for thousands of other networks NSF 网于是成为了成千上万其他网络的连接系统。

78. [D] As a backbone system 作为一个主干系统。

79. [C] Internet is the wired infrastructure on which web messages move. 英特网是一个连线基础设施，在这个设施上传递着网络信息。sign 符号；context 上下文，环境；leaflet 宣传小册。

80. [C] It began as a military communication system, which expanded into a government-

funded <u>civilian</u> research network. 英特网始于军用通讯系统,后拓展成为政府投资的民用研究网络。citizen 公民;resident 居民;amateur 业余的;civilian 民用的。

81. [A] the Internet is a user-financed system tying institutions of many sorts together <u>into</u> an "information superhighway." 英特网是用户投资的系统,将多种结构连接起来形成信息高速公路。tie...into 连接……而形成……

Part VI Translation

82. over him not to buy a car
83. Keeping sense of humor is contributive to
84. he had no choice but to confess his guilt
85. someone must are speaking ill of them
86. it difficult to resist the temptation of ice cream

2008 年 12 月 20 日大学英语六级（新题型）考试试题

Part Ⅰ　Writing（30 minutes）

Directions：*For this part，you are allowed 30 minutes to write a short essay entitled **How to Improve Students' Mental Health**. You should write at least 150 words following the outline given below.*

How to Improve Students' Mental Health

1. 大学生的心理健康十分重要
2. 因此，学校可以……
3. 我们自己应当……

Part Ⅱ　Reading Comprehension（Skimming and Scanning）（15 minutes）

Directions：*In this part，you will have 15 minutes to go over the passage quickly and answer the questions on **Answer Sheet 1**. For questions 1 - 7，choose the best answer from the four choices marked A），B），C）and D）. For questions 8 - 10，complete the sentences with the information given in the passage.*

Supersize Surprise

Ask anyone why there is an obesity epidemic and they will tell you that it's all down to eating too much and burning too few calories. That explanation appeals to common sense and has dominated efforts to get to the root of the obesity epidemic and reverse it. Yet obesity researchers are increasingly dissatisfied with it. Many now believe that something else must have changed in our environment to precipitate（促成）such dramatic rises in obesity over the past 40 years or so. Nobody is saying that the "big two" — reduced physical activity and increased availability of food — are not important contributors to the epidemic，but they cannot explain it all.

Earlier this year a review paper by 20 obesity experts set out the 7 most plausible alternative explanations for the epidemic. Here they are.

1. Not enough sleep

It is widely believed that sleep is for the brain，not the body. Could a shortage of shut-eye also be helping to make us fat?

Several large-scale studies suggest there may be a link. People who sleep less than 7 hours a night tend to have a higher body mass index than people who sleep more，according to data gathered by the US National Health and Nutrition Examination Survey. Similarly，the US Nurses' Health Study，which tracked 68,000 women for 16 years，found that those who slept an average of 5 hours a night gained more weight during the study period than women who slept 6 hours，who in turn gained more than those who slept 7.

It's well known that obesity impairs sleep，so perhaps people get fat first and sleep less afterwards. But the nurses' study suggests that it can work in the other direction too：sleep loss may precipitate weight gain.

Although getting figures is difficult, it appears that we really are sleeping less. In 1960 people in the US slept an average of 8.5 hours per night. A 2002 poll by the National Sleep Foundation suggests that the average has fallen to under 7 hours, and the decline is mirrored by the increase in obesity.

2. Climate control

We humans, like all warm-blooded animals, can keep our core body temperatures pretty much constant regardless of what's going on in the world around us. We do this by altering our metabolic（新陈代谢的）rate, shivering or sweating. Keeping warm and staying cool take energy unless we are in the "thermo-neutral zone", which is increasingly where we choose to live and work.

There is no denying that ambient temperatures（环境温度）have changed in the past few decades. Between 1970 and 2000, the average British home warmed from a chilly 13℃ to 18℃. In the US, the changes have been at the other end of the thermometer as the proportion of homes with air conditionings rose from 23% to 47% between 1978 and 1997. In the southern states — where obesity rates tend to be highest — the number of houses with air conditioning has shot up to 70% from 37% in 1978.

Could air conditioning in summer and heating in winter really make a difference to our weight? Sadly, there is some evidence that it does — at least with regard to heating. Studies show that in comfortable temperatures we use less energy.

3. Less smoking

Bad news: smokers really do tend to be thinner than the rest of us, and quitting really does pack on the pounds, though no one is sure why. It probably has something to do with the fact that nicotine（尼古丁）is an appetite suppressant and appears to up your metabolic rate.

Katherine Flegal and colleagues at the US National Center for Health Statistics in Hyattsville, Maryland, have calculated that people kicking the habit have been responsible for a small but significant portion of the US epidemic of fatness. From data collected around 1991 by the US National Health and Nutrition Examination Survey, they worked out that people who had quit in the previous decade were much more likely to be overweight than smokers and people who had never smoked. Among men, for example, nearly half of quitters were overweight compared with 37% of non-smokers and only 28% of smokers.

4. Genetic effects

Your chances of becoming fat may be set, at least in part, before you were even born. Children of obese mothers are much more likely to become obese themselves later in life. Offspring of mice fed a high-fat diet during pregnancy are much more likely to become fat than the offspring of identical mice fed a normal diet. Intriguingly, the effect persists for two or three generations. Grand-children of mice fed a high-fat diet grow up fat even if their own mother is fed normally — so your fate may have been sealed even before you were conceived.

5. A little older...

Some groups of people just happen to be fatter than others. Surveys carried out by the US National Center for Health Statistics found that adults aged 40 to 79 were around three times as likely to be obese as younger people. Non-white females also tend to fall at the fatter end of the spectrum: Mexican-American women are 30% more likely than white women to be obess, and black women have twice the risk.

In the US, these groups account for an increasing percentage of the population. Between 1970 and 2000 the US population aged 35 to 44 grew by 43%. The proportion of Hispanic-Americans also grew, from under 5% to 12.5% of the population, while the proportion of black Americans increased from 11% to 12.3%. These changes may account in part for the increased prevalence of obesity.

6. Mature mums

Mothers around the world are getting older. In the UK, the mean age for having a first child is 27.3, compared with 23.7 in 1970. Mean age at first birth in the US has also increased, rising from 21.4 in 1970 to 24.9 in 2000.

This would be neither here nor there if it weren't for the observation that having an older mother seems to be an independent risk factor for obesity. Results from the US National Heart, Lung and Blood Institute's study found that the odds of a child being obese increase about 14% for every five extra years of their mother's age, though why this should be so is not entirely clear.

Michael Symonds at the University of Nottingham, UK, found that first-born children have more fat than younger ones. As family size decreases, firstborns account for a greater share of the population. In 1964, British women gave birth to an average of 2.95 children; by 2005 that figure had fallen to 1.79. In the US in 1976, 9.6% of women in their 40s had had only one children; in 2004 it was 17.4%. This combination of older mothers and more single children could be contributing to the obesity epidemic.

7. Like marrying like

Just as people pair off according to looks, so they do for size. Lean people are more likely to marry lean and fat more likely to marry fat. On its own, like marrying like cannot account for any increase in obesity. But combined with others — particularly the fact that obesity is partly genetic, and that heavier people have more children — it amplifies the increase from other causes.

1. What is the passage mainly about?
   A) Effects of obesity on people's health.
   B) The link between lifestyle and obesity.
   C) New explanations for the obesity epidemic.
   D) Possible ways to combat the obesity epidemic
2. In the US Nurese' Health Study, women who slept an average of 7 hours a night _____.
   A) gained the least weight
   B) were inclined to eat less
   C) found their vigor enhanced
   D) were less susceptible to illness
3. The popular belief about obesity is that _____.
   A) it makes us sleepy
   B) it causes sleep loss
   C) it increases our appetite
   D) it results from lack of sleep
4. How does indoor heating affect our life?

A) It makes us stay indoors more.

B) It accelerates our metabolic rate.

C) It makes us feel more energetic.

D) It contributes to our weight gain.

5. What does the author say about the effect of nicotine on smokers?

    A) It threatens their health.

    B) It heightens their spirits.

    C) It suppresses their appetite.

    D) It slows down their metabolism.

6. Who are most likely to be overweight according to Katherine Flegal's study?

    A) Heavy smokers.

    B) Passive smokers.

    C) Those who never smoke.

    D) Those who quit smoking.

7. According to the US National Center for Health Statistics, the increased obesity in the US is result of _____.

    A) the growing number of smokers among young people

    B) the rising proportion of minorities in its population

    C) the increasing consumption of high-calorie foods

    D) the improving living standards of the poor people

8. According to the US National Heart, Lung and Blood Institute, the reason why older mothers' children tend to be obese remains _____.

9. According to Michael Symonds, one factor contributing to the obesity epidemic is the decrease of _____.

10. When two heavy people get married, chances of their children getting fat increase, because obesity is _____.

Part Ⅲ   Listening Comprehension（35 minutes）

Section A

Directions: *In this section, you will hear 8 short conversations and 2 long conversations. At the end of each conversation, one or more questions will be asked about what was said. Both the conversation and questions will be spoken only once. After each question there will be a pause. During the pause you must read the four choices marked A）, B）, C） and D）, and decide which is the best answer. Then mark the corresponding letter on Answer Sheet 2 with a single line through the center.*

11. A) He is quite easy to recognize.

    B) He is an outstanding speaker.

    C) He looks like a movie star.

    D) He looks young for his age.

12. A) Consult her dancing teacher.

    B) Take a more interesting class.

    C) Continue her dancing class.

    D) Improve her dancing skills.

13. A) The man did not believe what the woman said.

B) The man accompanied the woman to the hospital.

C) The woman may be suffering from repetitive strain injury.

D) The woman may not have followed the doctor's instructions.

14. A) They are not in style any more.

B) They have cost him far too much.

C) They no longer suit his eyesight.

D) They should be cleaned regularly.

15. A) He spilled his drink onto the floor.

B) He has just finished wiping the floor.

C) He was caught in a shower on his way home.

D) He rushed out of the bath to answer the phone.

16. A) Fixing some furniture.

B) Repairing the toy train.

C) Reading the instructions.

D) Assembling the bookcase.

17. A) Urge Jenny to spend more time on study.

B) Help Jenny to prepare for the coming exams.

C) Act towards Jenny in a more sensible way.

D) Send Jenny to a volleyball training center.

18. A) The building of the dam needs a large budget.

B) The proposed site is near the residential area.

C) The local people feel insecure about the dam.

D) The dam poses a threat to the local environment.

Questions 19 to 21 are based on the conversation you have just heard.

19. A) It saw the end of its booming years worldwide.

B) Its production and sales reached record levels.

C) It became popular in some foreign countries.

D) Its domestic market started to shrink rapidly.

20. A) They cost less.

B) They tasted better.

C) They were in fashion.

D) They were widely advertised.

21. A) It is sure to fluctuate.

B) It is bound to revive.

C) It will remain basically stable.

D) It will see no more monopoly

Questions 22 to 25 are based on the conversation you have just heard.

22. A) Organising protests.

B) Recruiting members.

C) Acting as its spokesman.

D) Saving endangered animals.

23. A) Anti-animal-abuse demonstrations.

B) Surveying the Atlantic Ocean floor.

C) Anti-nuclear campaigns.

D) Removing industrial waste.
24. A) By harassing them.
    B) By appealing to the public.
    C) By taking legal action.
    D) By resorting to force.
25. A) Doubtful.   B) Reserved.
    C) Indifferent.   D) Supportive.

Section B

Directions：*In this section，you will hear 3 short passages. At the end of each passage，you will hear some questions. Both the passage and questions will be spoken only once. After you hear a question，you must choose the best answer from the four choices marked A），B），C）and D）. Then mark the corresponding letter on **Answer Sheet 2** with a single line through the center.*

Passage One

Questions 26 to 28 are based on the passage you have just heard.

26. A) The air becomes still.
    B) The air pressure is low.
    C) The clouds block the sun.
    D) The sky appears brighter.
27. A) Ancient people were better at foretelling the weather.
    B) Sailors' saying about the weather are unreliable.
    C) People knew long ago how to predict the weather.
    D) It was easier to forecast the weather in the old days.
28. A) Weather forecast is getting more accurate today.
    B) People can predict the weather by their senses.
    C) Who are the real experts in weather forecast.
    D) Weather changes affect people's life remarkably

Passage Two

Questions 29 to 31 are based on the passage you have just heard.

29. A) They often feel insecure about their jobs.
    B) They are unable to decide what to do first .
    C) They are incompetent to fulfill their responsibilities.
    D) they feel burdened with numerous tasks every day
30. A) Analyze them rationally.
    B) Draw a detailed to-do list.
    C) Turn to others for help.
    D) Handle them one by one.
31. A) They have accomplished little.
    B) They feel utterly exhausted.
    C) They have worked out a way to relax.
    D) They no longer feel any sense of guilt.

Passage Three

Questions 32 to 35 are based on the passage you have just heard.

32. A) Their performance may improve.
    B) Their immune system may be reinforced.
    C) Their blood pressure may rise all of a sudden.
    D) Their physical development may be enhanced.

33. A) Improved mental functioning.
    B) Increased susceptibility to disease.
    C) Speeding up of blood circulation.
    D) Reduction of stress-related hormones.

34. A) Pretend to be in better shape.
    B) Have more physical exercise.
    C) Turn more often to friends for help.
    D) Pay more attention to bodily sensations.

35. A. Different approaches to coping with stress.
    B. Various causes for serious health problems.
    C. The relationship between stress and illness.
    D. New findings of medical research on stress.

Section C

Directions: *In this section, you will hear a passage three times. When the passage is read for the first time, you should listen carefully for its general idea. When the passage is read for the second time, you are required to fill in the blanks numbered from 36 to 43 with the exact words you have just heard. For blanks numbered from 44 to 46 you are required to fill in the missing information. For these blanks, you can either use the exact words you have just heard or write down the main points in you own words. Finally, when the passage is read for the third time, you should check what you have written.*

One of the most common images of an advanced, Western-style culture is that of a busy, traffic-filled city. Since their first (36) _____ on American roadways, automobiles have become a (37) _____ of progress, a source of thousands of jobs, and an almost inalienable right for citizens' personal freedom of movement. In recent (38) _____, our "love affair" with the car is being (39) _____ directly to the developing world, and it is increasingly (40) _____ that this transfer is leading to disaster.

America's almost complete dependence on automobiles has been a terrible mistake. As late as the 1950s, a large (41) _____ of the American public used mass transit. A (42) _____ of public policy decisions and corporate scheming saw to it that countless (43) _____ and efficient urban streetcar and intra-city rail systems were dismantled（拆除）. (44) _____. Our lives have been planned along a road grid — homes far from work, shopping far from everything, with ugly stretches of concrete and blacktop in between.

Development countries are copying Western-style transportation systems down to the last detail. (45) _____. Pollution control measures are either not strict or nonexistent, leading to choking clouds of smog. Gasoline still contains lead, which is extremely poisonous to humans. (46) _____.

In addition to pollution and traffic jams, auto safety is a critical issue in developing nations.

Part IV   Reading Comprehension (Reading in Depth) (25 minutes)

Section A

Directions: *In this section, there is a passage with 5 questions or incomplete sentences. Read the passage carefully. Then answer the questions or complete the statements in the fewest possible words. Please write your answers on* **Answer Sheet 2.**

Questions 47 to 51 are based on the following passage.

One of the major producers of athletic footwear, with 2002 sales of over $10 billion, is a company called Nike, with corporate headquarters in Beaverton, Oregon. *Forbes* magazine identified Nike's president, Philip Knight, as the 53rd-richest man in the world in 2004. But Nike has not always been a large multimillion-dollar organization. In fact, Knight started the company by selling shoes from the back of his car at track meets.

In the late 1950s Philip Knight was a middle-distance runner on the University of Oregon track team, coached by Bill Bowerman. One of the top track coaches in the U.S., Bowerman was also known for experimenting with the design of running shoes in an attempt to make them lighter and more shock-absorbent. After attending Oregon, Knight moved on to do graduate work at Stanford University; his MBA thesis was on marketing athletic shoes. Once he received his degree, Knight traveled to Japan to contact the Onitsuka Tiger Company, a manufacturer of athletic shoes. Knight convinced the company's officials of the potential for its product in the U.S. In 1963 he received his first shipment of Tiger shoes, 200 pairs in total.

In 1964, Knight and Bowerman contributed $500 each to form Blue Ribbon Sports, the predecessor of Nike. In the first few years, Knight distributed shoes out of his car at local track meets. The first employees hired by Knight were former college athletes. The company did not have the money to hire "experts", and there was no established athletic footwear industry in North America from which to recruit those knowledgeable in the field. In its early years the organization operated in an unconventional manner that characterized its innovative and entrepreneurial approach to the industry. Communication was informal; people discussed ideas and issues in the hallways, on a run, or over a beer. There was little task differentiation. There were no job descriptions, rigid reporting systems, or detailed rules and regulations. The team spirit and shared values of the athletes on Bowerman's teams carried over and provided the basis for the collegial style of management that characterized the early years of Nikes.

47. While serving as a track coach, Bowerman tried to design running shoes that were _____ _____.

48. During his visit to Japan, Knight convinced the officials of the Onitsuka Tiger Company that its product would have _____.

49. Blue Ribbon Sports was unable to hire experts due to the absence of _____ in North America.

50. In the early years of Nike, communication within the company was usually carried out _____.

51. What qualities of Bowerman's teams formed the basis of Nike's early management style? _____

Section B

Directions: *There are 2 passages in this section. Each passage is followed by some questions or unfinished statements. For each of them there are four choices marked A), B), C) and D). You should decide on the best choice and mark the corresponding letter on* **Answer Sheet 2** *with a single line through the center.*

Passage One

Questions 52 to 56 are based on the following passage.

Sustainable development is applied to just about everything from energy to clean water and economic growth, and as a result it has become difficult to question either the basic assumptions behind it or the way the concept is put to use. This is especially true in agriculture, where sustainable development is often taken as the sole measure of progress without a proper appreciation of historical and cultural perspectives.

To start with, it is important to remember that the nature of agriculture has changed markedly throughout history, and will continue to do so. Medieval agriculture in northern Europe fed, clothed and sheltered a predominantly rural society with a much lower population density than it is today. It had minimal effect on biodiversity, and any pollution it caused was typically localized. In terms of energy use and the nutrients (营养成分) captured in the product it was relatively inefficient.

Contrast this with farming since the start of the industrial revolution. Competion from overseas led farmers to specialize and increase yields. Throughout this period food became cheaper, safer and more reliable. However, these changes have also led to habitat (栖息地) loss and to diminishing biodiversity.

What's more, demand for animal products in developing countries is growing so fast that meeting it will require an extra 300 million tons of grain a year by 2050. Yet the growth of cities and industry is reducing the amount of water available for agriculture in many regions.

All this means that agriculture in the 21st century will have to be very different from how it was in the 20th. This will require radical thinking. For example, we need to move away from the idea that traditional practices are inevitably more sustainable than new ones. we also need to abandon the notion that agriculture can be "zero impact". The key will be to abandon the rather simple and static measures of sustainability, which centre on the need to maintain production without increasing damage.

Instead we need a more dynamic interpretation, one that looks at the pros and cons (正反两方面) of all the various ways land is used. There are many different ways to measure agricultural performance besides food yield: energy use, environmental costs, water purity, carbon footprint and biodiversity. It is clear, for example, that the carbon cost of transporting tomatoes from Spain to the UK is less than that of producing them in the UK with additional heating and lighting. But we do not know whether lower carbon footprints will always be better for biodiversity.

What is crucial is recognizing that sustainable agriculture is not just about sustainable food production.

52. How do people often measure progress in agriculture?
    A) By its productivity.
    B) By its sustainability.
    C) By its impact on the environment.
    D) By its contribution to economic growth.
53. Specialisation and the effort to increase yields have resulted in _____.

A) localised pollution　　　　B) the shrinking of farmland
C) competition from overseas　D) the decrease of biodiversity

54. What does the author think of traditional farming practices?
    A) They have remained the same over the centuries.
    B) They have not kept pace with population growth.
    C) They are not necessarily sustainable.
    D) They are environmentally friendly.

55. What will agriculture be like in the 21st century?
    A) It will go through radical changes.
    B) It will supply more animal products.
    C) It will abandon traditional farming practices.
    D) It will cause zero damage to the environment.

56. What is the author's purpose in writing this passage?
    A) To remind people of the need of sustainable development.
    B) To suggest ways of ensuring sustainable food production.
    C) To advance new criteria for measuring farming progress.
    D) To urge people to rethink what sustainable agriculture is.

Passage Two

Questions 57 to 61 are based on the following passage.

The percentage of immigrants (including those unlawfully present) in the United States has been creeping upward for years. At 12.6 percent, it is now higher than at any point since the mid-1920s.

We are not about to go back to the days when Congress openly worried about inferior races polluting America's bloodstream. But once again we are wondering whether we have too many of the wrong sort of newcomers. Their loudest critics argue that the new wave of immigrants cannot, and indeed do not want to, fit in as previous generations did.

We now know that these racist views were wrong. In time, Italians, Romanians and members of other so-called inferior races became exemplary Americans and contributed greatly, in ways too numerous to detail, to the building of this magnificent nation. There is no reason why these new immigrants should not have the same success.

Although children of Mexican immigrants do better, in terms of educational and professional attainment, than their parents, UCLA sociologist Edward Telles has found that the gains don't continue. Indeed, the fourth generation is marginally worse off than the third. James Jackson, of the University of Michigan, has found a similar trend among black Caribbean immigrants. Telles fears that Mexican-Americans may be fated to follow in the footsteps of American blacks — that large parts of the community may become mired (陷入) in a seemingly permanent state of poverty and underachievement. Like African-Americans, Mexican-Americans are increasingly relegated to (降入) segregated, substandard schools, and their dropout rate is the highest for any ethnic group in the country.

We have learned much about the foolish idea of excluding people on the presumption of the ethnic/racial inferiority. But what we have not yet learned is how to make the process of Americanization work for all. I am not talking about requiring people to learn English or to adopt American ways; those things happen pretty much on their own. But as arguments about immigration heat up the campaign trail, we also ought to ask some broader questions about assimilation, about how to ensure that people, once outsiders, don't forever remain marginalized within these shores.

That is a much larger question than what should happen with undocumented workers, or how best to secure the border, and it is one that affects not only newcomers but groups that have been here for generations. It will have more impact on our future than where we decide to set the admissions bar for the latest wave of would-be Americans. And it would be nice if we finally got the answer right.

57. How were immigrants viewed by U.S. Congress in the early days?
    A) They were of inferior races.
    B) They were a source of political corruption.
    C) They were a threat to the nation's security.
    D) They were part of the nation's bloodstream.
58. What does the author think of the new immigrants?
    A) They will be a dynamic workforce in the U.S.
    B) They can do just as well as their predecessors.
    C) They will be very disappointed on the new land.
    D) They may find it hard to fit into the mainstream.
59. What does Edward Telles' research say about Mexican-Americans?
    A) They may slowly improve from generation to generation.
    B) They will do better in terms of educational attainment.
    C) They will melt into the African-American community.
    D) They may forever remain poor and underachieving.
60. What should be done to help the new immigrants?
    A) Rid them of their inferiority complex.
    B) Urge them to adopt American customs.
    C) Prevent them from being marginalized.
    D) Teach them standard American English.
61. According to the author, the burning issue concerning immigration is _____.
    A) how to deal with people entering the U.S. without documents
    B) how to help immigrants to better fit into American society
    C) how to stop illegal immigrants from crossing the border
    D) how to limit the number of immigrants to enter the U.S.

Part V   Cloze (15 minutes)

Directions: *There are 20 blanks in the following passage. For each blank there are four choices marked A), B), C) and D) on the right side of the paper. You should choose the ONE that best fits into the passage. Then mark the corresponding letter on **Answer Sheet 2** with a single line through the centre.*

Individuals and businesses have legal protection for intellectual property they create and own. Intellectual properly __62__ from creative thinking and may include products, __63__ processes, and

62. A) retrieves   B) deviates
    C) results   D) departs
63. A) services   B) reserves
    C) assumptions   D) motions

ideas. Intellectual property is protected __64__ misappropriation (盗用). Misappropriation is taking the intellectual property of others without __65__ compensation and using it for monetary gain.

Legal protection is provided for the __66__ of intellectual property. The three common types of legal protection are patents, copyrights, and trademarks.

Patents provide exclusive use of inventions. If the U.S. Patent Office __67__ a patent, it is confirming that the intellectual property is __68__. The patent prevents others from making, using, or selling the invention without the owner's __69__ for a period of 20 years.

Copyrights are similar to patents __70__ that they are applied to artistic works. A copyright protects the creator of an __71__ artisitic or intellectual work, such as a song or a novel. A copyright gives the owner exclusive rights to copy, __72__, display, or perform the work. The copyright prevents others from using and selling the work. The __73__ of a copyright is typically the lifetime of the author __74__ an additional 70 years.

Trademarks are words, names, or symbols that identify the manufacturer of a product and __75__ it from similar goods of others. A servicemark is similar to a trademark __76__ is used to identify services. A trademark prevents others from using the __77__ or a similar word, name, or symbol to take advantage of the recognition and __78__ of the brand or to create confusion in the marketplace. __79__ registration, a trademark is usually granted for a period of ten years. It can be __80__ for additional ten-year periods indefinitely as __81__ as the mark's use continues.

64. A) for   B) with
    C) by   D) from
65. A) sound   B) partial
    C) due   D) random
66. A) users   B) owners
    C) masters   D) executives
67. A) affords   B) affiliates
    C) funds   D) grants
68. A) solemn   B) sober
    C) unique   D) universal
69. A) perspective B) permission
    C) conformity   D) consensus
70. A) except   B) besides
    C) beyond   D) despite
71. A) absolute   B) alternative
    C) original   D) orthodox
72. A) presume   B) stimulate
    C) nominate   D) distribute
73. A) range   B) length
    C) scale   D) extent
74. A) plus   B) versus
    C) via   D) until
75. A) distract   B) differ
    C) distinguish D) disconnect
76. A) or   B) but
    C) so   D) whereas
77. A) identical B) analogical
    C) literal   D) parallel
78. A) ambiguity B) utility
    C) popularity D) proximity
79. A) From   B) Over
    C) Before   D) Upon
80. A) recurred   B) renewed
    C) recalled   D) recovered
81. A) long   B) soon
    C) far   D) well

Part VI Translation (5 minutes)

Directions: *Complete the sentences by translating into English the Chinese given in brackets. Please write your translation on **Answer Sheet 2**.*

82. He designed the first suspension bridge，which _____ （把美观与功能完美地结合起来）.

83. It was very dark，but Mary seemed to _____ （本能地知道该走哪条路）.

84. I don't think it advisable that parents _____ （剥夺孩子们的自由）to spend their spare time as they wish.

85. Older adults who have a high level of daily activities have more energy and _____ （与不那么活跃的人相比死亡率要低）.

86. Your resume should attract a would-be boss's attention by demonstrating _____ （为什么你是某个特定职位的最佳人选）.

2008 年 12 月 20 日大学英语六级考试（新题型）试题
答案与解析

Part Ⅰ
Sample Writing

How to Improve Students' Mental Health

College students' mental health has become a matter of considerable public concern. According to a latest survey, no less than 30% of the youth are suffering from various mental problems, ranging from anxieties, depression to suicidal tendency.

As we all know, for most of the students, the major mental problems result from academic pressures or difficulty to communicate. Many students are disappointed to find that campus life is not as meaningful and colorful as they have expected. Obviously, it is necessary that effective actions should be taken to improve the situation. As for university authorities, they should do something to lessen the pressure from competitions and hold some activities to add the significance to students' daily life. Feeling relaxed and loved, they can master knowledge much more readily and learn more useful skills. On the other hand, more mental health hotlines should be set up so that students will have specialist to turn to when they feel confused.

As a college student, I think we should learn to take care of ourselves. By making more friends, we will build up our social support system to help us deal with various mental trouble; by reasonable arrangement of study schedule, we will feel less stressed; and by getting more actively involved with school activities, we will lead a happier campus life!

（华东理工大学　物流 071　田清羽）

Part Ⅱ

1. ［D］引言部分第二段：Earlier this year a review paper by 20 obesity experts set out the 7 most plausible alternative explanations for the epidemic（提出关于肥胖症的最合理的 7 种不同解释）. Here they are. 这一段点明了本文主题。

2. ［A］参见"Not enough sleep"部分第二段最后一句：... the US Nurses' Health Study ... found that those who slept an average of 5 hours a night gained more weight during the study period than women who slept 6 hours, who in turn gained more than those who slept 7.（研究表明……平均每晚睡眠五个小时的妇女在研究期间体重增长超过每晚六个小时的妇女，而后者体重增长又超过每晚睡七个小时的。）

3. ［B］根据"Not enough sleep"部分第三段第一句：It's well known that obesity impairs sleep（众所周知，肥胖损害睡眠），so perhaps people get fat first and sleep less afterwards. 由此可知，人们普遍相信，肥胖引起睡眠不足。

4. ［D］参见"Climate control"部分最后一段：Could air conditioning in summer and heating in winter really make a difference to our weight? Sadly, there is some evidence that it does — at least with regard to heating. Studies show that in comfortable temperatures we use less energy. 有证据表明空调的使用确影响体重，至少就供暖设备的使用而言。研究表明在气温舒适的环境下，我们消耗较少的能量。由此推知，供暖导致体重增加（contribute to weight gain）。

5. ［C］参见"Less smoking"部分第一段第一句：... nicotine is an appetite suppressant（尼古丁是食欲抑制剂）...

6. ［D］参见"Less smoking"部分第二段第二句：... people who had quit in the previous decade were much more likely to be overweight than smokers and people who had never smoked.

7. [B] "A little older..."部分第一段第三句提到"Non-white females also tend to fall at the fatter end of the spectrum（非白种女性都偏肥胖）"，第二段提到"In the US, these groups（即上文提到的 non-white minority groups）account for an increasing percentage of the population... These changes may account in part for the increased prevalence of obesity（少数人种人口增长的变化是肥胖增多的部分原因）。"

8. not entirely clear　参见"Mature mums"部分第二段第二句：Results from the US National Heart, Lung and Blood Institute's study found that the odds of a child being obese increase 14% for every five extra years of their mother's age（母亲生育年龄每增长五岁孩子肥胖的概率增长 14%），though why this should be so is not entirely clear。

9. family size　根据"Mature mums"部分第三段前两句：Michael Symonds at the University of Nottingham, UK, found that first-born children have more fat than younger ones. As family size decreases, firstborns account for a greater share of the population. 家庭缩小意味着头生子占总人口比例越来越多，而头生子又偏胖，可见导致肥胖的因素之一是家庭人口的减少。

10. partly genetic　参见"Like marrying like"部分第三、四句：On its own, like marrying like cannot account for any increase in obesity. But combined with others — particularly the fact that obesity is partly genetic... it amplifies the increase from other causes.（同类人结婚本身并不导致肥胖，但当两个肥胖者结婚——尤其是肥胖部分源自遗传因素，来自其他原因的肥胖概率就增大了。

Part Ⅲ

11. A　12. C　13. D　14. C　15. D　16. D　17. A　18. C　19. B　20. A
21. B　22. A　23. C　24. A　25. D　26. B　27. D　28. B　29. D　30. B
31. A　32. A　33. B　34. D　35. C
36. appearance　37. symbol　38. decades　39. exported
40. apparent　41. percentage　42. combination　43. convenient

44. Our air quality now suffers from the effects of pollutants emitted directly from our cars

45. The problems caused by motorized vehicles in the West are often magnified in developing nations

46. Movement in some cities comes to a virtual standstill as motorized traffic competes with bicycles and pedestrians

Part Ⅳ

47. lighter and more shock-absorbent　参见第二段第二句：One of the top track coaches in the U.S., Bowerman was also known for experimenting with（实验）the design of running shoes in an attempt to make them lighter and more shock-absorbent（更轻便更能吸收冲击力）。

48. potential in the US　参见第二段倒数第二、三句：...Knight traveled to Japan to contact the Onitsuka Tiger Company, a manufacturer of athletic shoes. Knight convinced the company's officials of the potential for its product in the U.S.（试图说服日本公司官员相信该运动鞋产品在美国的潜力）。

49. established athletic footwear　参见第三段第四句：The company did not have the money to hire "experts", and there was no established athletic footwear industry in North America from which to recruit those knowledgeable in the field.（运动鞋工业在北美尚未确立发展，无法从中聘请到资深专家。）

50. informally　参见第三段第五、六句：In its early years the organization（指 Nike 公司）operated in an unconventional manner（非常规的运作方式）that characterized its

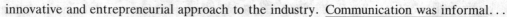

innovative and entrepreneurial approach to the industry. Communication was informal...

51. The team spirit and shared values of the athletes. 参见第三段最后一句：The team spirit and shared values of the athletes on Bowerman's teams carried over and provided the basis for the collegial style of management that characterized the early years of Nikes.（Bowerman团队中的运动员的团队精神与共享价值观传承下来，成为耐克公司早期管理风格的基础。）

52. [B] 细节理解题。参见第一段最后一句：This is especially true in agriculture, where sustainable development is often taken as the sole measure of progress（可持续性发展被看作是衡量进步的唯一标尺）。

53. [D] 细节理解题。参见第三段最后一句：However, these changes have also led to habitat loss and to diminishing biodiversity（这些变化导致生物栖息地丧失与物种多样性的减少）。"these changes"即前文提到的海外竞争导致农业劳动分工专业化（specialization）与产量的增加（increase yields）。

54. [C] 句意推断题。第五段第二、三句提到，"This will require radical thinking（激进大胆的想法）. For example, we need to move away from the idea that traditional practices are inevitably more sustainable than new ones（脱离那种传统农业做法比新方法更可持续的想法）."由此推知,作者认为传统农业实践未必更具可持续性（not necessarily sustainable）。故选C。

55. [A] 句意推断题。第五段第一句提到,21世纪的农业将与20世纪的农业截然不同（very different）,由此推知,21世纪的农业将经历重大变革（go through radical changes）。

56. [D] 全文主旨题。选项D含有文中多次出现的核心词为"sustainable development"、"agriculture"。

57. [A] 推断题。参见第二段第一句：We are not about to go back to the days when Congress openly worried about inferior races polluting America's bloodstream（国会公开表露关于劣等种族污染美国主流血脉的担忧）. 根据上下文提到的"newcomers"、"the new wave of immigrants"可知,劣等民族（inferior races）是指美国移民。故选A（美国国会早期将移民看作劣等民族）。

58. [B] 推断题。第二段最后一句与第三段第一句提到,最激进的批评家（loudest critics）认为,新一轮的移民不能、也不想像他们的先辈们那样融入（fit in）美国。但我们现在知道这些激进的观点是错误的。由此推知,作者认为新移民能够像他们一样适应融入美国社会。故选B。

59. [D] 细节理解题。第四段第五句提到,Telles担心的是,墨西哥裔美国人（新移民）可能步美国黑人的后尘,即大批社区移民永远陷入贫困与失败的泥潭（mired in a seemingly permanent state of poverty and underachieving）。故选D。

60. [C] 推断题。第五段最后一句提到,我们应该提出更事关大局的问题,比如关于社会同化问题（broader questions about assimilation）,关于如何保证曾是外来者的人们不会永远处于边缘化的状态（not forever remain marginalized）。由此推知,帮助新移民的方法是防止他们成为社会边缘人。

61. [B] 参见最后一段第一句：That is a much larger question than what should happen with undocumented workers, or how best to secure the border...（相比如何处理非法身份的工人、如何保证边境安全,这个问题更为重大。）句中"that"指上文提到的"ensure that people, once outsiders, don't forever remain marginalized（防止新移民边缘化,帮助他们融入美国社会）", "a much larger question"即本题干中所问及的"burning question concerning immigration"（关于移民的迫在眉睫的问题）。故选B。

62. ［C］Intellectual property <u>results from</u> creative thinking 知识财产起源于创造性思维；retrieve 意为"收回，找回"：retrieve the plane wreckage from the sea 从海中打捞飞机残骸；derive 意为"获取，派生"：derive pleasure from work 从工作中获得乐趣；depart 意为"离开"。

63. ［A］Intellectual property...may include products，<u>services</u>，processes and ideas 知识财产可以包括产品、服务、加工过程、想法。assumption 意为"假设"；reserve 意为"储备"；motion 意为"动作"。

64. ［D］Intellectual property is <u>protected from</u> misappropriation 知识财产受到保护以防被人盗用。protect...from 保护……不受……的伤害。

65. ［C］Misappropriation is taking the intellectual property of others without <u>due</u> compensation 盗用即使用他人知识财产而没付应付的补偿。due 意为"应得的，应归于的"；sound 意为"健全的"；partial 意为"部分的"；random 意为" 随机的"。

66. ［B］Legal protection is provided for the <u>owners</u> of intellectual property 人们为知识财产的所有人提供了法律保障。

67. ［D］<u>grant</u> a parent 授予专利权。grant 意为"（正式）授予，给予（学位、奖金、权利等）"；affiliate 意为"附属"：a hospital affiliated to Fudan University 复旦大学附属医院；fund 意为"资金，资助"：a foreign-funded company 外资企业。

68. ［C］...it（即 patent）is confirming that the intellectual property is <u>unique</u> 专利权就是确认某知识财产的独一无二性。unique 意为"独特的"；universal 意为"全球性的"；solemn 意为"严肃的"；sober 意为"清醒的"。

69. ［B］without the owner's <u>permission</u> 未经所有人许可。perspective 意为"视角"；conformity 意为"一致性，同一性"；consensus 意为"（大家）一致的意见，共识"。

70. ［A］Copyrights are similar to patents <u>except that</u> they are applied to artistic works. 版权类似于专利权，只是版权仅适用于艺术作品。except 意为"除了"。

71. ［C］A copyright protects the creator of an <u>original</u> artistic or intellectual work... 版权保护原创的艺术或知识性作品的创作者。absolute 意为"绝对的"；original 意为"原始的，原创的"；alternative 意为"二择一的"；orthodox 意为"正宗的（普遍接受到），正统的"。

72. ［D］A copyright gives the owner exclusive rights to copy，<u>distribute</u>，display or perform the work. 版权授予其拥有者作品复制、分销、展示、表演的独家权利。distribute 意为"分发，分销"；stimulate 意为"刺激"；presume 意为"假设"；nominate 意为"提名"。

73. ［B］The <u>length</u> of a copyright is typically the lifetime of the author <u>plus</u> additional 70 years. 版权期限一般是作者有生之年外加 70 年。length 意为"（时间或距离）长度"；range 意为"（波动的）范围"；scale 意为"规模"；extent 意为"程度"。

74. ［A］见上。plus 意为"加上"；versus 意为"比，相对于"；via 意为"通过"；until 意为"直到"。

75. ［C］<u>distinguish</u> it from similar goods of others 使它和其他同类产品区分开来。distract one's attention from...分散注意力；distinguish A from B 将 A 与 B 区分开来；differ from...与……不同；disconnect 意为"使分离"：disconnect our phone 切断电话。

76. ［B］A servicemark is similar to a trademark <u>but</u> is used to identify services. 服务商标类似于产品商标，但其目的是用于辨别服务。whereas 意为"而，然而（后接从句）"。

77. ［A］A trademark prevents others from using <u>identical</u> or similar word，name or symbol to take advantage of the recognition and <u>popularity</u> of the brand... 商标防止别人为了利用某品牌的认可度与知名度而使用一模一样的或雷同的词汇、名称、标识等。analogical 意为"类比的"；parallel 意为"平行的"；literal 意为"字面上的"。

78. ［C］见上。ambiguity 意为"模棱两可"；popularity 意为"普及，流行"；utility 意为"用途"；proximity 意为"接近"。

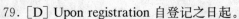

79. [D] Upon registration 自登记之日起。
80. [B] It can be renewed additional ten-year periods 商标可注册更新延长十年期限。
81. [A] as long as... 只要。

Part Ⅵ

82. made a perfect combination of beauty and function
83. know which way to take instinctively
84. (should) deprive children of their freedom
85. a lower death rate compared with relatively inactive people
86. why you would be the best candidate

上 篇
应试技巧 & 捷径训练

第一章 写 作

（Writing）

新六级考试写作部分要求考生 30 分钟内完成一篇不少于 150 字的短文。

分　值: 15 分

作文体裁: 以应用文、议论文为主,说明文较少。

题目形式: 带中文提示的三段式作文为主,少量图表作文。

作文内容: 多与大学生学习、生活相关,也涉及一些社会、环保方面的
热门话题。

一、应试技巧点津

四、六级虽已改为 710 分制,作文评卷仍以 15 分为满分,分为 14 分、11 分、8 分、5 分、2 分共 5 个评分档。阅卷教师根据作文总体印象(global impression)确定作文分档,适当上下浮动 1—2 分。阅卷老师对各分档的作文总体印象可概括如下:

14 分作文准确地道、可圈可点;

11 分作文清清爽爽、语病较少;

8 分作文马马虎虎、语病不少;

5 分作文糊里糊涂、错误低级;

2 分作文一塌糊涂、惨不忍睹。

高分作文并非遥不可及,考生在充分发挥原有语言水平的基础上,还要把握评分要点与阅卷心态,投其所好,以下 9 点考场秘籍争取做到 6 点就大功告成。

1. 尽量减少语法错误。洋教师看重文章的内容创意,而本土教师注重语言的准确性,最不能容忍"There's car runs fast"之类的低级语法错误。

2. 全文呈三段式结构——首尾简洁,中间翔实,主次分明。围绕三句中文提示展开,开门见山。

3. 中间段落要有层次感。用简单句形式表达主题句,主题句下含两个或三个分论点句,每个分论点通过举例或数据加以支撑,例子、数据要能说明问题。

段落结构示例:

Harmful Plastic Bags

主题句: Overusing plastic bags brings about **environmental hazards**. (核心词)

次主题句—1: Nicknamed "white pollution" in China, discarded plastic bags litter our cities, spoiling the beauty of living surroundings. (视觉污染)

次主题句—2: Besides, plastic bags are a waste of resources in that we use them once and throw them away. (浪费)

次主题句—3: Finally, most plastic bags may hang around for decades, refusing to decompose. As a result, rivers are choked, drains are blocked and soil is poisoned as well. Kill wildlife. (潜在危害)

4. 适当使用 besides、first、as a result 等连词、副词,突出上下文连贯性。

5. 适当使用设问句、倒装句、强调句、被动句、非谓语结构,突出句型多样性。

6. 尽量多用 go over、for the time being 等动词词组与固定搭配,行文更显地道。

7. 避免反复使用 important、good、useful 等词,否则词汇贫乏的弱点暴露无遗。

8. 有意识地用点深奥词语,显得你挺有水平,但没有把握不要乱用,以免弄巧成拙。

9. 注意字迹清晰、卷面整洁。你的作文会被扫描进电脑,阅卷老师在电脑上阅卷,眼睛十分辛苦,千万不要再以草书、小楷、墨团影响老师的心情!

二、训练方案优化

只要掌握 500 个高频词与 15 个常用句型并能应用自如,写出一篇 150 字的像样文章并非难事。所以,与其考前死背范文,不如积累好词好句,以不变应万变。下面为你提供的是:

(1) 常见作文开头、结尾、过渡句型,供你考前半小时浏览,做到胸有成竹。

(2) 常用词句的翻译练习——该练习既能帮助你检测自己作文中的常见语法错误,也能帮助你记忆好词好句以便考场活学活用。此外,还能助你应对六级新题型"汉译英",可谓一箭双雕。每天翻译 5 — 10 句,千万别偷懒!

(一)常用开头、结尾、扩展句背诵

常用开头句

——泛谈当今社会变化

● With the steady development of/rapid growth of..., great changes have taken place in our society/around us.

● The 20th century has seen/witnessed the rise and decline of...

——引用名言

● ...(Study hard and play hard) is an old proverb/saying. It still makes sense.

● One of the great men once remarked that... and now it still has its realistic significance.

——指出问题

● There is something very wrong with...(today's educational system) that...(puts so much emphasis on test scores)

● In recent years the issue of...(education system) has been brought to public attention.

● In the past decade there has been dramatic rise in...(drug addiction/divorce rate/teenage smoking)

——开门见山

● The truth is that.../There is no doubt that...

常用辩论句 & 段落扩展句

——逐项陈述原因

● It is easy to understand why...(young students take part-time jobs.) First, of course, there is the (money factor). But even more important is...(the sense of doing something that matters. Adolescents thrive on the sense of somebody is counting on them.)

● Why...? For one thing... For another...

● There are many causes for... But in general, they come down to three major ones. First of all... The primary cause is that...

——指出问题

● ...(Teenagers working) is not, in itself, a problem. Rather, problems occur when...(adults don't take their work seriously) Too often society fails to...(recognize the difficulties and conflicts that work raises for young people)...

——分析问题

- The factors for... （a sharp rise in the number of teenage smokers/drinkers）are quite complex. Some attribute it to... Many studies document that undesirable teenage behavior like smoking and drinking is... associated with...
- Our fault lies not so much with... （our economy or our politics）as with ourselves...

常用观点陈述句

- There is some measure of/an element of truth in the statement that.../Therefore, it is quite logical/reasonable to argue that...
- You have been exposed to this idea before, but this time pay more attention. It is important that this message get through loud and clear. The message ...
- A close look at history/recent events suggests that...
- It is a revealing fact that...

常用结尾句

——下结论

- In a word/In general/In short,.../So far, it is quite obvious that.../In summary,...
- From what has been discussed above, we can safely conclude that...

——讨论解决办法

- It is high time to put an end to the undesirable phenomenon of.../It is imperative that effective actions be taken to control/fight the tendency of.../Stricter measures should be taken to prevent.../Though the...（problem）seems very serious/tricky, it is temporary and can be cracked/solved through...
- If you are to..., try the strategies/proposals suggested above./It is worthwhile to...
- Laws must be laid down to... Only in this way, can we...

——展望未来

- With so much support from.../With great effort on the part of.../With so many advantages of..., there is no doubt that... in the near future.

——呼吁解决问题

- Enough is enough. So many acts of...（cheating on the exam）have been going on in universities that it is time to put an end to them.
- If we are succeed as a society in the new century, we had better/must... Not until... have been done away with, do we stand a chance.

图表描述套句

- The figure has almost doubled/tripled, as compared with that of last year.
- As indicated in the above pie chart（饼形图）/line graph（线形图）/bar graph（柱状图）,...
- According to a recent survey, the divorce rate rose by... over the last 5 years/soared to... in the year of...

（二）常用连词

连词是文章的黏合剂,可使行文紧凑连贯。

1. 表递进：too, also, furthermore, similarly, moreover, what's more...
2. 表示例：for instance, a case in point, take... as an example...

3．表复述：that is，in other words，in short...

4．表结论：so，therefore，thus，accordingly，consequently，as a result，hence，to sum up...

5．表让步：no doubt，although，to be sure，it is true that...

6．表原因：It's not that...but that...，because

7．表强调：indeed，in fact

8．表列举：in the first place，to begin with，secondly，finally

9．表对照：but，however，nevertheless，while，on the other hand，by contrast，on the contrary

（三）常用句型翻译

1．what...结构

（1）I didn't believe him. ＿＿＿＿＿＿＿＿＿＿＿＿＿＿＿＿＿（convince）起初我并不相信他的话，但读过这份报道后，我确信他说的是真的。

（2）＿＿＿＿＿＿＿（happen/experience）will make him a better person. 他所经历的一切将使他更加优秀。

（3）＿＿＿＿＿＿＿＿＿＿＿＿＿＿＿（realize，lethal）他们尚未意识到这种行为可能造成致命的后果。

Key：

（1）It was not until I read about this report that I was convinced what he said was true.

（2）What happened to him/What he has experienced

（3）What they failed to realize is that this behavior might be lethal.

2．倒装、强调、虚拟结构

（1）＿＿＿＿＿＿＿make friends with people like him. 我从未想到过要和他这样的人交朋友。（倒装）

（2）＿＿＿＿＿＿＿＿＿＿＿＿＿＿＿ controls our thinking. 直到 18 世纪，人们才意识到控制思维的是大脑，而不是心脏。（倒装）

（3）＿＿＿＿＿＿＿＿＿＿＿＿＿＿＿ what we have lost. 唯有此时，当你离我们远去，我们才体会到损失了什么。（倒装）

（4）＿＿＿＿＿＿＿＿＿＿，we ＿＿＿＿＿＿＿＿ in serious difficulties. 要不是你的经济资助，我们早陷入严重困境了。（虚拟，倒装）

（5）＿＿＿＿＿＿＿＿＿＿＿＿＿＿＿ sympathize with the poor. 正是她内心的痛苦，使她对穷人深感同情。（强调）

（6）＿＿＿＿＿＿＿＿＿＿，more important is your independent thinking ability. 忠告与帮助固然重要，更重要的是你个人的独立思考能力。（倒装）

Key：

（1）Never did it cross my mind to

（2）Not until 18th century did man realize that brain，rather than heart，

（3）Only now you are gone do we truly appreciate

（4）Had it not been for your financial support；would have been

（5）It was her inner suffering that made it possible for her to

（6）Dear as/though advice and help is

3．强势否定句

（1）Teachers ＿＿＿＿＿＿＿＿＿＿. 教师对学生越严格越好。

(2) It _____ that education plays a crucial role in economic development. 教育在经济发展中起着关键作用,这一点再怎么强调也不为过。

Key:

(1) cannot be too strict with their students

(2) cannot be too strongly emphasized

4. as.../with.... 句型

(1) _____ 学生越勤奋越好。(身份)

(2) I had to admit that she _____. 我不得不承认,她是个很在行的设计师。(身份)

(3) Naturally, _____. 中国地域辽阔,各地气候差异悬殊。(原因)

(4) _____, you will _____. 若不努力,你将一事无成。(条件)

Key:

(1) As a student, you cannot be too diligent.

(2) knew her business as a designer

(3) with such distances, the climate in China covers great extremes

(4) Without hard work; accomplish nothing

5. 比较结构

(1) Dad showed his love _____. 父亲的爱不是挂在嘴上,而是表现在行动上。

(2) I learned more _____. 我从他身上学到的东西远远超过书本知识。

(3) She is as _____. 她才貌双全。

(4) To be disabled is to _____, but far too often disabled people still _____. 身有残疾并不意味着低人一等,但残疾人生活受人主宰的情况仍比比皆是。

(5) The _____. 我们工作越努力,成果就越大。

Key:

(1) more by his actions than by his words

(2) from him than I could ever hope to learn from books

(3) brilliant as she is beautiful

(4) be no less human than anyone else; have their lives controlled/ruled by others

(5) harder we work, the better results we will get

6. there be 句型

(1) There is no _____.../no _____...无可否认/无可逃避

(2) There are _____ 有时

(3) There _____. 在许多情况下,勤奋比天分更重要。

(4) Of all the scientific workers of the 19 th century, _____

_____. 在 19 世纪的所有科研工作者中,没有人比达尔文取得更大的工作成就。

Key:

(1) denying that; escaping that

(2) times when...

(3) are many cases in which diligence is more important than talent

(4) there is no one who achieved a greater amount of work than Darwin.

7. 双重否定句

(1) Nothing is _____ . 没有不可能的事。

(2) There is nothing a standardized test measures _____ .
标准化测试所测量的,无非是你在下一次标准化测试中得多少分。

(3) There is _____ . 对于一名有求知欲的学生,任何知识都是可接受的。

Key：

(1) impossible

(2) other than your ability to score well on the next standardized test

(3) no body of knowledge inaccessible to a highly motivated student

8. 形式 it 句

(1) It should be noted that/It is _____ that... 值得注意的是/大家一致认为

It goes _____ 不用说,毫无疑问……

It is _____/_____ to do so. 这样做是明智的/失策的

(2) It's my firm/strong _____ that... 我坚信……

(3) Besides getting rid of boredom, daydreaming _____
_____ . 除了摆脱厌倦情绪,白日梦还使人更容易承受压力。

(4) _____are two ingredients to success. 强烈的学习动机和投入的时间是外语学习成功的两大因素。

Key：

(1) generally agreed that...

without saying that...

advisable to/ill-advised

(2) conviction

(3) makes it easier to endure stress

(4) When it comes to foreign language learning, strong motivation and time put in the learning process

9. 分词结构

(1) In our electronic age, _____ . 在我们这个电子时代,大人小孩都会整日泡在电视前,在舒适的家中享受休闲时光。(伴随)

(2) Both the management and the employees _____ . 劳资双方都以诚实合作的态度对待这次谈判,所以很快就达成了协议。(因果关系)

(3) Thanksgiving Day is _____ .
感恩节是家庭节日,通常由一顿丰盛的晚餐与阖家欢聚来庆祝。

(4) _____ , she immediately set about documenting the dead. 拿着两架相机和一台手提电脑,她马上开始记录死者身份。

Key：

(1) old and young alike can be couch potatoes, enjoying their entertainment from the comfort of home

(2) approached the negotiation with an honest and cooperative attitude, thus reaching an agreement quickly

(3) usually a family day, celebrated with big dinners and happy reunions

(4) Armed with two cameras and a laptop

10. 定语从句

(1) Three parts of our life have changed： _____

_____. 我们生活的三个方面发生了变化:工作方式、餐饮方式和娱乐方式。

(2) Many job seekers _____

_____. 对许多求职者来说,没有真实的资格证明,就无法再向前发展。

(3) The stepfather of Bill Clinton was a habitual drunkard, _____

_____. 克林顿的继父酗酒成性,导致家庭不和。

(4) He _____. 他在海德堡

待了一年,这座著名的大学城的学术气氛对他深有影响。

Key:

(1) the way we work, the way we eat and the way we entertain ourselves

(2) have reached a point where they cannot progress without formal qualifications

(3) which caused conflict in the family

(4) spent one year in Heidelburg, where he came under the intellectual influence of the famous university town

11. 状语从句

(1) _____, there is an opportunity to raise a healthy and happy child. 只要有耐心、爱心与责任心,就有机会培养出健康快乐的孩子。(条件)

(2) I carried an English book with me _____我随身带着一本英语书,有空就读。(目的)

(3) I was _____. 他的话让我感动得说不出话来。(因果)

(4) He said he _____. 他说等找到满意工作后再结婚。(时间先后)

Key:

(1) Where there is patience, love and commitment

(2) so that I could read it whenever I was free

(3) so moved by what he said to me that I could scarcely speak

(4) wouldn't get married until he found a satisfactory job

(四)大词难词翻译

用两三个大词点缀文章即可,适可而止,过多使用反而不好。

1. d_____/prove 证明

2. v_____/almost 几乎

3. p_____/regard sth as... 将……看做

4. supporter/a_____ 支持者

5. hold/h_____ a certain view 持有某观点

6. take advantage of/e_____ 利用

7. choice/o_____/a_____ 选择

8. a_____/about 大约

9. e_____/u_____/finally 最终

10. i_____/always 总是

Key:

1. demonstrate   2. virtually   3. perceive   4. advocate

5. harbor   6. exploit   7. option/alternative

8. approximately   9. eventually/ultimately

10. invariably

第二章　快速阅读
(Fast Reading — Skimming and Scanning)

快速阅读要求考生在 15 分钟内浏览一篇 900—1,200 字左右的文章并完成 10 道题。

文章体裁：说明文，一般带有标题、小标题，结构层次清晰。

文章内容：信息量大，涉及科普、环保、教育、文化、社会、心理、医药、产品介绍等内容。

题型 1：

4 道判断正误：若所给陈述句信息与文中内容相符，选 Y(Yes)；

若所给陈述句信息与文中内容矛盾，选 N (No)；

若所给陈述句信息文中未提及或找不到依据，选 NG(Not Given)。

6 道句子填空：根据文章内容，将句子补充完整。

题型 2 (2007 年 12 月新题型)：

7 道多项选择题和 3 道句子填空。

答案规律：4 道判断题中，2 个 Y 与 1 个 N，1 个 NG；或者 2 个 N 与 1 个 Y，1 个 NG。6 道句子填空中，一般只需填入 1—5 个词，多为文中原词。

一、应试技巧点津

快速阅读题是对略读(skimming)、寻读(scanning)等速读技能的测试，并不考你对文章的理解深度。要在规定时间内完成，千万不可逐字逐行阅读，也不要等读完文章后再做题。要学会边看题目边读文章的阅读方式。具体解题技巧如下：

1. 首先利用略读技能浏览文章标题(有的文章还带有几个小标题)与第一段，大致了解全文主旨。

2. 然后立刻阅读题目，找出题目中的信号词或核心词，以各小标题或者每段第一句(topic sentence)为向导，找到信号词或关键词所在的相关段落。快速阅读该段落，边读边找判断题目的信息依据。

信号词一般是人名、时间、数字(一眼即可从文中辨认)。

关键词一般是充当主语或宾语的名词。

2006/12 真题示例

[考题] Lance Bass wasn't able to go on a tour of space because of health problems.

[原文] Lance Bass of N Sync <u>was supposed to be the third</u> to make the $ 20 million trip, but he <u>did not join</u> the three-man crew as they blasted off on October 30, 2002, due to lack of payment. Probably the most incredible aspect of this proposed space tour was that NASA approved of it.

[解题步骤]

阅读题目，挑出信号词(Lance Bass)与关键词(health problems)

定位：根据信号词(Lance Bass)迅速定位于第二段。

寻读：使用 scanning 技巧，找到文中相关句"Lance Bass...didn't join the three-man crew...

due to lack of payment."

判断:题目中"because of health problems"与文中信息"lack of payment"相矛盾,故选[N]。

3. 注意做题的顺序性:出题顺序与原文顺序基本一致。看完一道题目应立即去找相关依据,然后再看下一道题。

4. 如果题目句子是对原文句子的同义转述,即用了近义词或近义结构,或者如果题目中的句子是对原文中几个句子的总结或推论,答案往往选[Y]。

2006/12 真题示例

[考题] The space agencies are reluctant to open up space to tourists.

[原文] In 1997, NASA published a report concluding that selling trips into space to private citizens could be worth billions of dollars. A Japanese report supports these findings, and projects that space tourism could be a ＄10 billion per year industry within the next two decades. The only obstacles to opening up space to tourists are the space agencies, who are concerned with safety and the development of a reliable, reusable launch vehicle.

[解题步骤]

阅读题目,挑出信号词(space agencies)与关键词(reluctant)

定位:根据信号词(space agencies)迅速定位于第四段。

寻读:找出原文相关句"The only obstacles to opening up space to tourists are the space agencies",题目中"reluctant to open up space travel"可由原文"obstacles to opening up space"(对游客开放太空旅游的障碍)推导出,故此题选[Y]。

5. 注意千万不要凭自己的背景知识去作逻辑推断。有些题目往往看上去很符合常识,也与文中信息相关,但是题目中的说法比原文的说法更具体、范围更小,仅从原文所给的信息来看,已无法进行准确的判断,这时答案最好选[NG]。

2006/12 真题示例

[考题] Two Australian billionaires have been placed on the waiting list for entering space as private passengers.

[解析] 本文只提到美国商人 Tito 和南非商人 Shuttleworth 尝试太空飞行的游客,并未提到"two Australian Billionaires",故选[NG]。

6. 后面六道句子补充题较为简单,主要根据题目中关键词或信号词找到原文中相关句,答案多为文中原句。

2006/12 真题示例

[考题] The prize for the winner in the fall 2001 NBC TV game show would have been _____ _____.

[原文] The Mir crash did cancel plans for a new reality-based game show from NBC, which was going to be called Destination Mir. The *Survivor*-like TV show was scheduled to air in fall 2001. Participants on the show were to go through training at Russia's cosmonaut (宇航员) training center, Star City. Each week, one of the participants would be eliminated from the show, with the winner receiving a trip to the Mir space station. The Mir crash has ruled out NBC's space plans for now. NASA is against beginning space tourism until the International Space Station is completed in 2006.

[解题步骤]

阅读题目,挑出信号词(the fall 2001)与关键词(NBC TV)

定位:从找到上一题答案的地方接着往下看,根据关键词迅速定位浏览"Space Accommodations"小节的第二段。

寻读：通过 scanning 技巧，找到文中相关句"Each week，one of the participants would be eliminated from the show，with the winner receiving a trip to the Mir space station."

判断：不难发现，题目中所缺的信息为"a trip to the Mir space station"。

7. 快速阅读语篇中含有少量超纲词，如 2006 年 12 月六级真题中的 suborbital，这种面孔陌生的词看上去深奥，但跳过去不读完全不影响做题，考生在考场上没必要为此恐慌。

二、训练方案优化

要做好快速阅读题，你必须：

1. 熟练掌握略读、寻读技巧——这点不难，只要仔细研读上面提供的解题技巧，再通过本书 8 套模拟题的训练，即可做到。

2. 积累 5,500 左右被动词汇量——这点挺难，短期内强化记忆大量生词是一件极具挑战的事，你需具备恒心、耐力、信心，并进行记忆术方面的训练，机械记忆与泛读识词并重。

第三章　听力理解
(Listening Comprehension)

改革后的六级考试听力比重明显加大,考生需在35分钟内完成四种不同题型的听力理解。

短 对 话：多项选择题,共8道,男女间一个来回的简短对话,对话后一个问句,类似改革前六级考试中的 short conversations,内容涉及衣食住行等一般日常交际活动。

长 对 话：多项选择题,两个长对话,各有6—9个对话来回,每个长对话后分别有3—4道选择题,类似以前的托福题。

短文理解：三段短文,共10道多选题,内容涉及教育、科普、文化、环保等多方面。

复合听写：同一语篇听三遍,填入7个缺失的单词与3个句子(不必与原文一模一样,但应符合原意)。

一、应试技巧点津

听力理解需要扎实的词汇、阅读、听力方面的基本功,此外临场反应因素与应试技巧也十分重要。

1. 放松镇定:即使前一晚上紧张失眠也不要紧,早上一杯浓咖啡足以帮你撑到考试结束。
2. 听前预测:拿到试卷马上阅读多选题选项,根据选项预测听力内容,重点关注相关性较大的选项。根据选项作听前预测,这一技巧,尤其适用于短对话。

二、复习方案优化

单词记忆可经三个月的短期强化完成,而听力技能则是冰冻三尺,非一日之寒,起点较低的考生至少需要五六个月的稳定训练方见成效。在训练中应注意以下几点:

1. 积累3,000左右的听力词汇量。听见一个单词或词组马上就能理解其意思,这就是你的听力词汇。听力词汇包括语音、语义方面的熟练掌握。
2. 首先精听。精听材料可以是精读课文磁带,也可以是历年六级真题听力材料。不要看听力文稿,应该逐字逐句作听写练习。完成1—2盘磁带的精听量,便可达到三大效果:

    纠正错误发音,熟悉外国人的发音特点;

    听力词汇量扎实增长;

    为复合式听写打下基础。

3. 然后泛听。推荐大家将《英语流行话题阅读——语境识词5500(MP3有声读物)》作为泛听材料,合上书,每天坚持听20分钟左右,听懂文章大意即可。坚持三个月,在增长文化背景知识的同时,你对较长语篇的听解能力也会大为提高。

三、复合式听写评分标准（共 10 分）

1. 复合式听写要求考生在听懂短文的基础上，用听到的原文填写空缺的单词，以及用听到的原文或用自己的语言正确地补全所缺信息。

2. 给分标准：

36 题至 43 题每题为 0.5 分。拼写完全正确的单词给 0.5 分，凡有错一律不给分，大小写错误忽略不计；44 题至 46 题每题满分为 2 分，答出内容且语言正确各得 1 分；完全没有答对问题得 0 分。

3. 扣分标准：

44 题至 46 题中凡有语言错误扣 0.5 分，每题语言错误扣分不超过 0.5 分，凡不得分部分如有语言错误不再重复扣分；44 题至 46 题中凡有与题目无关的信息扣 0.5 分；44 题至 46 题中如出现明显属于笔误造成的但不改变原意的拼写错误和大小写、标点符号错误，不扣分。

第四章 仔细阅读
（Reading in Depth）

第一节 简要回答问题

　　简要回答问题（Short Answer Questions）要求考生在15分钟内阅读一篇350—400词左右的短文，完成5个由不完整句子构成的或wh-疑问词提问的简要问答句。

题型特征： 5道简要问答题主要分为细节题、句意推论题与归纳题。其中以不完整句子为主，一般只需填入1—5个所缺词，难点在于所缺词不一定能从原文中直接找到，需要考生归纳推论。

测试重点： 考查考生对语篇的灵活理解以及语言精练表达能力。

一、应试技巧点津

1. 注意做题的顺序：5个问题的出题顺序与原文信息顺序基本一致。看完一道题目应立即去找相关依据，然后再看下一道题。
2. 根据细节题、句意推论题、归纳题等不同题型采取不同的做题策略。

2006/12 真题示例

[问题] Many people whose possessions were destroyed in natural disasters eventually considered their loss _____.

[原文] I've heard from and talked to many people who described how Mother Nature simplified their lives for them. They'd lost their home and many or all of their possessions through fires, floods, earthquakes, or some other disasters. Losing everything you own under such circumstances can be distressing, but the people I've heard from all <u>saw their loss, ultimately, as a blessing</u>.

[答案详解] as a blessing 本题为细节题，考查查找并阐明具体事实或细节的能力，答案一般在原文中可直接选出。参见上段原文最后一句：在这些情况下（自然灾难），失去所拥有的一切固然令人沮丧，但据我了解，那些人最终都将他们的损失看做是一种福分（as a blessing）。

2006/12 真题示例

[问题] What do we know about the author's house from the sentence "Gibbs and I did have a close call ..."(Lines 1-2, Para.4)?

[原文] Though we've never had a catastrophic loss such as that, Gibbs and I did <u>have a close</u> call shortly before we decided to simplify. At that time we lived in a fire zone. One night a firestorm raged through and destroyed over six hundred homes in our community. That tragedy gave us the opportunity to look objectively at the goods we'd accumulated.

[答案详解] It narrowly escaped the firestorm. 本题为句意推论题。"Gibbs and I did have a close call shortly before we decided to simplify." 一句意为："还没等我和吉波斯决定简化我们的生活，我们就经历了一场死里逃生的劫难。""have a close call"指"侥

幸逃脱。"下文提到,夫妇二人所在的居民区曾遭遇过一次火灾,六百多户人家的房屋财产被毁。那次悲剧使他们得以客观地看待自己囤积多年的那些财物,于是决定进行简化,抛弃一些无用之物。由此可推知该夫妇二人的房屋在那次火灾中幸免于难。

二、复习方案优化

1. 平时多读"闲书",中英文皆可,开卷有益,拓展知识面。
2. 可将精读课文后的阅读理解题作为操练材料,训练书面语的精练表达能力。

三、简答题评分标准(共5分)

1. 简答题要求学生在读懂文章的基础上,用正确简洁的语言回答问题。在评分的同时考虑内容和语言。每题满分为1分。
2. 给分标准:
   1分 — 答对问题,语言正确
   0.5分 — 答出部分内容,语言正确
   0分 — 没有答对问题
3. 扣分标准:
   (1) 语言错误扣0.5分,每题语言错误扣分不超过0.5分(如出现明显属于笔误造成的拼写错误和大小写、标点符号错误,不扣分);
   (2) 涉及无关内容的部分扣0.5分;若答案中有相互矛盾的内容,内容相互矛盾的部分皆不得分;
   (3) 照搬原句或原句中的大部分文字,语言不简洁,扣0.5分。

第二节　选择题型篇章阅读理解

> 　　多项选择题型的阅读理解是改革前的六级考试的"重量级"题型，但在改革后的六级中分量减半。
>
> **题　　量：**两篇阅读文章，共 10 道多项选择题。
>
> **考查重点：**考查学生对语篇主旨、长句理解、作者态度、字里行间之意的深度理解。

一、应试技巧点津

1. 对于基础不错、阅读速度较快的同学，可以先浏览原文再看题目，根据题目到原文中查找所需信息。

2. 对于基础不理想、阅读速度较慢的同学，应该边看题目边阅读文章。因为题目排列顺序与原文内容布局的次序基本吻合，考生可根据题目题干到原文中寻找信息。注意只需阅读题目题干部分，不必读四个选项，快速找出题干中的信号词或关键词。然后从头阅读原文，一遇到该信号词或关键词时，马上停下来仔细研读相关句，答案一般就是对那句话的同义转述或句意归纳、推论。

二、复习方案优化

1. 每日背单词，不必背出每个单词的拼写与用法，但要大致掌握词汇的核心意义与搭配意义。对自己进行量化管理，每日背 50 个左右。不要怕遗忘，遗忘是记忆的必经之路，这很正常；要有"记归记、忘归忘"的精神，贵在坚持。

2. 扩大阅读量，提高对词汇语境意义的灵活认知能力。通过词典机械记忆的单词，如果能在阅读中及时遭遇，便能巩固并加强记忆。

3. 加强精读，提高对长句、难句的理解能力。阅读理解考试中很多细节题考查的就是你的长句解读能力。

第五章　改错与完型填空
（Error Correction & Cloze）

> 　　短文改错（Error Correction）是改革前的六级考试中的经典题型，改革后的六级考试继续沿用，与完型填空一起用做二选一题型。
> **改错题考查重点**：考查考生对词性变化错误、句型结构错误、搭配错误、逻辑表达错误的辨识、借证能力。
> **完型填空考查重点**：测试考生对篇章的理解能力、使用词汇和语法结构的能力。（完型填空在四级考试中更为常见，详细介绍参见《大学英语四级 710 分预测卷》）

一、应试技巧点津

　　六级短文改错的语篇内容有一定理解难度，句子较长，结构也较为复杂，但错误都是典型的语法错误。历年真题规律性很强，有较强的可培训性。通过针对性训练，考生一般可答对 8 道题左右。

　　10 道题的错误类型主要分为：词法错误（2 — 3 题）；句法错误（5 — 6 题）；逻辑表达错误（1 — 2题）。历年六级真题错误类型如下：

1. 名词单复数混淆

　　［2003/12 真题］...There is no guarantee that plant breeders can continue to develop new, higher-yielding crop, but most researchers see...

　　［解析］crop → crops

2. 词性误用，尤其是同源的形容词与副词混淆

　　［2003/12 真题］Except for relative isolated trouble spots like present-day Somalia, and...

　　［解析］relative → relatively，过去分词 isolated 应由副词修饰。

　　［2006/12 真题］Now what started in schools across the country is playing itself on a nation stage and...

　　［解析］nation → national，名词 stage 应由形容词修饰。

　　［2001/6 真题］...population growth kept the number of clinical cases more or less constantly at 8 million a year.

　　［解析］constantly → constant

3. 代词指代错误

　　［2003/12 真题］The fast-growing population's demand for food, they warned, would soon exceed their supply...

　　［解析］their → its，its 指代单数名词 population's。

4. 冠词遗漏或冗余

　　［2001/6 真题］With occasional breaks for war, the rates of death and infection in the Europe and America dropped steadily...

　　［解析］in the Europe → in Europe

5. 介词搭配错误

　　［2006/12 真题］According to the survey, "reading is on the decline on every region, within every ethnic group，and at every educational level.

［解析］on every region → in every region

6. 序数词与基数词混淆

［2001/6 真题］. . . perhaps <u>one in every seventh deaths</u> in Europe's crowded cities. . .

［解析］seventh → seven

7. 动词固定搭配错误

［2002/1 真题］To understand how this transformation has taken place we must <u>briefly look up at</u> our ancient ancestors.

［解析］look up at → look at

8. 时态错误

［2003/12 真题］. . . more fertilizer and advanced growing practices <u>have more than double</u> corn and wheat yields in an experiment.

［解析］double → doubled，现在完成时构成为"have＋过去分词"。

［2006/12 真题］Our culture's decline in reading <u>begin well before</u> the existence of the Patriot Act.

［解析］begin → began，根据上下文应用一般过去时。

9. 主谓不一致

［2003/6 真题］<u>A diversity committee</u> composed of reporters，editors，and photographers <u>meets</u> regularly to value the Seattle Times' content. . .

［解析］meets → meet，该句强调集合名词 committee 中的个体，为复数概念，其后谓语也相应用复数形式。

10. 并列结构错误

［2006/12 真题］At the heart of the NEA survey is the belief in our democratic system depends on the leaders who can <u>think critically，analyze texts and writing</u> clearly.

［解析］writing → write，think、analyze、write 为三个并列谓语动词，均置于情态动词 can 之后，用动词原形。并列谓语动词形式错误。

11. 比较结构错误

注意观察形容词比较级形式、比较连词 than、as. . .as. . .，比较对象是否一致。

［2003/12 真题］Elsewhere，rice experts in the Philippines are producing a plant with <u>few stems and more seeds</u>. . .

［解析］few → fewer

12. 关系词或连词误用

［2002/6 真题］There are backward towns on the edge of Bombay or Brasilia，<u>just as though</u> there were on the edge of seventeenth-century London or early nineteenth-century Paris. <u>This</u> is new is the scale.

［解析］just as though→just as，just as 表示"正如"。

　　　　This → What，what 引导主语从句。

13. 非谓语动词形式错误，主要是现在分词与过去分词混淆

［2002/1 真题］<u>Viewing</u> biologically，the modern footballer is revealed as a member of a disguised hunting pack.

［解析］Viewing → Viewed. viewed 与逻辑主语 the modern footballer 含逻辑被动关系。

14. 逻辑表达错误

主要是由于错误使用了某形容词的反义词导致上下文语义相悖，考生须特别留意带前缀的形容词。

［2002/1 真题］If his aim is <u>inaccurate and he scores a goal</u>，he enjoys the hunter's triumph

of killing his prey.

［解析］inaccurate → accurate

［2003/6 真题］The underlying reason for the change is that for information to be <u>fair, appropriate, and subjective</u>, it should be reported by the same kind of population that reads it.

［解析］subjective → objective

二、复习方案优化

短文改错是集语篇阅读能力、词汇与语法知识为一体的综合测试题型。

1. 扩大阅读量，提高语篇理解能力与知识面。

2. 继续关注历年短文改错真题。

3. 巩固基本语法结构知识。

第六章 汉 译 英

(Translation)

改革后的六级翻译考题中,给出 5 个不完整的句子,要求考生在 5 分钟内根据所给汉语完成句子。

考查重点:词汇搭配用法;重点句型结构的应用。

一、应试技巧点津

汉译英测试学生的词汇、结构知识的活用能力,考的是词汇深度知识与语言应用基本功,其实并无太多应试技巧可言。

1. 首先要判断题目所用句型,准确套用。

2. 考场上要尽量仔细检查自己的拼写、时态、搭配,尽量不要犯低级语法错误。

2006/12 真题示例

〔题目〕72. If you had _____(听从了我的忠告,你就不会陷入麻烦).

〔解析〕本句考查虚拟结构用法:followed my advice, you would not have got into trouble.

二、翻译题评分标准(共 5 分)

1. 整体内容和语言均正确,得 1 分。

2. 结构正确,但整体意思不确切、信息不全或用词不当,得 0.5 分。

3. 整体意思正确但语言有错误,得 0.5 分。

4. 整体意思完全错误,即使结构正确也不得分。

5. 大小写错误及标点符号忽略不计。

三、复习方案优化

1. 掌握常用词的固定搭配与用法,不要只满足于了解词义。

2. 要积累至少 2,500 左右的复用性质词汇。写作中遇到不会写的词可以绕过,但翻译无路可退。

3. 积累常用句型结构,包括虚拟句、倒装句、状语从句、比较句、定语从句、同位语从句、被动句等等,其具体内容可参见第一章"写作"的翻译练习部分。

下 篇
实战演练 & 步步为"赢"

Test 1

Part Ⅰ Writing (30 minutes)

Directions: *For this part, you are allowed 30 minutes to write a short essay commenting on the value of beauty. You should write at least 150 words following the outline given below in Chinese.*

Is Beauty an Advantage?

1. 近年来不少大四学生就业前突击整容
2. 当今社会崇尚外表的舆论导向是导致上述现象的主要因素
3. 我对外表美的看法

Part Ⅱ Reading Comprehension (Skimming and Scanning) (15 minutes)

Directions: *In this part, you will have 15 minutes to go over the passage quickly and answer the questions on **Answer Sheet 1**. For questions 1 – 7, choose the best answer from the four choices marked A), B), C) and D). For questions 8 – 10 complete the sentences with the information given in the passage.*

The Science of Interruptions

In 2000, Gloria Mark was hired as a professor at the University of California. She would arrive at her desk in the morning, full of energy and ready to tackle her to-do list. No sooner had she started one task than a colleague would e-mail her with an urgent request; when she went to work on that, the phone would ring. At the end of the day, Mark had accomplished a fraction of what she set out to do.

Lots of people complain that office multitasking drives them nuts. But Mark studies how high-tech devices affect our behavior, so she was able to do more than complain: She set out to measure how nuts we've all become. She watched cubicle (办公室隔间) dwellers as they surfed the chaos of modern office life and found each employee spent only ten-and-a-half minutes on any given project before being interrupted. Each short project was itself fragmented into three-minute tasks, like answering e-mail messages or working on a sheet.

Mark's study also revealed that interruptions are often crucial to office work. The high-tech workers admitted that many of their daily distractions were essential to their jobs. When someone forwards you an urgent e-mail message, it's often something you really do need to see; if a mobile phone call breaks through, it might be the call that saves your hide.

For some computer engineers and academics, this realization has begun to raise an attractive possibility: Perhaps we can find an ideal middle ground. If high-tech work distractions are inevitable, maybe we can re-engineer them so we receive all of their benefits but few of their downsides.

The Birth of Multitasking

The science of interruptions began more than 100 years ago with the emergence of telegraph operators — the first high-stress, time-sensitive information-technology jobs. Psychologists discovered that if someone spoke to a telegraph operator while he was keying a message, the operator was

more likely to make errors. Later, psychologists determined that whenever workers needed to focus on a job that required the monitoring of data, presentation was all important. Using this knowledge, cockpits (驾驶舱) for fighter pilots were carefully designed so that each dial and meter could be read with just a glance.

Still, such issues seemed remote from the lives of everyday workers. Then, in the 1990s, computers began to experience a rapid increase in speed and power. "Multitasking" was born; instead of simply working on one program for hours at a time, a computer user works on several simultaneously. Office workers now stare at computer screens of overwhelming complexity, as they juggle (操纵) messages, text documents, PowerPoint presentations and web browsers. In the modern office we are all fighter pilots.

Effect of Multitasking: Computer-affected Behavior

Information is no longer a scarce resource — attention is. 20 years ago, an office worker had two types of communication technology: a phone, which required an instant answer, and postal mail, which took days. Now people have dozens of possibilities between these two poles.

The result is something like "continuous partial attention", which makes us so busy keeping an eye on everything that we never fully focus on anything. This can actually be a positive feeling, inasmuch as the constant email dinging makes us feel needed and desired. But what happens when you take that to the extreme? You get overwhelmed. Sanity lies in danger.

In 1997, Microsoft recruited Mary Czerwinski, who once worked in NASA's Human-computer Interaction Lab, to conduct basic research to find out how computers affect human behavior. She took 39 office workers and installed software on their computers that would record every mouse click. She discovered that computer users were as restless as hummingbirds. On average, they juggled eight windows at the same time. More astonishing, they would spend barely 20 seconds looking at one window before flipping to another.

Why constant shifting? In part it was because of the way computers are laid out. A computer offers very little visual real estate. A Microsoft Word document can cover almost an entire screen. Once you begin multitasking, a computer desktop quickly becomes buried in windows. When someone is interrupted, it takes just over 23 minutes to cycle back to the original task. Once their work becomes buried beneath a screenful of interruptions, office workers appear to forget what tasks they were originally pursuing. The central danger of interruptions is not the interruption at all, but the confusion they bring to our short-term memory.

Ways to Cope with Interruptions

When Mark and Czerwinski, working separately, looked at the desks of the people they were studying, they each noticed the same thing: Post-it notes. Workers would write brief reminders of the task they were supposed to be working on ("Test DA's PC, Waiting for AL..."). Then they would place them directly in their fields of vision, often in a circle around the edge of their computer screens.

These piecemeal efforts at coping pointed to ways that our high-tech tools could be engineered to be less distracting. Czerwinski also noticed many Microsoft people attached three monitors to their computers. They placed their applications on different screens — the email on the right side, a web browser on the right and their main work project in the middle — so that each application was read at a glance. When the ding on their email program went off, they just peek to the left to see the message.

The workers said this arrangement made them feel calmer. But did more screen area

actually help with cognition? To find out, Czerwinski had 15 volunteers sit in front of a regular size 38 cm monitor and complete a variety of tasks designed to challenge their concentration — a web search, some cutting and pasting, and memorizing phone numbers. Then the volunteers repeated the tasks using a computer with a massive 105 cm screen.

On the bigger screen, some people completed the tasks as much as 44% more quickly. In two decades of research, Czerwinski had never seen a single change to a computer system so significantly improve a user's productivity. The clearer your screen, the calmer your mind.

Looking for Better Interruptions

Mark compared the way people work when sitting in cubicles with how they work when they're at different locations and interact online. She discovered people working in cubicles suffer more interruptions, but they have better interruptions because their co-workers have a social sense of what they're doing. When you work next to others, they sense whether you're deeply immersed or relatively free to talk and interrupt you accordingly.

Why don't computers work this way? Instead of alerting us to email messages the instant they arrive, our machines could deliver them at optimum moments, when our brains are relaxed. Eric Horvitz at Microsoft is trying to do precisely that. He has been building automated reasoning systems equipped with artificial intelligence that observes a computer user's behavior and tries to predict the moment the user will be mentally free and ready to be interrupted.

(1,161 words)

1. As Mark's study indicated, many work distractions are _____.
   A) essential to high-tech jobs
   B) undesirable interruptions that should be avoided
   C) caused by urgent email messages
   D) damaging to office work efficiency
2. The birth of multitasking for ordinary workers could be traced to _____.
   A) the emergence of telegraph operators
   B) the job of fighter pilots
   C) the invention of first-generation computers
   D) the advances in computer power during the 1990s
3. Ordinary modern office workers are just like fighter pilots in that _____.
   A) both need to operate computers skillfully
   B) both have to monitor data of great complexity
   C) both have to read dials and meters with just a glance
   D) both have to juggle several programs simultaneously
4. What may happen to you if multitasking in your job goes to extreme?
   A) You get overwhelmed and might possibly go nuts.
   B) You can only pay partial attention to everything and so fail to do everything well.
   C) You get a positive feeling from being needed and desired.
   D) You become absent-minded.
5. According to Mary Czerwinski's research, computer users are constantly shifting from window to window, pausing _____ at each one.
   A) barely 20 seconds
   B) just over 23 minutes
   C) only ten and a half minutes

D) just a couple of seconds

6. Both Mark and Czerwinski noticed that some computer users relied on _____ to help them cope with distractions.
   A) enlarged screens for a clearer view
   B) Post-it notes as task reminders
   C) multiple monitors for multiple tasks
   D) user-friendly programs

7. Czerwinski found that by putting different applications on different screens, many Microsoft workers managed to _____.
   A) operate on a much more stable computer system
   B) make the best use of computer screens
   C) make their high-tech tools less distracting
   D) check their private male while doing their main work project

8. Czerwinski found that no other change to a computer system could more significantly improve a user's productivity than _____.

9. People who work next to each other in the same office have more but better interruptions than those who _____.

10. Eric Horvitz has been working on AI system that monitors a computer user's behavior and predicts _____.

Part Ⅲ Listening Comprehension (35 minutes)

Section A

Directions: In this section, you will hear 8 short conversations and 2 long conversations. At the end of each conversation, one or more questions will be asked about what was said. Both the conversation and questions will be spoken only once. After each question there will be a pause. During the pause you must read the four choices marked A), B), C) and D), and decide which is the best answer. Then mark the corresponding letter on **Answer Sheet 2** with a single line through the center.

11. A) The woman is being interviewed by a reporter.
    B) The woman is asking for a promotion.
    C) The woman is receiving an oral test.
    D) The woman is applying for a job.

12. A) He was struck by a tennis ball and got hurt in the head.
    B) His car was hit by another car.
    C) He had an accident on his way to hospital.
    D) While crossing the street, he was knocked down by a speeding car.

13. A) No medicine could solve the woman's problem.
    B) The woman was advised to choose the right foods.
    C) The woman should eat well-balanced meals to lose weight.
    D) Nothing could help the woman unless she went on diet.

14. A) She wants to have the blue sweater refunded.
    B) She wants to buy another sweater for her husband.
    C) She wants to change the sweater for a smaller one.
    D) She wants to have the blue sweater altered.

15. A) Women's liberty.
    C) Career planning for women.
    B) An important election.
    D) Women's rights in society.
16. A) To work in the flower beds.
    C) To work as a gardener.
    B) To clean the yard.
    D) To weed the garden.
17. A) To give each other a pleasant surprise.
    C) To avoid the crowds.
    B) To join the crowds.
    D) To get grocery bargains.
18. A) Classical music.
    C) Pop music.
    B) Folk music.
    D) All kinds of music.

Questions 19 to 22 are based on the conversation you have just heard.
19. A) About how to fill in the university application forms.
    B) About how to prepare for TOEFL.
    C) About the requirements for post-graduate programs.
    D) About tuition in Canadian universities.
20. A) GMAT and TOEFL.
    C) GMAT and IELTS.
    B) GRE and TOEFL or IELTS.
    D) GRE and GMAT.
21. A) In July or August.
    C) In October or November.
    B) In September or October.
    D) In November or December.
22. A) International students.
    B) Wealthy students.
    C) Mechanical engineering students.
    D) The top 5 students entering the program.

Questions 23 to 25 are based on the conversation you have just heard.
23. A) In fuel consumption.
    C) In taxi fares.
    B) In monthly payment.
    D) In tow truck fees.
24. A) She already has a used car.
    B) She loves her dear old car.
    C) She doesn't trust used-car dealers.
    D) She thinks used cars cost too much in maintenance.
25. A) They are sold when they are relatively new.
    B) They might not be well-maintained.
    C) They are cheaper than privately owned cars.
    D) They have as much wear and tear on them as on privately owned cars.

Section B
Directions: *In this section, you will hear 3 short passages. At the end of each passage, you will hear some questions. Both the passage and questions will be spoken only once. After you hear a question, you must choose the best answer from the four choices marked A), B), C) and D). Then mark the corresponding letter on* **Answer Sheet 2** *with a single line through the center.*

Passage One
Questions 26 to 29 are based on the passage you have just heard.
26. A) Because it symbolizes virginity.
    C) Because it signifies joy.
    B) Because it represents hope.
    D) Because it looks pure and beautiful.
27. A) Changes of social status.
    B) Funerals and weddings.

C) The occasion of Easter Sunday.　　　D) Flames of passion in new couples.

28. A) Because many Victorian brides believed in the myth of virginity.

　　B) Because white wedding dress were very expensive.

　　C) Because rich Victorian brides wore white wedding dress as a display of wealth.

　　D) Because white dress was associated with special occasions.

29. A) History of wedding dress.　　　　B) Appeal of white dress.

　　C) Origin of white wedding dress.　　D) The symbolic meaning of wedding dress.

Passage Two

Questions 30 to 32 are based on the passage you have just heard.

30. A) Because work can relieve most people of boredom.

　　B) Because work brings money and makes holidays affordable.

　　C) Because work brings us profound delights.

　　D) Because some work are very interesting.

31. A) Because they find some work exceedingly dull.

　　B) Because they find work less painful than idleness.

　　C) Because they have too much leisure and don't know how to kill time.

　　D) Because they have to work as hard as if they were poor.

32. A) Idleness is more painful than dull work.

　　B) The rich suffer more than the working people.

　　C) Work is desirable to everybody.

　　D) One must find some interesting work to do.

Passage Three

Questions 33 to 35 are based on the passage you have just heard.

33. A) He suggests charging a heavier fee for dog ownership.

　　B) He strongly objects to raising large, fierce dogs.

　　C) He objects to raising dogs as pets in cities.

　　D) He demands the dog owners to take better control of their dogs.

34. A) They are vain, selfish people.

　　B) They seem to have psychological trouble.

　　C) They are shy and cowardly.

　　D) They are inconsiderate about other people's needs.

35. A) City governments.　　　　　　　B) Lawmakers.

　　C) The citizens of the city.　　　　D) Dog owners.

Section C

Directions: *In this section, you will hear a passage three times. When the passage is read for the first time, you should listen carefully for its general idea. When the passage is read for the second time, you are required to fill in the blanks numbered from 36 to 43 with the exact words you have just heard. For blanks numbered from 44 to 46 you are required to fill in the missing information. For these blanks, you can either use the exact words you have just heard or write down the main points in your own words. Finally, when the passage is read for the third time, you should check what you have written.*

Perhaps only a little boy being trained to be a wizard at the Hogwards school magic could cast a spell so powerful as to create the biggest book launch ever. Wherever in the world the clock strikes midnight on June 20th, his followers will (36) _____ to get their paws on one copy of *Harry Potter and the Order of the Phoenix*. Bookshops will open in the middle of the night and (37) _____ firms are drafting in extra staff and bigger trucks. Related toys, games, DVDs and other merchandise will be everywhere. There will be no (38) _____ Potter-mania.

While an (39) _____ media is helping hype (宣传) the launch of Rowling's the fifth novel, about the most (40) _____ thing that publishers have organized is a reading by Ms. Rowling in London's Royal Albert Hall, to be broadcast as a live web cast. (41) _____ as it may seem, the guardians of the brand say that, to protect the Potter franchise (特权), they are trying to maintain a low (42) _____. Well, relatively low.

Ms. Rowling signed a contract in 1998 with Warner Brothers, giving the studio (43) _____ __ film, licensing, merchandising rights in return for what now appears to have been a steal: some $500,000. Warner (44) _____. Now she is wealthier than a queen — if you believe Britain's Sunday Times rich list. The process is self-generating: (45) _____ _____. Globally, the first four Harry Potter books have sold 200 million copies in 55 languages; the two movies have made over $1.8 billion at the box office. This is (46) _____ _____. In line with her wishes, Warner says it is being very careful about what it licenses and to whom.

Part IV　Reading Comprehension (Reading in Depth) (25 minutes)

Section A

Directions: *In this section, there is a short passage with 5 questions or incomplete statements. Read the passage carefully. Then answer the questions or complete the statements in the fewest possible words. Please write your answers on **Answer Sheet 2**.*

It is all very well to blame traffic jams, the cost of petrol and the quick pace of modern life, but manners on the roads are becoming terrible. Everybody knows that the nicest persons become monsters behind the wheel. It is all very well, again, to have a tiger in the tank, but to have one in the driver's seat is another matter altogether. You might tolerate the odd road monster, the rude and inconsiderate driver, but nowadays the well-mannered motorist is the exception to the rule. Perhaps the situation calls for a "Be Kind to Other Drivers" campaign, otherwise it may get completely out of hand.

Road politeness is not only good manners, but good sense too. It takes the most cool-headed and good-tempered of drivers to resist the temptation to revenge when subjected to uncivilized behavior. On the other hand, a little politeness goes a long way towards relieving the tensions of motoring. A friendly nod or a wave of acknowledgment in response to an act of politeness helps to create an atmosphere of goodwill and tolerance, which is so necessary in modern traffic conditions. But such acknowledgements of politeness are all too rare today. Many drivers don't even seem able to recognize politeness when they see it.

However, misplaced politeness can also be dangerous. Typical examples are the drivers who brakes violently to allow a car to emerge from a side street at some hazard to following traffic, when a few seconds later the road would be clear anyway; or the man who waves a child across a zebra crossing into the path of oncoming vehicles that may be unable to stop in time. The same goes for encouraging old ladies to cross the road whenever and wherever they care to. It always amazes me that the highways are not covered with the dead bodies of these grannies.

A veteran driver, whose manners are faultless, told me it would help if motorists learnt to filter correctly into traffic streams one at a time without causing the total blockage that give rise to bad temper. Unfortunately, modern motorists can't even learn to drive, let alone master the subtler aspects of boatmanship. Years ago the experts warned us that the car-ownership explosion would demand a lot more take-and-give on the part of all road users. It is high time for all of us to take this message to heart.

(400 words)

47. According to the passage, troubles on the road are primarily caused by _____.
48. What does the sentence "but the well-mannered motorist is the exception to the rule" imply?
   _____
49. Road politeness not only refers to the driver's civilized manners, but also means the driver's ability to _____ other drivers' behavior.
50. Encouraging old ladies to cross the street whenever and wherever they want to is a typical example of _____.
51. Experts have pointed out that in the face of car-ownership explosion, drivers should be ready to _____.

Section B
Directions: *There are 2 passages in this section. Each passage is followed by some questions or unfinished statements. For each of them there are four choices marked A), B), C) and D). You should decide on the best choice and mark the corresponding letter on **Answer Sheet 2** with a single line through the center.*

Passage One
Questions 52 to 56 are based on the following passage.

Pronouncing a language is a skill. Every person is expert in the skill of pronouncing his own language; but few are even moderately proficient at pronouncing foreign languages. The fundamental reason why people do not speak foreign languages very well is that they fail to grasp the true nature of the problem of learning to pronounce, and consequently never set about tackling it in the right way. Many people just fail to realize pronouncing a foreign language is a skill — one that needs careful training and one that can't be acquired by just leaving it to take care of itself. Even teachers tend to neglect the branch of study concerned with speaking the language. So the first point to make here is that English pronunciation must be taught; the teacher must be prepared to devote some lessen time to this. And by his whole attitude to the subject the teacher should get students to feel that here is a matter worthy of receiving close attention. So there should be occasions when other aspects of English such as grammar or spelling are allowed for the moment to take second place.

Apart from the time given to pronunciation, there are two more requirements for the teacher: knowledge and technique.

The teacher should be in possession of the necessary information. It is possible to get from books some idea of speech mechanics, to get a clear mental picture of the relationship between the sounds of different languages, between the speech habits of English people and those of the students. Unless the teacher has such a picture, any comments he may make on his students' pronunciation are unlikely to be of much use, and lesson time spent on pronunciation may well be wasted.

But it does not follow that the teacher can teach pronunciation successfully as soon as he has read the necessary books. It depends after that what he makes of his knowledge; and this is a matter of technique. Now the first and most important part of a language teacher's technique is his own performance, his ability to demonstrate the spoken language, in every detail of articulation as well as in fluent speaking, so that the students' latent capacity for imitation is given the fullest scope and encouragement. The teacher, then, should be as perfect a model in this respect as he can make himself. And to supplement his own performance, however satisfactory this may be, the modern teacher has at his disposal recordings and radio, to supply the authentic voices of native speakers.

(422 words)

52. What does the author actually say about pronouncing foreign languages?
  A) There are not many people who are even fairly good.
  B) Nobody is really an expert in the skill.
  C) There are even some people who are moderately proficient.
  D) Only a few people are really proficient.
53. The author argues that dealing with the problem of pronunciation in the wrong way is ____.
  A) a fundamental consequence of not speaking well
  B) a consequence of not understanding the problem correctly
  C) an obvious cause of not grasping the problem correctly
  D) not an obvious cause of speaking poorly
54. The value the student puts on correct speech habits depends on _____.
  A) how closely he attends to the matter
  B) whether it is English that is being taught
  C) his teacher's approach to pronunciation
  D) the importance normally given to grammar and spelling
55. How might the teacher find himself wasting lesson time?
  A) By spending lesson time on pronunciation.
  B) By not using books on speech mechanics on pronunciation.
  C) By not giving students a clear mental picture of the difference between sounds.
  D) By making ill-informed comments upon students' pronunciation.
56. What is the main point the author makes about the cultivation of the students' imitation capacity?
  A) It depends on the students' own effort.
  B) It relies on the teacher's technique to present speech models.
  C) The teacher himself must be a perfect speech model.
  D) The teacher must treat it as a matter of primary importance.

Passage Two
Questions 57 to 61 are based on the following passage.
Most growing plants contain much more water than all other materials combined. C. R. Darnes has suggested that it is as proper to term the plant a water structure as to call a house composed mainly of bricks as a brick building. It is certain that all the essential processes of plant growth and development occur in water. The mineral elements from the soil that are usable by the plant must be dissolved in the soil solution before they can be taken into the root. They are carried to all parts of the growing plant and are built into essential plant materials while in a dissolved state. The carbon dioxide (CO_2) from the air may enter the leaf as a gas but

is dissolved in the leaf before it is combined with a part of the water to form simple sugars — the base material from which the plant body is mainly built. Actively growing plant parts are generally 75 to 90 percent water. Structural parts of plants, such as woody stems no longer actively growing, may have much less water than growing tissues.

The actual amount of water in the plant at any one time, is only a very small part of what passes through it during its development. The processes of photosynthesis (光合作用), by which carbon dioxide and water are combined — in the presence of chlorophyll (叶绿素) and with energy derived from light — to form sugars, require that carbon dioxide from the air enter the plant. This occurs mainly in the leaf. The leaf surface is not solid but contains great numbers of minute openings, through which the carbon dioxide enters. The same structure that permits the one gas to enter the leaf, however, permits another gas — water vapor — to be lost from it. Since carbon dioxide is present in the air only in trace quantities (3 to 4 parts in 10,000 parts of air) and water vapor is near saturation in the air spaces within the leaf (at 80F, saturated air would contain about 186 parts of water vapor in 10,000 parts of air), the total amount of water vapor lost is many times the carbon dioxide intake. Actually because of wind and other factors, the loss of water in proportion to carbon dioxide intake may be even greater. Also, not all of the carbon dioxide that enters the leaf is synthesized into carbohydrates.

(398 words)

57. A growing plant needs water for all of the following except _____.
    A. forming sugars
    B. sustaining actively growing parts as well as woody stems
    C. absorbing mineral elements
    D. taking in carbon dioxide from the air

58. The essential function of photosynthesis in terms of plant needs is _____.
    A. to derive energy from light
    B. to preserve water
    C. to combine carbon dioxide with water
    D. to form sugars

59. The second paragraph uses facts to develop the idea that _____.
    A. a plant needs more water than is found in its composition
    B. a plant efficiently utilizes most of the water it absorbs
    C. the stronger the wind, the more water vapor the plant loses.
    D. carbon dioxide is the essential substance needed for plant development

60. According to the passage, which of the following statements is TRUE?
    A. The woody stems contain more water than the leaves.
    B. Only part of the carbon dioxide in the plants is synthesized.
    C. The mineral elements will not be absorbed by the plant unless dissolved in their roots.
    D. Air existing around the leaf is found to be saturated.

61. This passage mainly discusses _____.
    A. the functions of carbon dioxide and water
    B. the role of water in a growing plant
    C. the process of simple sugar formation
    D. the synthesis of water with carbon dioxide

Part Ⅴ Error Correction (15 minutes)

Directions: *This part consists of a short passage. In this passage, there are altogether 10 mistakes, one in each numbered line. You may have to change a word, add a word or delete a word. Mark out the mistakes and put the corrections in the blanks provided. If you change a word, cross it out and write the correct word in the corresponding blank. If you add a word, put an insertion mark (∧) in the right place and write the missing word in the blank. If you delete a word, cross it out and put a slash (/) in the blank.*

After more than 40 years of parallel development, the
information and life sciences — computing and biology — are
fusing into a single, powerful force that is the foundation for
the biotech century. Increasingly, the computer used to decode,   62. _____
manage and organize the vast amounts of genetic information
that will be raw resource of the new global economy.

The biotech century promises great riches: genetically
engineered plants and animal to feed a hungry population; genetically   63. _____
derived sources of energy and fiber to build a renewable society;
wonder drugs and genetic therapies to produce healthier babies,
eliminate suffering and extended human lifespan. But a question will   64. _____
gaunt us: at what cost?

The new genetic commerce raises more troubling issues than
any economic revolution in history. Will the artificial creation of cloned   65. _____
and transgenic animals mean the end of nature and substitution of a   66. _____
bio-industrial world? Will the mass release of thousands of genetically
engineered life forms into the environment cause catastrophic pollution
and reversible damage to the biosphere? What are the consequences of   67. _____
the world's gene pool become patented intellectual property, controlled   68. _____
exclusively by a handful of corporations? What will it mean to live in a
world where babies are genetically engineered in the womb, and that   69. _____
people are increasingly identified and stereotyped on the basis of their
genotype?

The debate is not about the science but about how we apply them.   70. _____
Until now the debate has engaged a very broad group of molecular   71. _____
biologists and government policy-makers, though the biotech
revolution affects us all. With the new technology flooding into our
lives, the moment has come for a much broader debate, one that involves
the whole society.

Part Ⅵ Translation (5 minutes)

Directions: *Complete the sentences by translating into English the Chinese given in brackets. Please write your translation on **Answer Sheet 2**.*

72. The announcement _____ （由于恶劣天气所有航班均已取消） greatly distressed the waiting passengers.

73. I failed the oral test again! _____ （要是我不那么紧张就好了！）

74. Patients with night eating syndrome often wake up multiple times during the night and are
_____（除非吃些东西，否则就无法入睡）.

75. It _____（直到去年）my sister, a chronic sleepwalker, found a doctor who could tell
her what her problem was and how to treat it.

76. It is unfair for those children _____（只能接受较差的教育）simply because they can't
afford to live in the middle-class neighborhoods with better schools.

Test 2

Part Ⅰ　Writing (30 minutes)

Directions: *For this part, you are allowed 30 minutes to write a short essay commenting on the pleasure of learning. You should write at least 150 words following the outline given below in Chinese.*

The Pleasure of Learning

1. 学习是一种乐趣
2. 学习的乐趣普遍存在(存在于书本学习、艺术欣赏、了解世界等多方面的学习之中)
3. 如何走出"学习是痛苦的"误区

Part Ⅱ　Reading Comprehension (Skimming and Scanning) (15 minutes)

Directions: *In this part, you will have 15 minutes to go over the passage quickly and answer the questions on **Answer Sheet 1**. For questions 1–7, choose the best answer from the four choices marked A), B), C) and D). For questions 8–10 complete the sentences with the information given in the passage.*

Flirt With Suicide

The life of David Woods was the stuff of an Australian boy's dream. He played professional rugby league football in a country that treats athletes as idols. At 29, he had a loving family, a girlfriend, a 3-month-old baby, plenty of money, everything to live for. And for inexplicable reasons, nothing to live for. On New Year's Eve, Woods called his mother to announce that he had signed a new contract with his team, Golden Coast, recalls his elder brother, Tony. The next morning, he ran a hose from the exhaust pipe to the window of his Mitsubishi sedan (轿车) and gasses himself. His family still has no idea why.

The death of David Woods came as a wake-up call to Australia, which is often voted as the ideal place to bring up kids. But the sun, the beaches and the sporting culture are the cheery backdrop to a disturbing trend: Young Australian men are now killing themselves at the rate of one a day — triple the rate of 30 years ago. Though most Australians aren't particularly suicidal, their boys are. In 1990 suicide surpassed car accidents as the leading cause of death among males aged 15 to 24. Fun-loving Australia is now far worse off than Asian nations known for strict discipline. The yearly suicide rate for young Australian males is 2.5 times higher than in Japan, Hong Kong, or Singapore.

Possible Causes for Suicide

Why boys? A nation of wide-open spaces and rugged individualism, Australia still idolizes the film star Gary Cooper model of masculinity: the strong, silent type who never complains, who always gets the job done. In recent years schools and social institutions have concentrated on creating new opportunities for equality for girls — while leaving troubled boys with the classic command of the Australian father: pull yourself together. It's past time to take a much closer look at the lives of young men, some researchers argue. "People think, 'My kids aren't doing drugs, my kids are safe at home'," says psychiatrist John Tiller of Melbourne University, who

studied 148 suicides and 206 attempts in the state of Victoria. "They are wrong."

The Haywards, a comfortably well-off family in Wyong, north of Sydney, figured they were dealing with the normal problems of troubled teenhood. Their son Mark had put up a poster of rock star Kurt Cobain, a 1994 suicide victim, along with a Cobain quote: "I hate myself and I want to die." "From the age of 12, Mark had his ups and downs — mood swings, depression and low self-esteem," says his father. The Haywards sent Mark to various counselors, none of whom warned that he had suicidal tendencies. By last year Mark was 19, fighting bouts (回合) of unemployment and a drug problem. He tried church, struggling to do the right thing. Last September he dropped out a detoxification (戒毒) program, and apologized to his parents. "I've let you down again." A few days later, his mother found Mark's body in bush-land near their home.

In retrospect, Mark Hayward's struggles were far from uncommon. The number of suicides tends to keep pace with the unemployment rate, which for Australians between 15 and 19 has risen from 19 percent in 1978, the first year data were collected, to 28 percent last year. Suicide is especially high among the most marginal: young Aboriginal (土著的) men, isolated by poverty, alcoholism and racism. As in other developed countries, Australian families have grown less cohesive in recent years, putting young men out into the world at an earlier age. Those who kill themselves often think "it'll make it easier for the parents by not being there".

The deeper mystery is why the universal anguish of growing up should have such particularly devastating effects in Australia. One answer is that the country allows easier access to guns than most other developed Asian countries. (One exception is neighboring New Zealand, where guns are as easy to find, and the suicide rate among young people is worse.) Australian boys tend to end their lives violently — by shooting or hanging. Girls, by contrast, often take an overdose of drugs, and are more often rescued.

Efforts to Tackle Suicide Problem

Educators now hope to teach adults to recognize youths troubled by suicidal depression. That is no easy task in a society that generally avoids introspection (反省). "Good services do exist in Australia," says child psychiatrist Marie Bashir, but "the Australian philosophy is: pull your socks up. Get out and play some sports."

To get Australia's attention, psychiatrist Tiller wants the government to sponsor a shock advertising campaign, similar to one that portrays the pain and guilt felt by survivors in drunk-driving accidents. The ads should make people aware of the threat, and urge them to get help for young people at risk.

The rising death toll has just begun to force suicide onto the nation's political agenda. Suicide now takes more lives than murder or AIDS. Brendan Nelson, a physician and backbencher in Parliament, recently called for the creation of a National Office for Young People to report to the prime minister on youth concerns. Slowly, Australians are overcoming the old fear of talking openly about a problem that has long been considered taboo. "We have one young person every day ending his life and possibly another four who are not reported as suicides but are killing themselves," says Clyde Begg of the Australian Community Research Organization. "Now, if we don't talk about that, we are neglecting our duties."

Tony Woods is talking now, but he wasn't always. The brother of the football player who gassed himself to death, Woods says he tried to take his own life at the age of 17 by slashing his wrists with a carving knife after breaking up with a girlfriend. Woods has made it his own mission to warn other boys that they may find themselves on the same dangerous path taken by his brother, David. Among other things, he plans to bring professional football players into schools to urge boys to seek counseling for their personal problems. "Boys can't communicate what they feel," says Woods. "They are socialized to be hard, tough, independent men who don't show their feelings. We need to tell them: You're worthwhile. Seek help... We need to teach boys to express themselves. We need to pick them up at 5 years old to prevent a problem in 15 years." It is the kind of simple advice, Tony Woods now believes, that his brother never heard.

(1,086 words)

1. What happened to David Woods on a New Year's Day?
   A) He died in a traffic accident.
   B) He broke up with his girl-friend.
   C) He lost his three-month-old baby.
   D) He killed himself with his car exhaust gases.
2. Recently, what forms a disturbing contrast with the cheery, sporting culture in Australia?
   A) An alarming suicide rate among young men.
   B) A rising unemployment rate in the middle class.
   C) An increasing number of youngsters dying from road accidents.
   D) A serious drug problem among rich kids.
3. Australian schools and social institutions may have contributed to the problem of suicide among boys by _____.
   A) putting too much pressure on the boys while giving girls much easier work to do
   B) focusing on giving girls more opportunities while leaving boys on their own
   C) making boys feel inferior to their female peers
   D) totally ignoring alcoholism and drug addiction among boys
4. Mark Haywards had been sent to hospital, but his counselors failed to warn his parents about his _____.
   A) intense worship for Kurt Cobain
   B) frequent mood swings
   C) suicidal tendencies
   D) very low self-esteem
5. Suicide rate is particularly high among young aboriginal men as they have to struggle against not only poverty but also _____.
   A) unemployment
   B) alcoholism and racism
   C) drug addiction
   D) threats to their personal safety
6. Growing pains are especially destructive in Australia, where _____.
   A) people idolize the strong, silent type of man who never complains
   B) people have unrealistically high expectations for young men
   C) there's an easer access to guns
   D) there's a high rate of divorce
7. Why is it difficult to teach Australian adults to recognize youths troubled by suicidal depression?
   A) Because the entire Australian society tend to avoid thinking about the problem.
   B) Because most Australian adults are uneducated.

C) Because lack of government subsidies hinders a countrywide awareness-raising campaign.

D) Because parents believe their kids are safe at home.

8. To help raise the public's awareness of the suicide problem, psychiatrist Tiller appealed to the government to organize _____.

9. _____ will be one of the political initiatives taken to tackle the suicide problem in Australia.

10. According to Tony Woods, the problem of suicide among young Australian men can be alleviated if boys _____.

Part Ⅲ   Listening Comprehension (35 minutes)

Section A

Directions: *In this section, you will hear 8 short conversations and 2 long conversations. At the end of each conversation, one or more questions will be asked about what was said. Both the conversation and questions will be spoken only once. After each question there will be a pause. During the pause you must read the four choices marked A), B), C) and D), and decide which is the best answer. Then mark the corresponding letter on **Answer Sheet 2** with a single line through the center.*

11. A) In her office.   B) In her handbag.
    C) In her car.   D) At home.

12. A) The husband is not so observant.
    B) The wife is annoyed at her husband's absent-mindedness.
    C) The husband hasn't told the truth.
    D) The husband felt surprised about her wife's new hairstyle.

13. A) She will fly directly to her destination.
    B) She must change at Jacksonville.
    C) She has to stay overnight at Albany.
    D) She will take a two-hour flight to Albany.

14. A) Enthusiastic.   B) Reluctant.
    C) Serious.   D) Cooperative

15. A) It's too windy.   B) The beaches are dirty.
    C) The air is polluted.   D) The people there are terribly rude.

16. A) He has too many dreams.
    B) He is too lazy to get out of bed.
    C) He doesn't have many good ideas.
    D) He doesn't put his ideas in practice.

17. A) The theater was too dark to see clearly.
    B) They went to the street corner at different times.
    C) The man went to the theater but the woman stayed at her apartment.
    D) They waited for each other at different places.

18. A) The credit hours required for an MPA degree.
    B) The basic requirements for entering Human Resources Department.
    C) Taking some optional courses in English.
    D) Getting extra credits for an MPA program.

Questions 19 to 22 are based on the conversation you have just heard.

19. A) Professor and student.   B) Classmates.
    C) Customer and shop assistant.   D) Colleagues.
20. A) The survey received a low rate of return.
    B) The sample selected was not representative.
    C) The questionnaires were too difficult.
    D) The results of the survey were against the public opinion.
21. A) Because he wants to collect information about the shoppers.
    B) Because people in the shopping mall have time to answer his questions.
    C) Because people in the shopping mall are more experienced than students.
    D) Because he can find various respondents in the shopping mall.
22. A) Because multiple choice questions are easier to design than long general ones.
    B) Because by asking multiple choice questions one can collect more detailed information.
    C) Because multiple choice questions require minimal effort to answer.
    D) Because almost all people are familiar with multiple choice questions.

Questions 23 to 25 are based on the conversation you have just heard.

23. A) Basketball and volleyball.   B) Swimming and tennis.
    C) Fitting training and swimming.   D) Weight-lifting and tennis.
24. A) 20 dollars.   B) 6 dollars and 50 cents.
    C) 5 dollars and 25 cents.   D) 4 dollars and 75 cents.
25. A) Because he is allocated to his own instructor.
    B) Because as a beginner he needs to be taught not to get hurt.
    C) Because the fitness training is cheap and safe.
    D) Because the season ticket is not available now.

Section B

Directions: *In this section, you will hear 3 short passages. At the end of each passage, you will hear some questions. Both the passage and questions will be spoken only once. After you hear a question, you must choose the best answer from the four choices marked A), B), C) and D). Then mark the corresponding letter on **Answer Sheet 2** with a single line through the center.*

Passage One
Questions 26 to 29 are based on the passage you have just heard.

26. A) To inform the job hunters of the opportunities available.
    B) To help design classified ads in the newspaper.
    C) To classify available jobs into various categories.
    D) To help job hunters write impressive application letters.
27. A) There is a fierce competition for the top-level jobs.
    B) There are so many people out of work.
    C) The job history is considered a good reflection of the job hunter.
    D) New graduates without work experience are unwanted.
28. A) To write an initial letter giving a full job history.
    B) To pass certain exams before applying for a job.
    C) To be able to read and write.
    D) To keep any detailed information until they came for an interview.

29. A) An aggressive comment on the company's practice.
    B) A sophisticated opinion about the organization one was trying to join.
    C) Something that would make one's application unique.
    D) A university diploma.

Passage Two
Questions 30 to 32 are based on the passage you have just heard.

30. A) To help children to get academic achievements.
    B) To offer children what they need to get a promotion.
    C) To equip children with social skills.
    D) To enable children to participate in extracurricular activities.
31. A) Fostering a healthy attitude in boys and girls.
    B) Giving children opportunity to make friends.
    C) Preparing children for the shock in adult society.
    D) Making children understand the aim of education.
32. A) Children are unfamiliar with each other's problems.
    B) Children are deprived of the opportunity to enter the adult world.
    C) There are too many segregated schools.
    D) Boys and girls do not study together and fail to know each other.

Passage Three
Questions 33 to 35 are based on the passage you have just heard.

33. A) Because students need individual attention.
    B) Because students need to be stimulated.
    C) Because students need exactly the same instruction.
    D) Because students don't know how to learn.
34. A) A practical knowledge of how the language works.
    B) A genuine interest in the language and thinking by themselves.
    C) Curiosity and conscious knowledge.
    D) Independent thinking.
35. A) Students learn by memorizing textbooks.
    B) Teachers teach by reciting lectures.
    C) Students should ask questions based on their own thinking.
    D) The linguistic knowledge is more important for teachers than the techniques of stimulating interest.

Section C
Directions: *In this section, you will hear a passage three times. When the passage is read for the first time, you should listen carefully for its general idea. When the passage is read for the second time, you are required to fill in the blanks numbered from 36 to 43 with the exact words you have just heard. For blanks numbered from 44 to 46 you are required to fill in the missing information. For these blanks, you can either use the exact words you have just heard or write down the main points in your own words. Finally, when the passage is read for the third time, you should check what you have written.*

When men and women get together, there are, in effect, two worlds — his and hers. They have different values, (36)_____, and habits. They play by different rules.

Some (37) _____ differences between men and women are biological. Women have larger (38) _____ and more frequent interaction between their brain's left and right hemispheres, which accounts for women's ability to have better verbal skills and (39) _____. Men have greater brain hemisphere (40) _____, which explains their skills for abstract reasoning and visual-spatial (41) _____. Different habits of men and women are explained by different roles in the process of (42) _____. Although life conditions have changed, both men and women tend to follow their biological (43) _____.

Men tend to retain a firm sense of direction. They need to trace the game, catch it, and find the way home, while women have a better peripheral (边缘的) vision that helps them (44)_____. Men's brains are programmed to hunting, (45)_____
_____.

When entering a room, men look for exits, estimating a possible threat, and ways of escape, (46)_____
_____. Men are able to sort out information and keep it in their head. The only way for women to stop thinking of the problems is to talk it over.

Part IV   Reading Comprehension (Reading in Depth) (25 minutes)
Section A
Directions: *In this section, there is a short passage with 5 questions or incomplete statements. Read the passage carefully. Then answer the questions or complete the statements in the fewest possible words. Please write your answers on* **Answer Sheet 2**.

To understand the importance of controlled observation in psychology, we look at a horse by the name of Hans. Hans could reason and "talk". Hans had been trained by a math teacher, Mr. Osten, to communicate by tapping forefoot and moving his head. A head nod meant yes, and a shake suggested no. Mr. Osten developed a code for verbal information in which each letter was represented by a pair of numbers. The letter A was coded as one tap, pause, one tap, and the letter I was three taps, pause, two taps. Once Hans learned to tap his foot or move his head when questioned, he was given simple problems and then fed a piece of bread or carrot for correct responses. By the end of his training, Hans could spell words, and he excelled in math. He became a hero in Germany — his picture was on wine bottles and toys.

An official commission examined the horse, testing him to see if he really did all the things claimed. They came away very impressed and issued a statement that there was no evidence of any intentional influence or aid on the part of Hans' questioners.

But there was one scientist who was not so sure that Hans was as intelligent as he had been portrayed. Oskar Pfungst, a sharp observer, had detected that Hans always faced his questioners. Pfungst hypothesized that this might have something to do with his math ability. The scientist set up a very simple experiment. He wrote numbers on a card and held them up one at a time, asking Hans to tap out the numbers written on each card. Half of the cards were held so that only Hans, not Pfungst himself, could see. Hans was his usual brilliant self, getting 92% of them correct. But for the numbers Pfungst could not see, Hans was no longer a brilliant horse, getting 8% correct.

Pfungst repeated the experiment over and over again with nearly the same results. He observed Hans with his other questioners. As soon as they stated the problem to Hans, most questioners would turn their head and upper body slightly. When the correct number of foot taps had been made by Hans, the questioner would move his head upward. Despite his years of work with the horse, Mr. Osten had never dreamed that Hans had learnt to "read" him. He felt angry and betrayed by the horse.

Thus we can see that experts sometimes can be wrong and that what sometimes seems to be the truth may be a false impression. Even experts can be fooled if they don't make appropriate use of research procedures to check their observations.

(447 words)

47. According to the passage, Hans, the horse, could "communicate" with people with his
_____ .

48. An official commission examined the horse and confirmed _____ .

49. Oskar Pfungst discovered that Hans performed badly in the math work when _____ .

50. According to Pfunst's experiment, Hans most probably did his work by _____ .

51. We learn from Hans' story that _____ is very important in observation.

Section B

Directions: *There are 2 passages in this section. Each passage is followed by some questions or unfinished statements. For each of them there are four choices marked A), B), C) and D). You should decide on the best choice and mark the corresponding letter on **Answer Sheet 2** with a single line through the center.*

Passage One
Questions 52 to 56 are based on the following passage.

Housing is recognized as a "socially determinant variable". In France, housing is the main item of expenditure in the family budget (accounting for an average of 29 percent), and many families would be unable to find decent housing without some help from the State. For a long time, the main problem was the housing shortage but in recent years the deterioration of housing conditions has been giving even greater cause for concern.

Despite extensive construction programs, the problem of housing for the most underprivileged population groups has not been solved. According to a recent report, between 2 and 3 million families had serious difficulties meeting their housing costs and were living in precarious and uncomfortable conditions.

Policies designed to address the housing problem have shifted over the past few decades from a macro-economic approach promoting construction to housing subsidies. The reasons for this shift can be traced to a determination to limit public spending and to avoid some of the adversary effects of macro-economic policies. The State has to some extent ceased to finance housing, especially the construction of new projects, with the result that the cost is now chiefly and directly borne by the family budget. Many underprivileged families, which were excluded from low-rent housing for various reasons such as selection of tenants, saturation of existing capacity or bankruptcy, had no alternative but to purchase their own home and were encouraged to do so without restraint by the then easy terms of housing loans. The housing sector thus contributed to the development of the "economy of indebtedness". It should indeed be emphasized that "widespread home ownership through borrowing could only be very harmful to low-income families."

In Belgium, the quality of housing, considered the prime indicator of housing deprivation, leaves much to be desired. Low-rent housing projects have been cut back as part of the austerity (缩减) policy which is pursued by the national and regional governments, and low-income households are finding it difficult to find somewhere to live. The number of homeless has also taken on alarming proportions. An estimated 3,000 persons spend nights in refuges, but the actual figure is probably much higher. Moreover, the number of homeless women and young persons is increasing.

(367 words)

52. In this passage the author mainly argues that housing _____.
  A) is a problem that can be solved socially
  B) is a heavy burden for most underprivileged families
  C) is a widespread problem in some European countries.
  D) changes with social conditions.

53. In recent years, _____ is the main problem with housing.
  A) the deterioration of housing conditions
  B) the shortage in housing
  C) the failures of construction programs
  D) the reduction of housing subsides

54. The main measures recently taken by the government to tackle the housing problem are _____.
  A) setting limits to public spending　　　B) restricting house purchasing.
  C) extensive construction projects　　　D) housing subsidies and easy bank loans

55. According to the passage, which of the following statements are NOT TRUE?
  A) Widespread house ownership through loans is not in the interests of underprivileged families.
  B) In spite of extensive construction projects, housing problems still exist.
  C) Many low-income families only have access to low-rent housing.
  D) In Belgium low-rent housing projects have been cut back as the governments try to control public spending.

56. The reduction of low-rent housing projects in Belgium has resulted in _____.
  A) an improvement in housing quality
  B) an alarming increase of homeless people
  C) an increase in house purchases
  D) a change in the government's policy

Passage Two
Questions 57 to 61 are based on the following passage.

Less than a year ago, a new generation of diet pills seemed to offer the long-sought answer to our chronic weight problems. Hundreds of thousands of pound-conscious Americans had discovered that a drug known as "fen-phen" could shut off huge appetites like magic, and the FDA had just approved a new drug, Redux, that did the same with fewer side effects. Redux would attract hundreds of thousands of new pill poppers within a few months.

But now the diet-drug revolution is facing a setback. Some of the nation's largest organizations, including Aetna US Healthcare and Prudential Healthcare, have begun cutting back or eliminating reimbursement (退还) for both pills. Diet chains like Jenny Craig are backing away from them too. Several states have restricted the use of fen-phen. Last week the Florida legislature banned new prescriptions and called on doctors to stop current patients from using the drug within 30 days; it also put a 90-day limit on Redux prescriptions. Even New Jersey doctor Shelton Levine, who boasted of Redux on TV and in his book, had stopped giving it to all but his most obese (重度肥胖的) patients.

The potentially fatal side effects can't be ignored. The FDA revealed that 82 patients had developed heart problems while on fen-phen, and that seven patients had come down with the same condition on Redux.

As if that were not bad enough, physicians reported a woman who had been taking fen-phen for less than a month died of hypertension (高血压). And an article in the *Journal of the American Medical Association* last month confirmed earlier reports that both fen-phen and Redux can cause brain damage in lab animals.

The findings led the *New England Journal* to publish an editorial advising doctors to prescribe drugs only for patients with severe obesity. Meanwhile, FDA asked drug-makers to put more explicit warnings on fen-phen and Redux labels. So far prescriptions for fen-phen have dropped 56%, and those for Redux 36%.

All that really does, however, is to bring the numbers down to where they should have been all along. Manufacturers said from the start that their pills offered a short-term therapy for the obese, not for people looking to fit into a smaller bathing suit. When limited to these very fat patients, the drugs make sense — because severe obesity carries its own dangers, including heart disease, diabetes, and stroke. Too often, however, Redux and fen-phen were sold to all comers, almost like candy. The current setback, says Levine, is a "roller coaster that never should have happened."

(406 words)

57. The new pills seemed to be a solution to _____.
   A) the problem of overweight that has obsessed Americans for a long time
   B) the problem that is of great weight and significance
   C) heart disease, diabetes, and stroke
   D) the side effects of weight-loss drugs

58. The underlined phrase in the first paragraph "pill poppers" most probably refers to _____.
   A) pill inventors   B) pill takers and abusers
   C) pill manufacturers   D) pill distributors

59. The statement "the diet-drug revolution is facing a setback" is supported by the following facts EXCEPT that _____.
   A) some health organizations and diet chains have suspended their support for the pills
   B) some states have forbidden or limited the prescriptions of the pills
   C) patients in Florida are advised to drop the use of fen-phen
   D) Sheldon Levine, a New Jersey doctor, recommended one of the pills on TV and in his book

60. According to the passage, the worst case that revealed the fatal side effects of the pills is _____.
   A) 82 patients on fen-phen have suffered heart trouble
   B) a woman patient on fen-phen died of hypertension
   C) the diet pills cause brain damage

D) 7 patients who had taken Redux developed heart defects

61. What can we infer from the last paragraph of the article?

A) The severely fat patients are threatened with potential illness.

B) The diet-pills have been sold to all comers without discrimination.

C) The diet-pills should not have been hailed as miraculous cures and then discarded as dangerous drugs.

D) The diet-pills were intended to a short-term cure for the very fat.

Part Ⅴ Error Correction (15 minutes)

Directions: *This part consists of a short passage. In this passage, there are altogether 10 mistakes, one in each numbered line. You may have to change a word, add a word or delete a word. Mark out the mistakes and put the corrections in the blanks provided. If you change a word, cross it out and write the correct word in the corresponding blank. If you add a word, put an insertion mark (∧) in the right place and write the missing word in the blank. If you delete a word, cross it out and put a slash (/) in the blank.*

If you had to sum up the problems of American health care in
two words, they would be "cost" and "coverage". The country spends
16% of its GDP on health. Yet a six of the population lacks medical   62. _____
coverage. Most Americans receive health insurance through their
employer. The government picks up the bill for the elder and the poor.   63. _____
But an estimating 47 million people fall through cracks — a number   64. _____
that is rising as premiums (保险金) soar.

Because so many people should be without medical coverage in   65. _____
the world's richest country is a disgrace. It spoils the lives of the
uninsured, who are unable to get access with affordable treatment at
an early age. And it casts a shadow of fear well beyond, to America's
middle classes who worry about not their jobs but their healthcare   66. _____
benefits as well. It is also grossly inefficient. Hospitals are forced,
by law, to help anyone who arrived in the emergency room.   67. _____
Since those with insurance coverage usually cannot pay for that car,   68. _____
the bill is passed on everyone else, driving up premiums. Higher
premiums, by turn, swell the ranks of the uninsured.   69. _____

Breaking that spiral would be a big step towards fixing American
healthcare. And it is one that politicians at last seem ready to get. Not   70. _____
in Washington, where reform is still stalled (延误) by an argument
between conservatives, who think more about consumer choice, with   71. _____
those on the left, who think government intervention is the answer.
Instead, state governors are taking the lead.

Part Ⅵ Translation (5 minutes)

Directions: *Complete the sentences by translating into English the Chinese given in brackets. Please write your translation on **Answer Sheet 2**.*

72. Just because a subject is difficult, _____ (并不意味着你学不好它).

73. At the end of my junior year of high school，I heard about _____（一项旨在使女孩对工科产生兴趣的暑期项目）.

74. _____（如果天气不那么潮湿），we would spend our holidays there.

75. They removed the over-excited witness _____（唯恐她扰乱法庭秩序）.

76. Many Americans look at the eyes of the people they are talking with，_____（认为这是表示尊重）.

Test 3

Part Ⅰ Writing (30 minutes)

Directions: *For this part, you are allowed 30 minutes to write a short essay commenting on the evaluation of teachers' performance done by the students. You should write at least 150 words following the outline given below in Chinese.*

Evaluation by Students

1. 不少大学让学生参与任课老师教学情况的测评
2. 对此改革措施校方、教师、学生的看法不一
3. 学生测评教师的益处以及可能产生的问题

Part Ⅱ Reading Comprehension (Skimming and Scanning) (15 minutes)

Directions: *In this part, you will have 15 minutes to go over the passage quickly and answer the questions on **Answer Sheet 1**. For questions 1 – 7, choose the best answer from the four choices marked A), B), C) and D). For questions 8 – 10 complete the sentences with the information given in the passage.*

The Wonderful World of Small

There's a quiet revolution going on, and its name is nanotechnology. A host of innovations are coming our way. Some seem almost magical, like the new material created in 2004 by Ray Baughman, a professor at the University of Texas. It's stronger than steel, transparent, very, very light. A hectare-size sheet would weigh just 280 grams.

When the professor announced that he hadn't decided what to call it, he started to get emails from around the world suggesting names. Since it was so light and strong, people started calling it "mithril"— the name of a highly prized type of armor used in *The Lord of Rings*.

There are other discoveries too — perhaps not so astounding, but practical and pleasant. Now there are socks that don't get smelly, pants that resist stains, windows that repel dirt and toilets that clean themselves. All this results from exploring the world of the very, very small.

Nano comes from the Greek word from dwarf. Usually nanotechnology is defined as the study and manipulation of matter smaller than 100 nanometers(纳米)— that's the scale of things like molecules and viruses. Ten hydrogen atoms pressed together against each other are just one nanometer long. And one million nanometers fit into a millimeter. Hard to grasp? Think of it this way: If everyone in Manila were a nanometer wide, the entire population, standing shoulder to shoulder, would fit on your thumbnail.

Stunning Uses of Nanotechnology

Like Alice in Wonderland, researchers in Nanoland find themselves in a world where old rules don't apply. Small things behave differently. This is behind several innovations, including the self-cleaning toilet. The toilet bowl is sealed with a super-smooth glaze(涂层) that has microscopic holes under 30 nanometers. Because they're smaller than bacteria or other tiny particles, there's not enough room for dirt to get stuck in the surface. Flushing is basically all the work you have to do.

Researchers in Nanoland are also making really, really small things with astonishing properties — like the carbon nanotube. Chris Papadopoulos of the University of Victoria, says, "The carbon nanotube is the poster boy for nanotechnology."

In your pencil, carbon, in the form of graphite (石墨), is soft and easily broken. But a carbon nanotube is tough as nails — much tougher in fact. It's very thin sheet graphite that's formed into a tube. These tiny straw-like cylinders, which can be as small as half a nanometer wide, are up to 100 times stronger than steel and six times lighter. They are the hardest, stiffest, strongest materials known and are among the world's best conductors of heat and electricity. They can carry some 1,000 times more electricity current than copper wire. Everybody wants them, but until now they've been in short supply and pricey. The current annual production, worldwide, is only 300 kilograms. At $860 a gram, carbon nanotubes cost 50 times more than gold.

When it comes to finding uses for carbon nanotubes, the range is huge. The National Research Council Canada (NRC) is looking at harnessing their strength by embedding them in construction materials, among other applications. The Boeing Company thinks nanotubes may be the source of futute improvements for high-performance aircraft. Some of the most stunning uses come out of Ray Baughman's research. Employing what he calls the "ancient technology of spinning", Baughman and his team developed a way of spinning carbon nanotubes into fibers that are four times tougher than spider silk, the toughest natural filament (细丝). Since they also conduct electricity, the futuristic yarns could be woven into "smart" clothing that stores electricity, is potentially bulletproof and incorporates sensors capable of adjusting the temperature of garment. The fibers could also be made into cables for suspension bridges much longer than any we have now.

And then there are Baughman's superstrong, superlight sheets. Papadopoulos explains that one of the reasons scientists are excited by the sheets is that they would make ideal solar sails. He says, "With a solar sail, you are allowing the pressure of the sun's light to propel you through space the same way wind powers a sailboat." But there is also something in this for the earthbound traveler. Using an ordinary microwave oven, Baughman's team was able to weld one of his sheets between two pieces of plexiglass (树脂玻璃). Afterwards, it still conducted electricity and remained transparent. One idea, therefore, is to put these sheets in windshields of the car and run current through them to defrost car windows.

Medicine and Nanotechnology

Many disease-causing bacteria and viruses are nano size. So only nanotechnology would offer us ways of fighting back. Nucryst Pharmaceuticals has come up with a winning formula that combines nanoscience with old-fashioned folk wisdom. The ancient Greeks used silver to promote healing and prevent infection, but the treatment took a back seat when antibiotics came on the scene. Nucryst has revived and improved on the old cure by coating a burn-and-wound bandage with nano-size silver particles that are more reactive than the bulk form of metal. They penetrate into the skin and work steadily. As a result, burn victims can have their dressings changed as little as once a week. Before Nucryst, such dressings had to be changed several times a day, a painful procedure that involved removing a healing cream.

In 2004, Nucryst produced over three million bandages, and its sales topped $30 million. 70% of chronic-wound patients who were not healing at the expected rate got better with the use of these bandages.

Copy Nature with Nanotechnology

With new instruments that reveal natural structures down to the last atom, nanotechnologists' ability to copy nature has taken off. When Bharat Bhushan, a mechanical engineering professor at Ohio State University, wanted to make a super-smooth surface, he decided to copy lotus leaves. Scientists have long known that the leaves shed water very well: They're waxy and covered with tiny nano-size bumps, so water rolls off. Bhushan succeeded in making a polymer (聚合体) sheet that was equally smooth. "If you applied it to glass, you could have windows that don't need washing." says Bhushan.

Hicham Fenniri, a chemistry professor at the Univeristy of Alberta, took a similar tack to make artificial joints act more like natural ones. The body recognizes an artificial hip or knee as foreign and may reject it. In most cases, the implant can become loose and painful and has to be replaced. But Fenniri has made a nanotube coating for the artificial joint. It's a very good imitation of collagen (胶原质), a natural protein that is part of bone. As a result, the coating attracts bone cells. This is important because bone growth helps integrate an artificial joint into the body. Says Fenirri, "You need to attract the right cells to the right places, right away. Speed is essential when incorporating an artificial joint into the body."

(1,146 words)

1. In 2004, Prof. Professor Baughman invented _____.
   A) a hectare-size sheet of super-strong steel
   B) a super-strong, super-light material using nanotechnology
   C) a magical material as strong as the prized armor in *The Lord of Rings*
   D) a new transparent material as strong as steel

2. How is nanotechnology usually defined?
   A) The study of the very small things such as molecules, bacteria and viruses.
   B) The manipulation of matter under 30 nanometers.
   C) The study of matter no bigger than 100 nanometers.
   D) The invention of astounding products such as stain-resistant pants and self-cleaning toilets.

3. _____ is not only the hardest, stiffest material ever known, but also one of the world's best conductor of heat and electricity.
   A) Sheet graphite   B) Steel   C) Copper   D) Carbon nanotube

4. Due to its very low production, carbon nanotubes is _____ times more expensive than gold.
   A) 100 times   B) to times   C) 300 times   D) 1000 times

5. What is National Research Council Canada trying to do with carbon nanotubes?
   A) To build strong nanotube-embedded construction materials.
   B) To spin carbon nanotubes into toughest fibers.
   C) To make tough nanotube pencils.
   D) To build high-performance aircraft with carbon nanotubes as materials.

6. The tough fibers made from carbon nanotubes could be made into _____.
   A) bulletproof windows
   B) smart garments that can test body temperature
   C) solar sails
   D) cables for very long suspension bridges

7. Baughman's super-strong, super-light, transparent sheet can be inserted in the windshields to help to _____.

A) deforest car windows with running current

B) strengthen window-shields

C) keep car windows from getting stained

D) make wind-shields shining bright

8. The burn-and-wound bandages coated with nano-size silver particles are a typical example of _____.

9. According to Prof. Bhushan, we could have stain-resistant window glass by using super-smooth polymer sheets, which are produced by _____.

10. The artificial joint with _____, being a good imitation of natural bone protein, can attract bone cells and become quickly incorporated into the body.

Part III   Listening Comprehension (35 minutes)

Section A

Directions: *In this section, you will hear 8 short conversations and 2 long conversations. At the end of each conversation, one or more questions will be asked about what was said. Both the conversation and questions will be spoken only once. After each question there will be a pause. During the pause you must read the four choices marked A), B), C) and D), and decide which is the best answer. Then mark the corresponding letter on **Answer Sheet 2** with a single line through the center.*

11. A) She is not good at writing.　　　　　　B) She is probably upset.

　　C) She has called to talk about her problem.　D) She has found out what's troubling her.

12. A) Most people enjoy visiting museums.

　　B) Most of them need a special discount to save money.

　　C) There might be varied opinions.

　　D) They should not miss the opportunity.

13. A) He has just bought a property there.

　　B) His rich uncle asked him to take care of his property there.

　　C) He has been left a big fortune there.

　　D) He wishes to make a fortune there one day.

14. A) Play golf.　　　　　　　　　　　　　B) Play tennis.

　　C) Stay home.　　　　　　　　　　　　　D) Go boating.

15. A) Rome.　　　　　　　　　　　　　　　B) London.

　　C) Madrid.　　　　　　　　　　　　　　D) Paris.

16. A) At the west end of a street.　　　　　　B) To the east of the traffic light.

　　C) Just behind a brown-brick building.　　D) On the west side of a square.

17. A) She has to read a lot of literature books.

　　B) She has failed to meet the deadline for her reading assignment again.

　　C) The Eastern Literature books are too difficult to understand.

　　D) She feels regretful that she has been taking a wrong course.

18. A) They will ask Mr. Smith paint their house.

　　B) They will paint their house on their own.

　　C) They will hire someone to paint the house.

　　D) They will buy their neighbor's newly painted house.

Questions 19 to 22 are based on the conversation you have just heard.

19. A) In a library.   B) On a bus.
    C) In a supermarket.   D) At a newspaper shop.
20. A) Majorca.   B) Palma.   C) Geneva.   D) Iletas.
21. A) Don't get too familiar with the hotel staff.
    B) Book the hotel right away.
    C) Keep a check on your spending.
    D) Don't sit down at a bar.
22. A) She bumped into someone while crossing the street.
    B) She narrowly escaped an accident.
    C) She got run over.
    D) She lost her way.

Questions 23 to 25 are based on the conversation you have just heard.

23. A) Because she owned a car.
    B) Because she drove so well.
    C) Because it was her childhood dream.
    D) Because she liked the handsome uniforms of the taxi drivers.
24. A) Driving at night.   B) Developing a sense of direction.
    C) Coping with nasty people.   D) Learning to judge distance.
25. A) Meeting various people.   B) Getting generous tips.
    C) Being outdoors.   D) Seeing interesting sights in the city.

Section B

Directions: *In this section, you will hear 3 short passages. At the end of each passage, you will hear some questions. Both the passage and questions will be spoken only once. After you hear a question, you must choose the best answer from the four choices marked A), B), C) and D). Then mark the corresponding letter on* **Answer Sheet 2** *with a single line through the center.*

Passage One

Questions 26 to 29 are based on the passage you have just heard.

26. A) They extend their water pipes.
    B) They give out faint cries.
    C) They make noises to drive insects away.
    D) They become as elastic as rubber bands.
27. A) Healthy plants.   B) Quiet plants.
    C) Well-watered plants.   D) Thirsty plants.
28. A) They can buzz in to kill.
    B) They can hear the dry plants' cries.
    C) They can imitate the plants' crying.
    D) They can attack healthy plants in dry, hot weather.
29. A) They could drive the insects away.
    B) They could keep the plants well-watered.
    C) They could build devices to trap insects.
    D) They could protect the plants from severe droughts.

Passage Two

Questions 30 to 32 are based on the passage you have just heard.

30. A) He is a professional pickpocket.
    B) He is an undercover policeman.
    C) He is interested in traveling.
    D) He is interested in documenting pickpocket skills.

31. A) He hoped to prove himself the best pickpocket in the world.
    B) He wanted to master different stealing skills around the world.
    C) He wanted to compile a book on thievery skills around the world.
    D) He intended to find out the best pickpocket skill in the world.

32. A) He tried to warn bus riders of pickpockets.
    B) He filmed how pickpockets targeted bus riders.
    C) He stole a wad of money from a well-dressed Italian man.
    D) He got acquainted with two skillful pickpockets.

Passage Three

Questions 33 to 35 are based on the passage you have just heard.

33. A) How leadership differs in small and large groups.
    B) Different ways in which a person become a leader.
    C) Different leadership roles.
    D) How social groups determine who will lead them.

34. A) Emotional support.   B) Technical guidance.
    C) Strict discipline.   D) Personal affection.

35. A) To maintain stable group relationship.
    B) To give orders and see to the attainment of group goals.
    C) To offer sympathy for group members in difficulty.
    D) To smooth tension and conflict among group members.

Section C

Directions: *In this section, you will hear a passage three times. When the passage is read for the first time, you should listen carefully for its general idea. When the passage is read for the second time, you are required to fill in the blanks numbered from 36 to 43 with the exact words you have just heard. For blanks numbered from 44 to 46 you are required to fill in the missing information. For these blanks, you can either use the exact words you have just heard or write down the main points in your own words. Finally, when the passage is read for the third time, you should check what you have written.*

Modern life is stressful. The noise and the fast pace of the city take their (36) _____ on the spirit. Everybody knows this, but the sad (37) _____ is how poorly many people deal with it. They attempt to escape from noise into more noise and the empty moments are filled with the (38) _____ noises of electronic entertainment. Many city (39) _____ escape on weekends to country cottage, but they take the city with them, and spend their afternoons out on the lake listening to the (40) _____ of an outboard motor.

The seventeenth century French (41) _____ Pascal said "All man's miseries derive from not being able to sit quietly in a room alone." Sitting quietly and doing nothing is the (42) _____ of the oldest medical practice in the world, Buddhist meditation (冥想). People

need the healing force of quiet and (43) _____. We all need to take a breath, and slow down. It may be (44) _____

_____.

Whenever I visit New York, I am struck by how much everyone seems to be in a rush. (45) _____

_____. This is all the more reason why they need to find quiet and peace outside of work. (46) _____

_____?

It could be that Pascal knew that, too, because he also said "The eternal silence of these infinite spaces frightens me."

Part Ⅳ Reading Comprehension (Reading in Depth) (25 minutes)

Section A

Directions: *In this section, there is a short passage with 5 questions or incomplete statements. Read the passage carefully. Then answer the questions or complete the statements in the fewest possible words. Please write your answers on Answer Sheet 2.*

Successful business tends to continue implementing the ideas that made them successful. But in a rapidly changing world, ideas often become outdated overnight. What worked in the past won't necessarily work in the future. In order to thrive in the future, you must constantly create new ideas for every aspect of your business. In fact, you must continually generate new ideas just to keep your head above water. Businesses that are not creative about their future may not survive.

Although Bill Gates is the most successful man on the planet, he did not anticipate the Internet. Now he is scrambling to catch up. If Bill Gates can miss a major aspect of his industry, it can happen to you in your industry. Your business needs to continually innovate and create its future. Gates now is constantly worried about the future of Microsoft. Here's what he said in a recent interview in the *US News World Report*: "Will we be replaced tomorrow? No. In a very short time frame, Microsoft is an incredibly strong company. But when you look to the two-to-three-year time frame, I don't think anyone can say with a straight face that any technology company has a guaranteed position. Not Intel, not Microsoft, not Compaq, not Dell, take any of your favorites. And that's totally honest."

Yet many remember that in 1985 the Cabbage Patch Kids were the best-selling toys on the market. But after Coleco Industries introduced their sensational line of dolls they became complacent and didn't create any new toys worth mentioning. As a result, Coleco went bankrupt in 1988.

The most successful businesses survive in the long term because they constantly reassess their situations and reinvest themselves accordingly. The 3M Company has a 15% rule: Employees are encouraged to spend 15% of their time developing new ideas on any project they desire. It's no surprise, then, that 3M has been around since 1902.

Most businesses are not willing to tear apart last year's model of success and build a new one. Here's a familiar analogy to explain why they are lulled into complacency. Imagine that your business is like a pot of lobster. To cook lobster, you put them into a pot of warm water and gradually turn up the heat. The lobsters don't realize they are being cooked because the process is so gradual. As a result, they become complacent and die without a struggle. However,

if you throw a lobster into the pot when the water is boiling, it will desperately try to escape. This lobster is not lulled by a slowly changing environment. It realizes instantly that it's in a bad environment and takes immediate action to change its status.

47. The passage conveys the message that the way for a company to keep out of financial difficulty is to _____.

48. Why is Gates constantly worried about the future of Microsoft?

    _____

49. The case of _____ suggests that complacency and lack of creation will ruin a company.

50. According to the passage, the long-term success of the 3M Company lies in _____.

51. The analogy of "cooking a lobster in a pot" illustrate that in a slowly changing environment _____.

Section B

Directions: *There are 2 passages in this section. Each passage is followed by some questions or unfinished statements. For each of them there are four choices marked A), B), C) and D). You should decide on the best choice and mark the corresponding letter on **Answer Sheet 2** with a single line through the center.*

Passage One
Questions 52 to 56 are based on the following passage.

The tragic impact of the modern city on the human being has killed his sense of aesthetics, the material benefits of a wealthy society have diverted his attention from his city and its cultural potentials to the products of science and technology: washing machines, central heating, TV sets, computers and cars.

He is a car driver and reluctant to walk. Without adequate parking facilities, the streets are littered with cars. Congestion (堵塞) has become the predominant factor in his environment, and statistics suggest that two cars per household may make matters worse.

Meanwhile, insult is added to injury by "land value". The value of land results from its use. When its use is intensified, its value rises. "Putting land to its highest and best use" becomes the principal economic standard in urban growth. This speculative approach and the pressure of increasing population leads to the "vertical" growth of cities with the result that people are forced to adjust themselves to congestion to maintain these relatively artificial land values. Paradoxically the remedy for removing congestion is to create more of it. Partial decentralization in the form of large development units away from the traditional town centers only shifts the disease of congestion round the town center.

It is within our power to build better cities and revive the pride of their citizens, but we shall have to stop operating on the fringe of the problem. We shall have radically to re-plan them to achieve a rational density of population. We shall have to provide them what can be called minimum "psychological elbow room". One of the ingredients of this will be proper transportation plans. These will have to be an integral part of the overall planning process which in itself is a scientific process where facts are essential. We must collect all and complete information about the city or the town, if we want to plan effectively.

We must not forget that cities are built by people, and that their form and shape should be subject to the will of the people. Scientific methods of data collection and analysis will indicate trends, but they will not direct action. Scientific methods are only an instrument. The "man-

educated" man, the human, will have to set the target, and using the results obtained by science, take upon himself the final shaping of his environment. He will have to use his moral sense of responsibility to the community and future generations.

(408 words)

52. The main concern of the passage is with _____.
   A) city congestion   B) city planning
   C) decentralization   D) land values in cities

53. We know from the first paragraph that people in old times _____.
   A) were more enthusiastic about the development of science and technology
   B) had a stronger sense of beauty
   C) over-dependent on labor saving devices
   D) paid more attention to material benefits

54. The dramatic increase of land value in cities _____.
   A) is a desirable result of economic development
   B) brings about greater opportunities for land dealers
   C) lead to an efficient, positive use of land in the form of vertical growth
   D) is annoyingly artificial and meaningless

55. Partial decentralization may _____.
   A) eventually solve the problem of city congestion
   B) relieve the strain on the city facilities
   C) decrease the land value in the town center
   D) bring the same problem of congestion to the suburban areas

56. According to the author, the re-modeling of cities should take into account all of the following except _____.
   A) the benefits of future generations   B) the will and the pride of the city dwellers
   C) the psychological needs of land owners D) proper transportation plans

Passage Two
Questions 57 to 61 are based on the following passage.

Recent stories in the newspapers and magazines suggest that teaching and research contradict each other, that research plays too prominent a part in academic promotions, and that teaching is badly underemphasized. There is an element of truth in these statements, but they also ignore deeper and more important relationships.

Research experience is an essential element of hearing and promotion at a research university because it is the emphasis on research that distinguishes such a university from an arts college. Some professors, however, neglect teaching for research and that presents a problem.

Most research universities reward outstanding teaching, but the greatest recognition is usually given to achievements in research. Part of the reason is the difficulty of judging teaching. A highly responsible and tough professor is usually appreciated by top students who want to be challenged but disliked by those whose records are less impressive. The mild professor usually gets high overall ratings, but there is a sense of disappointment on the part of the best students. Thus, a university trying to promote professors primarily on the basis of teaching qualities would have to confront this confusion.

As modern science moves faster, two forces are exerted on professors: one is the time needed to keep up with the profession; the other is the time needed to teach. The training of new scientists requires outstanding teaching at the research university as well as the arts college. Although scientists are usually made in the elementary schools, scientists can be lost by poor teaching at the college and graduate school levels. The solution is not to separate teaching and research but to recognize that the combination is difficult but vital. It is time for universities to reserve the title of professor for those willing to profess, willing to be an earnest part of the community of scholars. Professors unwilling to teach can be called "distinguished research investigators" or something else.

The pace of modern science makes it increasingly difficult to be a great researcher and a great teacher. Yet many are described in just those terms. Those who say we can separate teaching and research simply do not understand the system, but those who say the problem will disappear are not fulfilling their responsibilities.

(369 words)

57. What point does the author intend to put across in the first paragraph?
   A) Teaching and research are two contradictory fields.
   B) Research can never be overemphasized.
   C) The relationship between research and teaching should not be simplified.
   D) It is not right to overestimate the importance of teaching.
58. Research universities still attach importance to research in academic promotions partly because _____.
   A) professors with academic achievements are usually responsible and tough
   B) it is difficult to conduct objective evaluation of teaching quality
   C) top students who want to be challenged appreciate research professors
   D) research helps to improve the effectiveness of teaching
59. Which of the following statements can we know from the fourth paragraph?
   A) Distinguished professors at research universities should focus on research only.
   B) The separation of teaching from research may affect the quality of future scientists.
   C) It is vitally important to improve teaching in elementary schools in order to train new scientists.
   D) It is impossible to combine research with teaching due to the rapid development of modern science.
60. The underlined word "profess" in the fourth paragraph most likely means _____.
   A) do academic research   B) teach
   C) do field work   D) investigate
61. The problem mentioned in the last paragraph refers to _____.
   A) the separation of teaching from research
   B) raising the status of academic research
   C) professors' reluctance to teach
   D) the combination of teaching and research

Part V Error Correction (15 minutes)

Directions: *This part consists of a short passage. In this passage, there are altogether 10 mistakes, one in each numbered line. You may have to change a word, add a word or delete a word. Mark out the mistakes and put the corrections in the blanks provided. If you change a word, cross it out and write the correct word in the corresponding blank. If you add a word, put an insertion mark (∧) in the right place and write the missing word in the blank. If you delete a*

word, cross it out and put a slash (/) in the blank.

American higher education stands on the brink of chaos.
Never have so many spent so long learning so little. The present
crisis stems from the increasing widespread acceptance among   62. _____
faculty and administrators of the fatal educational principle
which a student should not be required to do any academic work   63. _____
that displeases him. If a student prefers not to study science or history
or literature, he has allowed to attain his degree without studying any   64. _____
science, history, or literature.

In America the attempt is being made to provide students
with what is advised as a liberal education without requiring by them 65. _____
the necessary self-discipline and hard work. Students have been led to
believe they can achieve without effort, that all they need to do is skip
light-heartedly down the merry road to learning. Fortunately, that road 66. _____
is no more than a detour (弯路) to the dead end of ignorance.

We must realize that becoming an educated person is a
difficult, demanded enterprise. Just as anyone who regards intense   67. _____
physical training as a source of delight would be thought a fool, for
we all know how much pain such training involves, but anyone who   68. _____
speaks intense mental exertion as a source of joy ought to be thought   69. _____
equally foolish, for such effort also involves pain. It is painful to have
one's ignorance exposing and frustrating to be baffled by intellectual 70. _____
subtleties. Of course, there can be joy in learning as there can be in sport.
But in both cases a joy is the result of overcoming challenges and can't 71. _____
be experienced without toil.

Part VI Translation (5 minutes)

Directions: *Complete the sentences by translating into English the Chinese given in brackets.
Please write your translation on **Answer Sheet 2**.*

72. _____(这些年来当我发现自己处于困境时)，I'd try what Dad suggested — search
deep within myself for strength.

73. SARS _____ (三年前大概占据了各家报纸的头版头条)，but it wasn't the only
weird disease on the World Health Organization's radar screen.

74. We were greatly relieved to learn that _____(所有紧急事务都已处理完毕).

75. The government was faced with the demand that the tax _____(尽快废除).

76. When you purchase a car, keep in mind _____(你购买的不仅仅是一堆金属与橡胶)；
you are buying into service departments and manufactures who care about your safety.

Test 4

Part Ⅰ Writing (30 minutes)

Directions: *For this part, you are allowed 30 minutes to write a short essay commenting on the latest change in the postgraduate craze. You should write at least 150 words following the outline given below in Chinese.*

Post-graduate Craze Cools Off

No. of Post-graduate Test Takers in Shanghai

Year	Number of Applicants	Margin
2002	59,816	
2003	79,299	+32.6%
2004	84,611	+6.7%
2005	99,548	+1.8%
2006	101,607	+2.1%
2007	95,045	−6.5%

1. 考研人数在持续上涨 10 年后于 2007 年开始减少。
2. 考研热降温的原因。(收费改革;研究生就业难;用人单位重视工作经验)
3. 我们应该如何选择。

Part Ⅱ Reading Comprehension (Skimming and Scanning) (15 minutes)

Directions: *In this part, you will have 15 minutes to go over the passage quickly and answer the questions on Answer Sheet 1. For questions 1 – 7, choose the best answer from the four choices marked A), B), C) and D). For questions 8 – 10 complete the sentences with the information given in the passage.*

Where Have All the People Gone?

Germans are getting used to a new kind of immigrant. In 1998, a pack of wolves crossed the Neisse River on the Polish-German border. In the empty landscape of eastern Saxony, dotted with abandoned mines and declining villages, the wolves found plenty of deer and few humans. Five years later, a second pack split from the original, so there're now two families of wolves in the region. A hundred years ago, a growing land-hungry population killed off the last of Germany's wolves. Today, it's the local humans whose numbers are under threat.

Villages are empty, thanks to the region's low birth rate and rural flight. Home to 22 of the world's 25 lowest fertility rate countries, Europe will lose 30 million people by 2030, even with continued immigration. The biggest population decline will hit rural Europe. As Italians, Spaniards, Germans and others produce barely three-fifths of children needed to maintain status quo, and as rural flight sucks people into Europe's suburbs and cities, the countryside will lose a quarter of its population. The implications of this demographic (人口的) change will be far-reaching.

Environmental Changes

The postcard view of Europe is of a continent where every scrap of land has long been farmed, fenced off and settled. But the continent of the future may look rather different. Big parts of Europe will renaturalize. Bears are back in Austria. In Swiss Alpine valleys, farms have been receding and forests are growing back. In parts of France and Germany, wildcats and wolves have re-established their ranges.

The shrub and forest that grows on abandoned land might be good for deer and wolves, but is vastly less species-rich than traditional farming, with its pastures, ponds and hedges. Once shrub covers everything, you lose the meadow habitat. All the flowers, herbs, birds, and butterflies disappear. A new forest doesn't get diverse until a couple of hundred years old.

All this is not necessarily an environmentalist's dream it might seem. Take the Greek village of Prastos. An ancient hill town, Prastos once had 1,000 residents, most of them working the land. Now only a dozen left, most in their 60s and 70s. The school has been closed since 1988. Sunday church bells no longer ring. Without farmers to tend the fields, rain has washed away the once fertile soil. As in much of Greece, land that has been orchards and pasture for some 2,000 years is now covered with dry shrub that, in summer, frequently catches fire.

Varied Pictures of Rural Depopulation

Rural depopulation is not new. Thousands of villages like Prastos dot Europe, the result of a century or more of emigration, industrialization, and agricultural mechanization. But this time it's different because never has the rural birth rate so low. In the past, a farmer could usually find at least one of his offspring to take over the land. Today, the chances are that he has only a single son or daughter, usually working in the city and rarely willing to return. In Italy, more than 40% of the country's 1.9 million farmers are at least 65 years old. Once they die out, many of their farms will join the 6 million hectares — one third of Italy's farmland — that has already been abandoned.

Rising economic pressures, especially from reduced government subsidies, will amplify the trend. One third of Europe's farmland is marginal, from the cold northern plains to the dry Mediterranean (地中海) hills. Most of these farmers rely on EU subsides, since it's cheaper to import food from abroad. Without subsidies, some of the most scenic European landscapes wouldn't survive. In the Austrian or Swiss Alps, defined for centuries by orchards, cows, high mountain pastures, the steep valleys are labor-intensive to farm, with subsidies paying up to 90% of the cost. Across the border in France and Italy, subsidies have been reduced for mountain farming. Since then, across the southern Alps, villages have emptied and forests have grown back in. Outside the range of subsidies, in Bulgaria, Romania and Ukraine, big tracts of land are returning to wild.

Big Challenges

The truth is varied and interesting. While many rural regions of Europe are emptying out, others will experience something of a renaissance. Already, attractive areas within driving distance of prosperous cities are seeing robust revivals, driven by urban flight and an in-flooding of childless retirees. Contrast that with less-favored areas, from the Spanish interior to eastern Europe. These face dying villages, abandoned farms and changes in the land not seen for generations. Both types of regions will have to cope with steeply ageing population and its accompanying health and service needs. Rural Europe is the laboratory of demographic changes.

For governments, the challenge has been to develop policies that slow the demographic decline or attract new residents. In some places such as Britain and France, large parts of countryside are reviving as increasingly wealthy urban middle class in search of second homes recolonises villages and farms. Villages in central Italy are counting on tourism to revive their town, turning farmhouses into hostels for tourists and hikers.

But once baby boomers start dying out around 2020, populations will start to decline so sharply that there simply won't be enough people to reinvent itself. It's simply unclear how long current government policies can put off the inevitable.

"We are now talking about civilized depopulation. We just have to make sure that old people we leave behind are taken care of." Says Mats Johansson of Royal Institute of Technology in Stockholm. The biggest challenge is finding creative ways to keep up services for the rising proportion of seniors. When the Austrian village of Klaus, thinly spread over the Alpine foothills, decided it could no longer afford a regular public bus service, the community set up a public taxi-on-demand service for the aged. In thinly populated Lapland where doctors are few and far between, tech-savvy Finns the rising demand for specialized health care with a service that uses videoconferencing and the Internet for remote medical examination.

Another pioneer is the village of Aguaviva, one of rapidly depopulating areas in Spain. In 2000, Mayor Manznanares began offering free air-fares and housing for foreign families to settle in Aguaviva. Now the mud-brown town of about 600 has 130 Argentine and Romanian immigrants, and the town's only school has 54 pupils. Immigration was one solution to the problem. But most foreign immigrants continue to prefer cities. And within Europe migration only exports the problem. Western European look towards eastern Europe as a source for migrants, yet those countries have ultra-low birth rates of their own.

Now the increasingly worried European governments are developing policies to make people have more children, from better childcare to monthly stipends (津贴) linked to family size. But while these measures might raise the birth rate slightly, across the much of the ageing continent there are just too few potential parents around.

(1,150 words)

1. What happened to Germany's wolves a hundred years ago?
   A) They were starved to death as all the deer got killed off.
   B) They got killed off with more and more people competing for land.
   C) They were driven cross the Nessie River on the Polish-German border.
   D) They went extinct in the harsh winter.
2. The current rural depopulation in Europe is mainly the result of _____.
   A) low birth rate and rural flight   B) industrialization
   C) agricultural mechanization   D) continued emigration to America
3. With rural depopulation, the general view of Europe is likely to change from cultivated farmland to _____.
   A) meadows covered with flowers and herbs
   B) large species-rich forests
   C) vast wasteland with few signs of life
   D) growing shrubs and forests with only a few species of wildlife
4. As more and more fields lie unattended, much of the rural Greece is plagued with _____.
   A) loss of civilized life   B) serious food shortage
   C) environmental hazards   D) fierce wild animals
5. Largely because of very low birth rate, _____ of farmland in Italy has already been

abandoned.

    A) a quarter   B) a third

    C) more than 40%   D) three-fifths

6. The trend of rural depopulation in Europe is fueled by the economic pressures mainly arising from _____.

    A) inflation   B) rising rate of unemployment

    C) rising prices of imports   D) reduced financial support from the government

7. Despite the trend of rural depopulation, some attractive rural regions not far from cities are experiencing population growth, _____.

    A) as more and more childless seniors pour in from cities

    B) thanks to government policies to attract new residents

    C) as a result of baby booming

    D) as more and more immigrants come to settle

8. The governments' polices to attract new residents and slow depopulation process might become futile once _____.

9. _____ are two examples of finding creative ways to keeping up services for the rapidly aging population in rural Europe.

10. The mayor of a Spanish town once tried to use free air passage and housing to _____.

Part Ⅲ   Listening Comprehension (35 minutes)

Section A

Directions: *In this section, you will hear 8 short conversations and 2 long conversations. At the end of each conversation, one or more questions will be asked about what was said. Both the conversation and questions will be spoken only once. After each question there will be a pause. During the pause you must read the four choices marked A), B), C) and D), and decide which is the best answer. Then mark the corresponding letter on **Answer Sheet 2** with a single line through the center.*

11. A) She is not to blame.   B) She will accept the responsibility.

    C) It was her fault.   D) She will be more careful next time.

12. A) She is scornful.   B) She is sympathetic.

    C) She is angry.   D) She's disappointed.

13. A) She likes the job of a cleaner because it's simple.

    B) She thinks it's important to have a good job from the beginning.

    C) She hates to be a cleaner because it's low-paid.

    D) She would work as a cleaner in summer if she has to.

14. A) She has to resign from the company for her poor sales performance.

    B) She has been granted leave for a month.

    C) She has been dismissed by the company.

    D) She has been offered a new job.

15. A) Public means of transportation are much faster and cheaper.

    B) The man thinks going by subway is much safer than by taxi.

    C) Parking is becoming a big problem.

    D) The woman doesn't agree with the man.

16. A) It failed for lack of funds.

B) It ended up fairly successful.

C) It was suspended for the land dispute.

D) It was difficult to complete and had to be stopped.

17. A) Go out with the man for lunch.   B) Share her yogurt with the man.

    C) Have a sandwich for lunch.   D) Eat what she brought with.

18. A) It'll cost him a lot of money.

B) He isn't serious about going.

C) Other people will pay for his air-fare and supplies.

D) He is excited and can't wait to go.

Questions 19 to 22 are based on the conversation you have just heard.

19. A) In an office.   B) In a supermarket.

    C) In an hospital.   D) In a classroom.

20. A) Six packets.   B) Three packets.

    C) Nine packets.   D) Twelve packets.

21. A) A heavy smoker.   B) A light smoker.

    C) A chain-smoker.   D) A second-hand smoker.

22. A) Because she wanted to save money for her marriage.

B) Because her boyfriend persuaded her to give up smoking.

C) Because second-hand smoking was ruining her daughter's health.

D) Because she was going to have a baby.

Questions 23 to 25 are based on the conversation you have just heard.

23. A) About which house to buy.

B) About which school to send their children to.

C) About whether to buy the sailing-boat.

D) About how to decorate the new house.

24. A) Because he enjoys traveling from home to office everyday.

B) Because the city air is polluted.

C) Because he doesn't like the crowded houses and strange neighbors in the city.

D) Because he has a romantic feeling about nature.

25. A) London.   B) East Colchester.

    C) In the town center.   D) Near the village.

Section B

Directions: *In this section, you will hear 3 short passages. At the end of each passage, you will hear some questions. Both the passage and questions will be spoken only once. After you hear a question, you must choose the best answer from the four choices marked A), B), C) and D). Then mark the corresponding letter on* **Answer Sheet 2** *with a single line through the center.*

Passage One

Questions 26 to 29 are based on the passage you have just heard.

26. A) To introduce the categories of books in the US libraries.

B) To explain roles of different US libraries.

C) To define the circulation system of US libraries.

D) To demonstrate the importance of US libraries.

27. A) Because books could be lent to everyone.
    B) Because books could be lent at no costs.
    C) Because books were lent to students and faculty.
    D) Because books were lent on a paid membership basis.
28. A) To provide readers with comfortable reading rooms.
    B) To provide adults with opportunities of further education.
    C) To collect and store books.
    D) To serve the community's cultural and recreational needs.
29. A) Service.   B) Function.   C) Readership.   D) Ownership.

Passage Two
Questions 30 to 32 are based on the passage you have just heard.
30. A) The color of the dog.
    B) The price of the dog.
    C) Whether the dog will fit the environment.
    D) Whether the dog will get along with other pets in the house.
31. A) It must be trained so it won't bite.
    B) It demands more food and space.
    C) It costs more money to keep.
    D) It needs more love and care from the master.
32. A) They are less likely to run away.
    B) It is easier for their master to train them to perform specific tasks.
    C) They are less likely to be shy with other pets in the house.
    D) It's easier for them to form a relationship with their masters.

Passage Three
Questions 33 to 35 are based on the passage you have just heard.
33. A) The number of their accounts.
    B) Withholding client information.
    C) Being mysterious to the outsiders.
    D) Attracting wealthy foreign clients.
34. A) Most clients would go bankrupt.
    B) The Swiss banks would be sued.
    C) The Swiss banks would quickly go bankrupt.
    D) Some clients would face charges for their improper acts.
35. A) To tighten up banking rules.   B) To eliminate illegal acts.
    C) To cancel the secrecy system.   D) To protect clients' interests.

Section C
Directions: *In this section, you will hear a passage three times. When the passage is read for the first time, you should listen carefully for its general idea. When the passage is read for the second time, you are required to fill in the blanks numbered from 36 to 43 with the exact words you have just heard. For blanks numbered from 44 to 46 you are required to fill in the missing information. For these blanks, you can either use the exact words you have just heard or write down the main points in your own words. Finally, when the passage is read for the third time, you should check what you have written.*

The term "Learning Disabilities" means a disorder in one or more of the basic psychological processes involved in understanding or in using language, spoken or written. The disorder may (36) _____ itself in an imperfect ability to listen, think, speak, read, write, spell, or to do mathematical (37) _____ , including conditions such as perceptual disabilities, brain injury, (38) _____ brain dysfunction and dyslexia (诵读困难). The term does not include learning problems that are primarily the result of (39) _____ or hearing disabilities, of mental delay, of emotional (40) _____ , or of environmental, cultural, or economic disadvantage. Learning disabilities can be (41) _____ by things that happen before or during birth. For example, a mother may have an (42) _____ , such as German measles. Or a baby does not get enough (43) _____ while it is being born. Sometimes a childhood illness, such as meningitis (脑膜炎), can cause learning disabilities.

Who have learning disabilities? (44) _____ .
What are the health concerns of people with learning disabilities? (45) _____
_____ . Are people with learning disabilities at risk of abuse? (46) _____
_____ .

Part Ⅳ   Reading Comprehension (Reading in Depth) (25 minutes)

Section A

Directions: *In this section, there is a short passage with 5 questions or incomplete statements. Read the passage carefully. Then answer the questions or complete the statements in the fewest possible words. Please write your answers on **Answer Sheet 2**.*

It's a rough world out there. Step outside and you could break a leg slipping on your doormat. Light up the stove and you could burn down the house. Luckily, if the doormat or stove failed to warn of coming disaster, a successful lawsuit might compensate you for your troubles. Or so the thinking has gone since the early 1980s, when juries began holding more companies liable for their customers' misfortunes.

Feeling threatened, companies responded by writing ever-longer warning labels, trying to anticipate every possible accident. Today, stepladders carry labels several inches long that warn, among other things, that you might — surprise! — fall off. The label on a child's batman cape cautions that toy "does not enable user to fly".

While warnings are often appropriate and necessary — the dangers of drug interactions, for instance — and many are required by state or federal regulations, it isn't clear that they actually protect the manufacturers and sellers from liability if a customer is injured. About 50 percent of the companies lose when injured customers take them to court.

Now the tide appears to be turning. As personal injury claims continue as before, some courts are beginning to side with defendants, especially in cases where a warning label probably wouldn't have changed anything. In May, Julie Nimmons, president of Schutt Sportswear in Illinois, successfully fought a lawsuit involving a football player who was paralyzed in a game while wearing a Schutt helmet. "We're really sorry he has become paralyzed, but helmets aren't designed to prevent those kinds of injuries," says Nimmons. The jury agreed that the nature of the game, not the helmet, was the reason for the athlete's injury. At the same time, the American Law Institute — a group of judges, lawyers, and academics whose recommendations carry substantial weight — issued new guidelines stating that companies need not warn customers of various dangers or bombard (轰炸) them with a lengthy list of possible ones. "Important information can get buries in a sea of trivialities." says a law professor at Cornell Law School who helped draft the new guidelines. "The information on products might actually be provided for the benefit of customers and not as protection against legal liability."

(365 words)

47. In the 1980s, when accidents happened, injured customers could _____.
48. Manufacturers mentioned in the passage were obliged to make the best of warning labels so as to _____.
49. The case of Schutt helmet demonstrated that recently some injury claims _____.
50. According to the American Law Institute, the warnings on products should not be intended for legal protection but for _____.
51. What is the author's attitude toward the issue of product warnings?

_____

Section B

Directions: *There are 2 passages in this section. Each passage is followed by some questions or unfinished statements. For each of them there are four choices marked A), B), C) and D). You should decide on the best choice and mark the corresponding letter on **Answer Sheet 2** with a single line through the center.*

Passage One
Questions 52 to 56 are based on the following passage.

The essential problem of man in a computerized age remains the same as it has always been. That problem is not solely how to be more productive, more comfortable, but how to be more sensitive, more sensible, more alive. The computer makes possible a gigantic leap in human proficiency; it demolishes the fences around the practical and even the theoretical intelligence. But the question persists and indeed grows whether the computer will make it easier or harder for human beings to know how they really are, to identify their real problems, to respond more fully to beauty, to place adequate value on life, and to make their world safer than it is now.

Electronic brains can reduce the profusion (繁多) of dead ends involved in research. But they can't connect a man to the things he has to be connected to: the reality of pain in others; the possibilities of creative growth in himself; the memory of the race and the rights of the next generation.

The reason why these matters are important in a computerized age is that there may be a tendency to mistake data for wisdom, just as there has always been a tendency to confuse logic with values, and intelligence with insight. Unobstructed access to facts can produce unlimited good only if it is matched by the desire and ability to find out what they mean and where they would lead.

Facts are terrible things if left spreading and unattended. They are too easily regarded as evaluated certainties rather than as the rawest of raw materials trying to be processed into the texture of logic. It requires a very unusual mind to undertake the analysis of a fact. The computer can provide a correct number, but it may be an irrelevant number until judgment is pronounced.

To the extent, then, that man fails to make the distinction between the intermediate

operations of electronic intelligence and the ultimate responsibilities of human decision and conscience, the computer could prove an irrelevance. It could obscure man's awareness of the need to come to terms with himself. It may foster the illusion that he is asking fundamental questions when actually he is asking only functional ones. It may be regarded as a substitute for intelligence instead of an extension of it. It may promote undue confidence in concrete answers.

If we begin with certainties, we shall end in doubts, but if we begin with doubts, and we are patient with them, we shall end in certainties.

(417 words)

52. From the first two paragraphs we may infer that the author thinks one of the computer's limitations is that _____.
    A) it can not improve human proficiency
    B) it is not creative and productive enough
    C) it fails to break the boundary of the practical and theoretical intelligence
    D) it fails to make people more alert to real problems in human society

53. In a computerized age, which one of the following should be given priority to?
    A) Data.   B) Wisdom.   C) Intelligence.   D) Logic.

54. By saying that "Facts are terrible things if left spreading and unattended", the author aims to _____.
    A) point out that the abundance of facts may be harmful to human intellect
    B) illustrate the necessity of always attending to facts
    C) show the importance of using human judgment in the computerized age
    D) tell that facts are always irrelevant and needed to be connected

55. The author sees the computer as _____.
    A) a substitute for human intelligence
    B) a means to help people reach concrete answers
    C) something that can inspire people to ask fundamental questions
    D) something that is of merely subsidiary function

56. Which of the following best describes the author's attitude towards computer?
    A) Enthusiastic.   B) Approving.
    C) Critical.   D) Neutral.

Passage Two
Questions 57 to 61 are based on the following passage.

Cultural norms so completely surround people, so permeate thought and action, that we never recognize the assumptions on which our lives rest. If birds were suddenly endowed with scientific curiosity they might examine many things, but the sky itself would be overlooked as a suitable subject; if fish were to become curious about the world, it would never occur to them to begin by investigating water. For birds and fish would take the sky and sea for granted, unaware of their profound influence because they comprise the medium for every act. Human beings, in a similar way, occupy a symbolic universe governed by codes that are unconsciously acquired and automatically different from the ways people conduct their affairs in other cultures.

As long as people remain blind to the sources of cultural norms, they are imprisoned within them. These cultural frames of reference are no less confining simply because they cannot be seen or touched. Whether it is an individual mentality that keeps an individual out of contact with his neighbors, or a collective mentality that separates neighbors of different cultures, both are forms of blindness that limit what can be experienced and what can be learned from others.

It would seem that everywhere people would desire to break out of the boundaries of their own worlds. Their ability to react sensitively to a wider spectrum of events and peoples requires an overcoming of such cultural parochialism. But, in fact, few attain this broader vision. Some have little opportunity for wider cultural experiences, though this condition should change as the movement of people accelerates. Others do not try to widen their experience because they prefer the old and familiar, seek from their affairs only further confirmation of the correctness of their own values. Still others avoid such experiences because they feel it dangerous to probe too deeply into the personal or cultural unconscious. Exposure may reveal how arbitrary many cultural norms are; such exposure might force people to acquire new bases for interpreting events. And even for those who do seek actively to enlarge the variety of human beings to communicate with, there are still difficulties.

Cultural near-sightedness persists not merely because of inertia and habit, but chiefly because it is so difficult to overcome. One acquires a personality and a culture in childhood, long before he is capable of comprehending either of them. To survive, each person masters the perceptual orientations, cognitive biases, and communicative habits of his own culture. But once mastered, objective assessment of these cultural processes is awkward, since the same mechanisms that are being evaluated must be used in making the evaluations.

(437 words)

57. The examples of birds and fish are used to _____.
   A) indicate that animals also have their respective cultures
   B) explain that human beings occupy a symbolic universe as birds and fish occupy the sky and the sea.
   C) illustrate that human beings are unaware of the cultural codes governing them
   D) demonstrate the similarity between man, birds, and fish in their ways of thinking
58. The underlined word "parochialism" in the third paragraph can best be replaced by _____.
   A) open-mindedness   B) provincialism
   B) colonialism   D) optimism
59. Which of the following statements is TRUE according to the passage?
   A) Individual and collective mentalities might prevent communication with others.
   B) People in different cultures may be governed by the same cultural norms.
   C) If cultural norms are something tangible, they won't be so confining.
   D) People's visions will be enlarged if only they know that cultural differences exist.
60. Which of the following can be inferred from the last paragraph?
   A) Everyone would like to widen their cultural scope if they can.
   B) The obstacles to overcoming cultural parochialism lie in mainly people's habitual way of thinking.
   C) As long as one is brought up in a certain culture, he cannot be without bias in making cultural evaluations.
   D) Childhood is an important stage in comprehending culture.
61. Which of the following might be the best title for the passage?
   A) How to Overcome Cultural Near-sightedness
   B) Different Cultural Norms
   C) Harms of Cultural Blindness
   D) Deep-rooted Cultural Near-sighted

Part Ⅴ　Error Correction (15 minutes)

Directions: *This part consists of a short passage. In this passage, there are altogether 10 mistakes, one in each numbered line. You may have to change a word, add a word or delete a word. Mark out the mistakes and put the corrections in the blanks provided. If you change a word, cross it out and write the correct word in the corresponding blank. If you add a word, put an insertion mark (∧) in the right place and write the missing word in the blank. If you delete a word, cross it out and put a slash (/) in the blank.*

Earthquakes are probably one of the most frightening and
destructive happenings of nature that man experiences. They
have caused the death of many human beings, much suffering
and greatly damage to property. Today, the study of earthquake　　　62. _____
has grown greatly with scientists all over the world　　　63. _____
investigating the causes of earthquakes. Scientists hope that their
studies will improve ways of predicting earthquakes and also
develop ways to reduce its destructive effects.　　　64. _____

The scientific study of earthquakes is fairly new. Until the
18th century many factual descriptions of earthquakes were　　　65. _____
recorded. In general, people did not understand the cause of
earthquakes. Many believe they were a punishment from God　　　66. _____
and a warning for them to repent (忏悔). One early theory was
that earthquakes were caused by air rushed out the caves deep in the　　　67. _____
interior of the earth.

On Nov. 1, 1755, a serious earthquake occurred near Lisbon,
Portugal. Shocks from the quake had felt in many parts of the world.　　　68. _____
After the quake, Portuguese priests were asked to observe and to
make written records. These records were the first system attempt　　　69. _____
to document the effects of an earthquake. Since that time, detailed
records have been kept to almost every major earthquakes.　　　70. _____

Currently, scientists are making studies to enable them to
predict earthquakes. But at the present time, the ability to predict the
time, place, and size of earthquakes are very limited.　　　71. _____

Part Ⅵ　Translation (5 minutes)

Directions: *Complete the sentences by translating into English the Chinese given in brackets. Please write your translation on **Answer Sheet 2**.*

72. Indeed, it _____ (正是总裁在投资问题上的仓促决定) eventually led to the bankruptcy of our corporation.

73. All his friends congratulated him _____ (听说他获得了演讲比赛一等奖).

74. The question _____ (是否该坦白交代) has troubled him for a week.

75. The technology in new automobiles changes so rapidly _____ (以至于今天的车比五年前生产的车要先进得多).

76. The fire was gaining on us, and there was _____ (除了祈祷外我们无能为力).

Test 5

Part I   Writing (30 minutes)

Directions: *For this part, you are allowed 30 minutes to write a composition on the title: Is Long Holiday Necessary? You should write at least 150 words following the outline given below in Chinese.*

Is Long Holiday Necessary

1. 对于长假是否必要，不同的人有不同的看法
2. 我认为长假是必要的，因为……
3. 如何度长假

Part II   Reading Comprehension (Skimming and Scanning) (15 minutes)

Directions: *In this part, you will have 15 minutes to go over the passage quickly and answer the questions on **Answer Sheet 1**. For questions 1–7, choose the best answer from the four choices marked A), B), C) and D). For questions 8–10 complete the sentences with the information given in the passage.*

Economizing of the Poor

Comprehending Economizing of the Poor

Walking down the aisles of a supermarket, low-income shoppers must consider a number of factors including quantity, price, quality and nutritional differences when selecting food products. Food-purchase decisions by the poor often entail balances among taste, preference and quality factors — either real or perceived — to meet spending constraints. Within broad product categories such as cereal, cheese, meat and poultry, and fruits and vegetables, shoppers can choose among many substitutable products. Low-income shoppers can extend their food dollars in a number of ways. They may shop in discount food stores; they may purchase and consume less food than higher-income shoppers; they may purchase low-priced (and possibly lower quality) food products; or they may rely on some combination of all three. A better understanding of how the poor economize in food spending addresses important policy questions raised by researchers, nutrition educators, and food-assistance program managers.

The Correlation between the Location and Price

Whether the poor face significantly different food prices due to where they shop for food remains an unresolved empirical question. Extensive research over the years has tried to answer the question — Do the poor pay less for food? The Economic Research Service (ERS) in 1997 received the results of studies comparing price differences in grocery stores across different income levels and combined these with current census data on the distribution of low-income households by urbanization type. The ERS study concluded that, in general, the poor face higher prices due to their greater representation in urban and rural areas (as opposed to suburban areas), where food prices tend to be higher.

Higher Prices but Less Spending

Based on results from household surveys, ERS also found that despite facing higher prices, low-income shoppers spend less than higher-income shoppers for food purchased in food stores. Due to their level of aggregation and lack of in-store sales and promotion information, such surveys shed little light on the economizing practices of households. To learn more about how low-income shoppers spend less for food despite facing higher prices, we obtained food-store purchase data that incorporate per-capita quantity and expenditure-measure equivalents (household measures adjusted for household size) across income levels.

The Main Economizing Practices

The resulting comparisons describe how individuals with different levels of income vary in their food-spending patterns. By using actual transaction data, detailed information about the product purchased (for example, price, product description, package size, and brand name) as well as the condition of purchase (promotion, coupon, or sale item) was obtained. From these, the average unit cost (per ounce, per pound) for each item was calculated. Low-income shoppers may use four primary economizing practices to reduce their food spending. First, they may purchase a greater proportion of discounted products. Second, they may purchase more private-label products (generic or store brand) versus brand products than higher-income shoppers buy. Third, they may take advantage of volume discounts by purchasing larger package sizes. Fourth, they may purchase a less-expensive food product within a product class. Although quality differences such as freshness, convenience and taste often contribute to prices differences, differences in nutritional quality are also evident.

More Spending on Promotional Items

The use of promotions is measured by comparing the percentage of expenditures and quantities of each product purchased on promotion (manufacturers' coupons, store coupons, store sales, and other promotions). For random-weight cheese, fruit, vegetables and meat in 1998, low-income households (less than $ 25, 000 per year) spent a greater share of expenditures for products on promotion than other households. (This is also true for quantities purchased on promotion.) For poultry, however, middle-income households spent about the same percentage on promotion as low-income households (36% versus 35%, respectively). For both groups, spending for promotion items was at least five percentage points more than spending by the high-income group.

Among fixed-weight products, promotion-spending patterns differed. Low-income shoppers purchased the lowest share of total ready-to-eat (RTE) cereal on promotion. This result may be explained by other economizing practices in this product category — such as purchasing a larger percentage of private-label products, which are on promotion less often but have lower non-sale prices than the brand-name alternatives. Low-income households spent 11.5% of their RTE cereal expenditures on private-label cereals, while the higher-income households spent lower shares, with those shares decreasing with increasing income levels. A similar pattern is found for the quantities of private-label RTE cereal purchased.

Choice of Package Size

Choice of package size also enables those in low-income households to economize by purchasing larger packages, which often have lower per-unit prices than smaller packages. However, data on expenditure shares for RTE cereal and packaged cheese show that low-income households' purchases of large packages of RTE cereal were less than such purchases by other households in 1998. In 1998, households earning $ 50, 000 or more spent 23.1% of cereal purchases on large packages, compared with 15.8% by the low-income group. A similar pattern was found for fixed-weight cheese products.

In fact, low-income households had the lowest proportion of large-package purchase of all income groups. This behavior has three possible explanations: Low-income shoppers do not have access to stores that sell large packages; they cannot afford to store staple products, and they perceive that the cost of storing large packages is higher than the savings from the volume discount. A combination of these constraints likely accounts for much of the observed difference in package size quantities purchased and expenditures on those packages by the different income groups.

Low-income shoppers may also be economizing by purchasing a less costly combination of fruit and vegetable product types. On average, low-income households paid 11.5% less per pound for vegetables than high-income households, and 9.6% less per pound for fruit. This price measurement is a function of the quality and expenditures that each household type devotes to fruits and vegetables. Overall, low-income households purchased 3.3% less fruits and vegetables (by weight) per person than high-income households, but they paid 13% less. This implies that these households are choosing less expensive fruits and vegetables, which saves a lot for them.

(1,005 words)

1. In order to _____, low-income shopped must base their food purchase decisions on a number of factors such as quantity, quality and price differences.
   A) keep up with the Joneses
   B) save shopping time
   C) meet financial constraints
   D) answer policy questions raised by food-assistance managers
2. According to an ERS study, low-income shoppers generally face higher food prices as _____.
   A) they tend to shop in nearby grocery stores instead of large shopping malls
   B) there is no escape of inflation problems
   C) they have no easy access to in-store sales and promotion information
   D) most of them live in urban and rural areas where food is higher priced
3. By _____, researchers found out about economizing practices of the poor in buying food.
   A) comparing price differences in grocery stores across different income levels
   B) analyzing current census data on the distribution of low-income households
   C) analyzing actual food transaction data across the income levels
   D) observing how the poor doing their shopping in supermarkets
4. Besides quality differences in freshness, convenience and taste, _____ also plays an obvious role in determining food prices.
   A) store locations   B) production costs
   C) nutritional quality differences   D) packaging costs
5. In 1998, low-income households was found to spend a greater share of expenditures for _____ than other households.
   A) fixed-weight on promotion
   B) random-weight fruit, vegetables and meat products on promotion
   C) large-package products on promotion
   D) total ready-to-eat cereal on promotion

6. As one of economizing measures, low-income households spent _____ of their ERT cereal expenditures on private-label cereal products.

    A) 23.1%   B) 15.8%   C) 11.5%   D) 9.6%

7. _____ can benefit low-income households in theory, but it seldom works in practice.

    A) The purchase of large-package products

    B) The purchase of private-label products

    C) The purchase of promotion items

    D) The purchase of discounted items

8. Higher-income households purchased less _____ RTE cereal than low-income households.

9. There are three possible explanations for the contradiction of the assumption of large-package purchase: transportation, _____ limitations.

10. Low-income shoppers may gain _____ on fruit and vegetable products.

Part Ⅲ   Listening Comprehension (35 minutes)

Section A

Directions: *In this section, you will hear 8 short conversations and 2 long conversations. At the end of each conversation, one or more questions will be asked about what was said. Both the conversation and questions will be spoken only once. After each question there will be a pause. During the pause you must read the four choices marked A), B), C) and D), and decide which is the best answer. Then mark the corresponding letter on Answer Sheet 2 with a single line through the center.*

11. A) She'll go to visit her aunt.

    B) She has an important appointment with a friend she has not seen for years.

    C) She thinks the traffic in New York is heavy on weekdays.

    D) She'll have a visitor.

12. A) He's excited that his mother-in-law is coming.

    B) He's thinking about quite a number of things.

    C) He's not feeling well lately.

    D) He's looking for a new apartment.

13. A) An apartment building.   B) A stadium.

    C) A theater.   D) A race-track.

14. A) The students should return to classes.

    B) There should be more issues to vote on.

    C) More students should come to the meetings.

    D) Last night's meeting was badly managed.

15. A) Ask the man to choose a gift for her.

    B) Decide on the wrapping paper for the gift.

    C) Go to Customer Service.

    D) Wrap the gift herself.

16. A) He has been asked to join the committee.

    B) He would like to take the woman's place on the committee.

    C) There are not many people interested in working on the committee.

    D) The woman should ask him to find a replacement.

17. A) The man hates to go to any barbecues indoors.
    B) The guests should be cooperative during a barbecue.
    C) The woman thinks they shouldn't spend too much time going to barbecues.
    D) The weather spoiled the last barbecue.
18. A) He made a sudden turn.
    B) He tried to avoid hitting the truck.
    C) He was pursued by the running dog.
    D) A girl riding a bike crashed into his car.

Questions 19 to 22 are based on the conversation you have just heard.

19. A) A comparison between conscious and unconscious behavior patterns.
    B) Recent developments in psychology research.
    C) Reasons for certain behavior patterns.
    D) Reasons for being late.
20. A) He feels angry.
    B) He wants to be noticed.
    C) He's reluctant to meet his friends.
    D) He's very nervous.
21. A) He's late for social occasions but not for work.
    B) He's a quiet person but likes to make grand entrances.
    C) He expects others to be on time but is usually late himself.
    D) He loses pay for being late for work but doesn't mind it.
22. A) Trying to let Mark know about his problem.
    B) Helping Mark relax and be more comfortable in a group.
    C) Waiting fifteen minutes and then leaving without Mark.
    D) Telling Mark to come earlier than the planned meeting time.

Questions 23 to 25 are based on the conversation you have just heard.

23. A) Collecting objects on the beach.   B) Creating models of different shapes.
    C) Mapping currents in the ocean.   D) Tracking water pollution.
24. A) An interesting piece of wood.   B) A bottle with a message inside.
    C) A pair of sneakers.   D) A piece of modern sculpture.
25. A) A storm can hardly change the direction of an ocean current.
    B) The loss of sneakers in the storm put the company in the financial difficulty.
    C) Not all useful experiments are planned ahead of time.
    D) Computers cannot always predict the effects of ocean storms.

Section B

Directions: *In this section, you will hear 3 short passages. At the end of each passage, you will hear some questions. Both the passage and questions will be spoken only once. After you hear a question, you must choose the best answer from the four choices marked A), B), C) and D). Then mark the corresponding letter on* **Answer Sheet 2** *with a single line through the center.*

Passage One
Questions 26 to 29 are based on the passage you have just heard.
26. A) Fire prevent.   B) Pest control.

C) House construction.   D) Toxic chemicals.

27. A) It's cheaper.   B) It's safer.

     C) It's quicker.   D) It's readily available.

28. A) To keep the heat inside.   B) To prevent insects from escaping.

     C) To reduce the risk of fire.   D) To keep the wood dry.

29. A) To show that the new method will not cause fire.

     B) To point out the danger of the old method.

     C) To explain a step in the new treatment.

     D) To indicate the good quality of construction wood.

Passage Two

Questions 30 to 32 are based on the passage you have just heard.

30. A) To commemorate a historic flight.

     B) To try out eight new balloons.

     C) To recruit balloonists from all over the United States.

     D) To test whether helium（氦气）balloons are better than hot-air balloons.

31. A) They may find it difficult to inflate their balloons.

     B) Their balloons are potentially explosive and dangerous.

     C) Their flight patterns could be uncertain due to the wind.

     D) They'll suffer financial loss if some balloons can't take off.

32. A) They're expensive.

     B) They're much faster than hydrogen balloons.

     C) They are more frequently used in the United States.

     D) They're a lot safer than hot-air balloons.

Passage Three

Questions 33 to 35 are based on the passage you have just heard.

33. A) Because they can't afford to.

     B) Because they prefer the apartments near their workplace.

     C) Because a mobile home is more convenient as they move from place to place.

     D) Because small houses are easy to redesign.

34. A) Because many old houses in the bad part of the town are not inhabited.

     B) Because old houses are much cheaper.

     C) Because many older couples sell their houses after their children leave.

     D) Because more and more people are choosing to rent comfortable apartments.

35. A) They have to furnish their own houses.

     B) They have to do their own maintenance.

     C) They will find it difficult to make the rest of payment.

     D) They will find it difficult to dispose of their old-style furniture.

Section C

Directions: *In this section, you will hear a passage three times. When the passage is read for the first time, you should listen carefully for its general idea. When the passage is read for the second time, you are required to fill in the blanks numbered from 36 to 43 with the exact words you have just heard. For blanks numbered from 44 to 46 you are required to fill in the missing information. For these blanks, you can either use the exact words you have just heard or write* *down the main points in your own words. Finally, when the passage is read for the third time, you should check what written.*

Packaging is the design and production of physical container for a product, which in fact becomes a part of total utility of the product. The consumer sees often the package and the contents as a whole, and his (36) _____ decision is influenced by the package. For example, the consumer may not be able to (37) _____ between two similar perfumes, but he or she will choose one in the more (38) _____ package. In recent years, the marketing (39) _____ of packaging has been increasingly recognized by enterprises. Today packaging has truly become a major (40) _____ force in the struggle for markets domestically and abroad.

However, over-packaging has also arisen as a noteworthy (41) _____. It's said that the public and Congressional concern about (42) _____ packaging started because Senator Hart discovered that the boxes of biscuits consumed by his family were becoming higher and narrower, with a (43) _____ of net weight from 12 to 10.5 ounces, without any reduction in price. There were still twelve biscuits, but they had been reduced in size. (44) _____ _____. As the package journals show week by week, there is never any hesitation in introducing a new size and shape of box or bottle. (45) _____ _____, but no one in the trade comments unfavorably on the huge costs incurred by endless changes of package sizes that are used for improving a product's market position. (46) _____ _____, according to the Environmental Protection Agency in Washington.

Part Ⅳ Reading Comprehension (Reading in Depth) (25 minutes)
Section A
Directions: *In this section, there is a short passage with 5 questions or incomplete statements. Read the passage carefully. Then answer the questions or complete the statements in the fewest possible words. Please write your answers on* **Answer Sheet 2***.*

When you stop smoking, you're likely to feel tense, nervous, irritable, anxious — even eat more. You may think it's purely psychological, but it's also physical. It's caused by your body craving nicotine — physically craving nicotine. And Habitrol can help relieve those cravings.

Habitrol is a nicotine patch, available only by prescription from your doctor. It replaces some of the nicotine you're not getting from cigarettes and helps lessen the effects of your withdrawal symptoms. When used as part of a comprehensive behavioral smoking cessation program, Habitrol has been clinically proven to increase the chances of quitting smoking in the critical first three months. That's when the nicotine withdrawal symptoms force many people back to smoking.

Remember how stressed out, anxious and burdensome you felt the last time you tried to quit? And how you thought it was purely psychological and there was nothing that could help you? Well, now you know it's also physical and there is something that can help you. Habitrol.

Habitrol is a drug indicated as an aid to smoking cessation for the relief of nicotine withdrawal symptoms. Its effectiveness has been established only as part of a comprehensive behavioral smoking cessation program. It won't work for everyone. In studies during the first 3 months after quitting, Habitrol has been shown to increase the chances of stopping smoking.

Long-term studies of Habitrol haven't been conducted. It shouldn't be used for more than 3 months.

Habitrol, like cigarettes, contains nicotine, so stop smoking completely before starting Habitrol. And do not smoke or use anything with nicotine while on it. If you're pregnant or nursing (nicotine could cause fatal harm) or have heart disease, or other conditions, ask your doctor about other ways to stop smoking. If you're taking prescription medicine or under a doctor's care, ask your doctor about the potential risks of Habitrol. Habitrol hasn't been studied in pregnant women or in patients under 18. Used and unused Habitrol systems should be kept out of the reach of children and pets.

(335 words)

47. Giving up smoking in the first few months will make smokers have a stronger desire _____.

48. Not stated but implied in the first two paragraphs is that stopping smoking can be a(n) _____ for you.

49. What is the function of Habitrol in quitting smoking?
_____

50. Habitrol is very effective for increasing the chances of stopping smoking _____.

51. Since Habitrol contains nicotine, it can only be used in those who _____.

Section B

Directions: *There are 2 passages in this section. Each passage is followed by some questions or unfinished statements. For each of them there are four choices marked A), B), C) and D). You should decide on the best choice and mark the corresponding letter on **Answer Sheet 2** with a single line through the center.*

Passage One

Questions 52 to 56 are based on the following passage.

France might be described as an "all-round" country, one that has achieved results of equal importance in many diverse branches of artistic and intellectual activity. Most of great nations of Europe excel (胜过) in some special branch of art or of thought, Italy in the plastic arts, Germany in philosophy and music, England in poetry and the sciences. France, on the contrary, has produced philosophers, musicians, painters, scientists, without any noticeable specialization of her effort. The French ideal has always been the man who has a good all-round knowledge better still, an all-round understanding; it is the ideal of general culture as opposed to specialization. This is the ideal reflected in the education France provides for her children. By studying this education we in England may learn a few things useful to ourselves even though, perhaps indeed because, the French system is very different from our own in its aims, its organization and its results. The French child, too, the raw material of this education, is unlike the English child and differences in the raw material may well account for differences in the processes employed.

The French child, boy or girl, gives one the impression of being intellectually more precocious (早熟的) than the product of the chillier English climate. This precocity is encouraged by his upbringing among adults, not in a nursery. English parents readily adapt their conversation to the child's point of view and interest themselves more in his games and childish preoccupations. The English are, as regards national character, younger than the French, or, to put it another way, there is in England no deep division between the life of the child and that of the grown man. The art of talking to children in the kind of language they understand is so much an English art that most of the French children's favorite books are translations from the English. French parents, on the other hand, do their best to develop the child's intelligence as rapidly as possible. They have little patience with childish ideas even if they do not go so far as to look upon childhood as an unfortunate but necessary prelude (序言) to adult life. Not that they need to force the child, for he usually leads himself willingly to the process, and enjoys the effect of his unexpectedly clever remarks and of his keen judgment of men and things. It is not without significance that the French mother instead of appealing to the child's heart by asking him to be good appeals to his reason by asking him to be wise. Reasonableness is looked for early in France, and the age of reason is fixed at seven years.

(445 words)

52. The author considers that France _____.
    A) specialized in the ideal of general culture
    B) favors the ideal of general culture
    C) is a specialist country as compared with other countries.
    D) cannot help being a specialist country
53. In comparing French and English education, the author indicates that _____.
    A) the main differences are in the children
    B) the French child needs far more training
    C) a great deal can be learnt by both countries
    D) differences should not be looked for only in the methods
54. The passage suggests that the French child _____.
    A) only associates with adults   B) is as he is because of the climate
    C) is not treated as a child   D) is forced to behave like an adult
55. In Paragraph 2, what is said about books _____.
    A) is not in any sense a contradiction
    B) appears to be somewhat contradictory
    C) suggests that French parents like English children's books
    D) suggests that French parents find these books educational
56. With what conclusion, regarding French mother, is the reader left?
    A) They equate goodness with reason.
    B) They identify wisdom with reasonableness.
    C) They know how to appeal to what is best in their sons.
    D) They are the most significant influence in their son's lives.

Passage Two
Questions 57 to 61 are based on the following passage.
    The desire for achievement is one of life's great mysteries. Social scientists have devoted lifetimes to studying the drives that spur us out of bed in the morning, compel us to work or study hard and spark all manner of human endeavor. Indeed, a textbook actually documents 32 distinct theories of human motivation.
    Given this diversity of thought, it's easy to forget that for a half century, American society has been dominated by the psychological school known as behaviorism, or Skinnerian psychology. Although behaviorism and its fundamental principle of "positive reinforcement"

have long since lost their way in academic circles, the Skinnerian legacy remains powerful in every field of daily life, from the home and classroom to the workplace. Don't want to take the trash out? Do it, and you can go to the movies on Friday night. Not in the mood for work? Keep plugging away, and you might get a bonus. Not interested in calculus? Strive for an A in the class, and you'll make the honor roll. The theory may be bankrupt, but incentives and rewards are so much a part of American culture that it's hard to imagine life without them.

Yet that's exactly what a growing group of researchers are advocating against today. A steady stream of research has found that rather than encouraging motivation and productivity, rewards actually can undermine genuine interest and diminish performance. "Our society is caught in a whopping paradox," asserts Alfie Kohn, author of the new book published by Rewards (Houghton Mifflin), which surveys recent research in the effectiveness of rewards. "We complain loudly about declining productivity, the crisis of our school and the distorted values of our children. But the very strategy we use to solve those problems — dangling rewards like incentive plans and grade and candy bars in front of people — is partly responsible for the fix we're in."

It's a tough argument to make in a culture that celebrates the spoils of success. Yet study after study shows that people tend to perform worse, to give up more easily and to lose interest more quickly when a reward is involved. Children who are given treats for doing artwork, for example, lose their initial love of art within weeks. Teenagers who are promised a reward for tutoring youngsters don't teach as enthusiastically as tutors offered nothing. And chief executive officers who have been awarded long-term incentive plans have often steered their companies toward lower returns.

(407 words)

57. According to behaviorism, all human actions _____.
    A) are of a great mystery   B) have no bearing on human drives
    C) are supposed to be highly motivated   D) are based on stimulus and response
58. Behaviorism basically believes in _____.
    A) motivation   B) performance   C) rewards   D) human factors
59. From the passage, it can be inferred that _____.
    A) rewards are highly effective in America
    B) rewards are not much sought-after in academic circles
    C) rewards have long lost their appeal in American society
    D) Americans are addicted to rewards
60. Recent research findings prove that _____.
    A) rewards can result in low productivity
    B) behaviorism is still influential in America
    C) positive reinforcement still work wonders
    D) there is a crisis of values in American school
61. The children's behavior in the last paragraph _____.
    A) can be best explained by behaviorism
    B) can be linked to Pavlov's dogs
    C) shows that rewards may well kill desire
    D) serves to provide evidence to behaviorism

Part Ⅴ **Cloze** (**15 minutes**)

Directions: *There are 20 blanks in the following passage. For each blank there are four choices marked A), B), C) and D) on the right side of the paper. You should choose the ONE that best fits into the passage. Then mark the corresponding letter on **Answer Sheet 2** with a single line through the center.*

There are no bad foods, only bad diets. So say many nutritionists, who ___62___ the demonization (妖魔化) of some foods as junk. On the evidence, there are an awful lot of bad diets around. A recent nationwide weigh-in of 11-year-olds ___63___ that at a fifth were obese and since being weighed was voluntary and larger children were less ___64___ to step on the scales, this was no doubt an underestimate.

So Ofcom, the communications watchdog, has ___65___ that it may be time for a little food demonization after all. In the following few months it is to bring in a ban ___66___ advertising foods that contain lots of fat or sugar during TV shows that ___67___ particularly to children. And brand advertising, where no particular products is mentioned, will be ___68___. The basic idea is popular with parents, who see it as an easier option than using the off switch.

There are also worries about the specific foods ___69___. Ofcom is using a "nutrient-

profiling scheme", in which foods are ___70___ points for their good qualities (containing fruit or vegetables, say) and penalized for bad ones (lots of salt, sugar or fat). But the calculations are ___71___ on a 100g-portion of the food, so condiments (佐料) such as Marmite and ketchup, which are never ___72___ in such large quantities, are out. And nutritionally valueless foods containing fat and sugar substitutes may pass muster, ___73___ nutritionally dense staples

such as some cheese will not. ___74___ breast milk

for sale, it would be banned, ___75___ it is too high in fat and sugar.

Sweden and Norway, which have the usual Scandinavian ___76___ for public health, get

62.	A. argue for	B. stand for
	C. object to	D. stick to
63.	A. reveals	B. demonstrates
	C. illustrates	D. appreciates
64.	A. possible	B. probable
	C. likely	D. potential
65.	A. determined	B. decided
	C. proposed	D. doubted
66.	A. for	B. with
	C. against	D. on
67.	A. attracts	B. replies
	C. attributes	D. appeals
68.	A. exempt	B. immune
	C. excused	D. impaired
69.	A. oriented	B. confirmed
	C. targeted	D. presented
70.	A. rewarded	B. awarded
	C. allowed	D. ascribed
71.	A. focused	B. based
	C. relied	D. carried
72.	A. resumed	B. assumed
	C. presumed	D. consumed
73.	A. as	B. while
	C. though	D. since
74.	A. Were	B. When
	C. Had	D. If
75.	A. and	B. for
	C. but	D. so
76.	A. devotion	B. commit

round these definitional difficulties ___77___ banning all advertising to children. The immediate impact on food industry in Britain will anyway be ___78___, as these newly dubbed junk foods are not often heavily advertised. But there is more at ___79___ than the food industry's interests. Anyone cutting out entire food groups is likely to suffer vitamin and mineral ___80___. Many girls already avoid dairy products for fear of gaining weight, and giving them another reason to ___81___ themselves is a bad idea.

C. enthusiasm   D. emotion

77. A. on   B. for
    C. by   D. at

78. A. enormous   B. limited
    C. impressive   D. vague

79. A. stake   B. cost
    C. least   D. last

80. A. deficiencies   B. poisoning
    C. shortage   D. efficiency

81. A. hurt   B. starve
    C. mistreat   D. injure

Part Ⅵ　Translation（5 minutes）

Directions：*Complete the sentences by translating into English the Chinese given in brackets. Please write your translation on **Answer Sheet 2**.*

82. She has applied to the university _____（延长她对牛津大学的访问时间）.

83. _____（正如人们所预料的那样），the response to the question was very mixed.

84. A foreign language _____（是服务于人的一种有用的工具），we should do our best to have a good command of it.

85. Once they had fame, fortune, secure futures; _____（如今只剩下贫穷）.

86. My sister _____（计划在一年之内拿到一个文学硕士学位）.

Test 6

Part Ⅰ   Writing（30 minutes）

Directions：*For this part，you are allowed 30 minutes to write a composition on the title*：*How to Treat Our Aging Population? You should write at least 150 words following the outline given below in Chinese.*

How to Treat Our Aging Population

1. 中国已渐渐步入老龄化社会（65 岁以上的老年人已占全国人口的 7%）
2. 我认为应如何对待老年人群（社会关爱与福利制度，家庭温暖，社区服务……）
3. 我的结论

Part Ⅱ   Reading Comprehension（Skimming and Scanning）（15 minutes）

Directions：*In this part，you will have 15 minutes to go over the passage quickly and answer the questions on* **Answer Sheet 1**. *For questions 1 - 7，choose the best answer from the four choices marked A），B），C）and D）. For questions 8 - 10 complete the sentences with the information given in the passage.*

The Geodesic Dome（圆顶屋）— the House of the Future?

R. Buckminster Fuller spent much of the early 20 th century looking for ways to improve human shelter by applying modern technological know-how to shelter construction, making shelter more comfortable and efficient, and more economically available to a greater number of people.

After acquiring some experience in the building industry and discovering the traditional practices and perceptions which severely limit changes and improvements in construction practices, Fuller carefully examined and improved interior structure equipment, including the toilet, the shower, and the bathroom as a whole. He studied structure shells, and devised a number of alternatives, each less expensive, lighter, and stronger than traditional wood, brick, and stone buildings.

In 1944, the United States suffered a serious housing shortage. Government officials knew that Fuller had developed a prototype of family dwelling which could be produced rapidly, using the same equipment which had previously built war-time airplanes. They could be "installed" anywhere, the way a telephone is installed, and with little additional difficulty. When one official flew to Wichita, Kansas to see this house, which Beech Aircraft and Fuller built, the man reportedly gasped, "My God! This is the house of the future!"

Soon, unsolicited checks poured in from people who wanted to purchase this new kind of house, but Fuller was never able to get it into full production. This was due to many obstacles such as only union contractors were able to hook the houses up to water, power and sewers in many cities. However, because the houses were already wired and had the plumbing installed by the aircraft company, many construction trade unions made it clear that they would not work on the houses. There were also in-house differences between Fuller and the stockholders. Fuller did not feel the house design was complete; there were problems he wanted to fix. But the stockholders wanted to move ahead. However, the main obstruction was obtaining the financing

for the tooling costs, which were purposefully not included in the negotiations with investors. No bank would finance the project with union problems and stockholder battles.

After the war, Fuller's efforts focused on the problem of how to build a shelter which is so lightweight that it can be delivered by air. Shelter should be mobile which would require great breakthroughs in the weight-reduction of the materials. Technology would have to follow nature's design as seen by the spider's web which can float in a hurricane because of its high strength-to-weight ratio. New shelter would have to be designed that assimilates these principles and that was Fuller's intent.

One of the ways Buckminster Fuller would describe the differences in strength between a rectangle and a triangle would be apply pressure to both structures. The rectangle would fold up and be unstable but the triangle withstands the pressure and is much more rigid — in fact the triangle is twice as strong. This principle directed his studies toward creating a new architectural design, the geodesic dome, based also upon his idea of "doing more with less". Fuller discovered that if a spherical structure was created from triangles, it would have incomparable strength.

The sphere uses the "doing more with less" principle in that it encloses the largest volume of interior space with the least amount of surface area thus saving on materials and cost. Fuller reintroduced the idea that when the sphere's diameter is doubled it will quadruple its square footage and produce eight times the volume.

The spherical (球形的) structure of a dome is one of the most efficient interior atmospheres for human dwellings because air and energy are allowed to circulate without obstruction. This enables heating and cooling to occur naturally. Geodesic shelters have been built all around the world in different climates and temperatures and still they have proven to be the most efficient human shelter one can find.

More specifically, the dome is energy efficient for many reasons: Its decreased surface area requires less building materials; exposure to cold in the winter and heat in the summer is decreased because, being spherical, there is the least surface area per unity of volume per structure; the curved-in interior creates a natural airflow that allows the hot or cool air to flow evenly throughout the dome with the help of return air ducts; extreme wind turbulence is lessened because the winds that contribute to heat loss flow smoothly around the dome; it acts like a type of giant down-pointing headlight reflector and reflects and concentrates interior heat. This helps prevent radiant heat loss.

The net annual energy savings for a dome owner is 30% more than normal rectilinear (直线的) homes according to the Oregon Dome Co. This is quite an improvement and helps save the environment from wasted energy. Domes have been designed by Fuller and others to withstand high winds and extreme temperatures as seen in the Polar Regions.

Many dome manufacturers offer various designs in geodesic dome housing with little assembly time required. Some houses can be assembled in less than a day with others taking up to six months. Many also come in dome kits that buyers can build themselves or with the help of friends.

R. Buckminster Fuller's first worldwide acceptance by the architectural community occurred with the 1954 Triennale where his cardboard dome was displayed for the first time. The Milan Triennale was established to stage international exhibitions aimed to present the most innovative accomplishments in the fields of design, crafts, architecture and city planning.

The theme for 1954 was Life between Artifact and Nature: Design and the Environmental Challenge, which fit in perfectly with Fuller's work. Fuller had begun efforts towards the development of a Comprehensive Anticipatory Design Science, which he defined as, "the effective application of the principles of science to the conscious design of our total environment in order to help make the Earth's limited resources meet the needs of all humanity without disrupting the ecological processes of the planet." The cardboard shelter that was part of his exhibit could be easily shipped and assembled with the directions printed right on the cardboard. The 42-foot paper board Geodesic was installed in old Sforza garden in Milan and came away with the highest award, the Grand Premio.

(1,036 words)

1. For a good part of the early 20th century, Fuller was devoted to _____.
   A) making shelter more comfortable and efficient, and less expensive
   B) learning modern technology in shelter construction
   C) acquiring some experiences in building industry
   D) discovering traditions in construction practices worldwide

2. In 1944, government officials saw great promise in the family dwelling designed by Fuller because _____.
   A) it could improve housing conditions of the ordinary people
   B) it could be produced rapidly and installed easily
   C) it was mobile and convenient to live in
   D) it was strong and weather-resistant

3. Fuller's new design of house in 1944 failed to go into production mainly because of _____.
   A) intervention from aircraft companies
   B) the disagreements between Fuller and shareholders
   C) obstructions from construction trade unions
   D) financing difficulties

4. After WWII, Fuller became interested in building a new shelter _____.
   A) with a low strength-to-weight ratio
   B) that is both strong and light enough to be air-delivered
   C) that is tough enough to survive a hurricane
   D) in the shape of spider's web

5. Fuller created the geodesic dome, a new architectural design that _____.
   A) is shaped like a triangle
   B) occupies a great amount of ground area
   C) is built from rectangles
   D) follows the principle of "doing more with less"

6. What makes geodesic domes environmentally friendly structures?
   A) They produce less waste water.
   B) They require much less expensive construction materials.
   C) They are energy efficient.
   D) They can resist high winds and extreme temperatures.

7. Every year, a dome owner may spend _____ less in energy expenditure than a normal rectilinear home one.
   A) 10%　　　　　　B) 20%　　　　　　C) 30%　　　　　　D) 40%

8. Besides the feature of "doing more with less", the spherical structure of dome can also allow natural _____ without obstruction.

9. It has been proved that the geodesic dome is _____ human shelter.

10. Fuller won _____ in 1954 for his achievement in the 42-foot cardboard shelter.

Part III Listening Comprehension (35 minutes)

Section A

Directions: *In this section, you will hear 8 short conversations and 2 long conversations. At the end of each conversation, one or more questions will be asked about what was said. Both the conversation and questions will be spoken only once. After each question there will be a pause. During the pause you must read the four choices marked A), B), C) and D), and decide which is the best answer. Then mark the corresponding letter on* **Answer Sheet 2** *with a single line through the center.*

11. A) At the airport.
    C) At a hotel.
    B) In a travel agency.
    D) In a restaurant.

12. A) His only daughter is dying.
    B) His mother died some time ago.
    C) He failed to take good care of his daughter.
    D) He neglected his sick wife because of heavy work duties.

13. A) He wears blue jeans when exercising.
    B) He hasn't bought new pants for a while.
    C) He has bought plenty of new blue jeans recently.
    D) He has gained weight lately.

14. A) She knows a larger apartment he can rent.
    B) She is used to living in a large apartment.
    C) She knows the man's neighbor is moving out.
    D) The man should go and see her apartment.

15. A) Their parents cut back the loan.
    B) They can't pay the rent for the month.
    C) The woman's boss refused to give her a raise.
    D) They have overspent during their holiday trip.

16. A) Move his plants away from the window.
    B) Water the plants more often.
    C) Let the plants have more sunlight.
    D) Let her take care of the plants for a while.

17. A) To remind him of the data he should take to the conference.
    B) To see if he has time to attend the conference.
    C) To inform him of the latest arrangements about the conference.
    D) To help him prepare for the coming conference.

18. A) She feels excited.
    C) She is indifferent.
    B) She feels surprised.
    D) She is a little annoyed.

Questions 19 to 22 are based on the conversation you have just heard.

19. A) He worked as a sales-assistant in a clothing shop.
    B) He was the manager of a clothing shop.
    C) He worked in a laundry.
    D) He was a lifeguard in a swimming pool.

20. A) She had four months free before she went to college.
    B) Her working place was near where she lived.
    C) She was unqualified for anything.
    D) She needed the money.
21. A) They were all above thirty years old.
    B) All the workmates were tough to her.
    C) The oldest workmate was kind to her.
    D) She got along quite well with all the workmates.
22. A) She washed nurses' aprons and surgeons' caps.
    B) She pressed surgeons' caps and nurses' aprons.
    C) She folded surgeons' caps and nurses' aprons into knife-edged creases.
    D) She steamed the clothes of the surgeons and nurses.

Questions 23 to 25 are based on the conversation you have just heard.
23. A) To improve his skating techniques.
    B) To visit his sister in New Mexico.
    C) To take a vacation.
    D) To learn to ski in Albuquerque.
24. A) She went there last year.
    B) Her sister works there.
    C) She lives only thirty minutes away from there.
    D) She goes there on regular business trips.
25. A) The high altitude.   B) The unpredictable climate.
    C) The extreme temperatures.   D) The wild animals.

Section B
Directions: *In this section, you will hear 3 short passages. At the end of each passage, you will hear some questions. Both the passage and questions will be spoken only once. After you hear a question, you must choose the best answer from the four choices marked A), B), C) and D). Then mark the corresponding letter on **Answer Sheet 2** with a single line through the center.*

Passage One
Questions 26 to 29 are based on the passage you have just heard.
26. A) A comparison of fish as a cold-blooded animal with warm-blooded animals.
    B) The difference between water animals and land animals.
    C) The importance of fish to human beings.
    D) How water has affected the development of fish.
27. A) It can't be compressed.   B) It's often polluted.
    C) Its temperature often fluctuates. D) It limits their size.
28. A) A whale.   B) A snail.
    C) A snake.   D) A human.
29. A) Its skeleton.   B) Its shape.
    C) Its senses.   D) Its body temperature.

Passage Two

Questions 30 to 32 are based on the passage you have just heard.

30. A) Speak very slowly but loudly.
    B) Ask questions frequently.
    C) Vary pitch, volume and speed of speech.
    D) Keep the speech clear and concise.
31. A) Use a good microphone.   B) Use smaller rooms.
    C) Remain the same in the volume.   D) Not to shout.
32. A) By raising pitch.   B) By pausing.
    C) By lowering registers.   D) By using gestures.

Passage Three

Questions 33 to 35 are based on the passage you have just heard.

33. A) Fuel-efficient cars.   B) Air pollution caused by cars.
    C) History of Automobile developments. D) Electric-powered cars.
34. A) They're cheaper and simpler to drive.
    B) They are faster.
    C) They cause littler air pollution.
    D) They have a brighter future.
35. A) It's small and not comfortable to sit in.
    B) It can't go long distance without recharging.
    C) The batteries are expensive to build.
    D) It costs a lot to have batteries recharged.

Section C

Directions: *In this section, you will hear a passage three times. When the passage is read for the first time, you should listen carefully for its general idea. When the passage is read for the second time, you are required to fill in the blanks numbered from 36 to 43 with the exact words you have just heard. For blanks numbered from 44 to 46 you are required to fill in the missing information. For these blanks, you can either use the exact words you have just heard or write down the main points in your own words. Finally, when the passage is read for the third time, you should check what you have written.*

It is no accident that more and more people are educating their children at home. Home schooling in the United States is no longer an (36) _____ or unorganized movement. Today's schools and day care centers are in serious trouble, despite the many (37) _____ individuals who teach in public schools or who care for children. Fewer and fewer children are receiving the (38) _____ attention, values, and skills they need in order to (39) _____. Tied together with this is the fact that many children today spend very little (40) _____ time with their parents. Family life is fast becoming (41) _____. Home schooling is an attempt to return the family to children—the children who (42) _____ long for the loving authority that only parents can give, the children who will not resent their parents' (43) _____ and correction.

There are many good reasons why parents home-school their children. (44) _____

_____. Some couples home-school for religious and moral reasons. (45) _____

_____

_____. Some couples home-school simply to solidify their own sense of family togetherness. (46) _____
_____. These reasons — and there are surely many others — are both understandable and justified.

Part IV   Reading Comprehension（Reading in Depth）（25 minutes）

Section A

Directions: *In this section, there is a short passage with 5 questions or incomplete statements. Read the passage carefully. Then answer the questions or complete the statements in the fewest possible words. Please write your answers on **Answer Sheet 2**.*

The importance of and focus on the interview in the work of the print and broadcast journalist is reflected in several books that have been written on the topic. Most of these books, as well as several chapters, mainly in, but not limited to, journalism and broadcasting handbooks and reporting texts, stress the "how-to" aspects of journalistic interviewing rather than the conceptual aspects of the interview, its context and implications. Much of the "how-to" material is based on personal experiences and general impressions. As we know, in journalism as in other fields, much can be learned from the systematic study of professional practice. Such study brings together evidence from which broad generalized principles can be developed.

There is, as has been suggested, a growing body of research literature in journalism and broadcasting, but very little significant attention has been devoted to the study of the interview itself. On the other hand, many general texts as well as numerous research articles on interviewing in fields other than journalism have been written. Many of these books and articles present the theoretical and empirical aspects of the interview as well as the training of the interviewers. Unhappily, this plentiful general literature about interviewing pays little attention to the journalistic interview. The fact that the general literature on interviewing does not deal with the journalistic interview seems to be surprising for two reasons. First, it seems likely that most people in modern Western societies are more familiar, at least in a positive manner, with journalistic interviewing than with any other form of interviewing. Most of us are provably somewhat familiar with the clinical interview, such as that conducted by physicians and psychologists. In these situations the professional person or interviewer is interested in getting information necessary for the diagnosis and treatment of the person seeking help. Another familiar situation is the job interview. However, very few of us have actually been interviewed personally by the mass media, particularly by television. And yet, we have a vivid acquaintance with the journalistic interview by virtue of our roles as readers, listeners, and viewers. Even so, true understanding of the journalistic interview, especially television interviews, requires thoughtful analysis and even study, as this book indicates.

(369 words)

47. The main idea of the first paragraph is that importance should be attached to the systematic study of _____.
48. Much research has been done on interviews in general but journalistic interviewing as a specific field has unfortunately _____.
49. Westerners are familiar with the journalistic interview but most of them may not have been _____.

50. Who is the interviewee in a clinical interview?

   _____

51. The passage is most likely a part of a _____ .

Section B

Directions: *There are 2 passages in this section. Each passage is followed by some questions or unfinished statements. For each of them there are four choices marked A), B), C) and D). You should decide on the best choice and mark the corresponding letter on **Answer Sheet 2** with a single line through the centre.*

Passage One

Questions 52 to 56 are based on the following passage.

Low self-esteem pops up regularly in academic reports as an explanation for all sorts of violence, from hate crimes and street crimes to terrorism. But despite the popularity of the explanation, not much evidence backs it up. In a recent issue of *Psychological Review*, three researchers examine this literature at length and conclude that a much stronger link connects high self-esteem to violence. "It is difficult to maintain belief in the low self-esteem view after seeing that the more violent groups are generally the ones with higher self-esteem." write Roy Baumeister of Case Western Reserve University and Laura Smart and Joseph Boden of the University of Virginia.

The conventional view is that people without self-esteem try to gain it by hurting others. The researchers find that violence is much more often the work of people with unrealistically high self-esteem attacking others who challenge their self-image. Under this umbrella come bullies, rapists, racists, psychopaths and members of street gangs and organized crime.

The study concludes: Certain forms of high self-esteem seem to increase one's proneness to violence. An uncritical endorsement of the cultural value of self-esteem may therefore be counterproductive and even dangerous. The societal pursuit of high self-esteem for everyone may literally end up doing considerable harm. "As for prison programs intended to make violent convicts feel better about themselves, "perhaps it would be better to try instilling modesty and humility." the researchers wrote.

In an interview with the Boston Globe, Baumeister said he believed the "self-promoting establishment" was starting to crumble. "What would work better for the country is to forget about self-esteem and concentrate on self-control." he said. In the schools, this would mean turning away from psychic boosterism and emphasizing self-esteem as a by-product of real achievement, not as an end in itself. The self-esteem movement, still entrenched in schools of education, is deeply implicated in the dumbing down of our schools, and in the disguised equality behind the idea that it is a terrible psychic blow if one student does any better or any worse than another. Let's hope it is indeed crumbling.

(362 words)

52. The researchers find that there are stronger connections between _____ .
   A) low self-esteem and violence   B) low self-control and violence
   C) high self-image and violence   D) high self-control and violence
53. Traditionally, it is believed that people without self-esteem _____ .
   A) are usually the targets of organized crime
   B) are less violent than those with unrealistically high self-esteem

C) are more likely to hurt others to gain self-esteem

D) always resort to violence when their self-image is challenged

54. The conclusions from the study indicate that _____.

    A) the pursuit of high self-esteem is a trend of modern living

    B) what is beneficial for the country is self-control rather than self-esteem

    C) it is productive to promote the traditional culture value of self-esteem

    D) modesty and humility should be emphasized to avoid harmful effect of high self-esteem

55. Nowadays in the schools _____.

    A) self-esteem is emphasized as the ultimate goal of one's pursuit

    B) the self-esteem movement has lost its momentum

    C) the idea of self-esteem boosts real achievement

    D) emphasis in self-esteem helps to promote the idea of equality

56. The researchers would most probably agree with the following EXCEPT _____.

    A) prisons should change their present practice

    B) school should change their concepts of self-esteem

    C) the tradition view is beginning to lose ground

    D) self-esteem should be promoted and encouraged

Passage Two

Questions 57 to 61 are based on the following passage.

By 2030, people over 65 in Germany, the world's third-largest economy, will account for almost half the adult population, compared with one-fifth now. And unless the country's birth rate recovers from its present low of 1.3 per woman, over the same period its population of under 35 will shrink about twice as fast as the older population will grow. The net result will be that the total population, now 82 m, will decline to 70 m - 73 m. The number of people of working age will fall by a full quarter, from 40 m today to 30 m.

The German demographics(人口统计) are far from exceptional. In Japan, the world's second-largest economy, the population will peak in 2005, at around 125 m. By 2050, according to the more pessimistic government forecasts, the population will have shrunk to around 95 m. Long before that, around 2030, the share of the over-65's in the adult population will have grown to about half. And the birth rate in Japan, as in Germany, is down to 1.3 per woman. The figures are pretty much the same for most other developed countries, and for a good many emerging ones, especially China.

Life expectancy — and with it the number of older people — has been going up steadily for 300 years. But the decline in the number of young people is something new. The only developed country that has so far avoided this fate is America. But even there the birth rate is well below replacement level, and the proportion of older people in the adult population will rise steeply in the next 30 years.

All this means that winning the support of older people will become a political imperative (需要) in every developed country. Pensions have already become a regular election issue. There is also a growing debate about the desirability of immigration to maintain the population and workforce. Together these two issues are transforming the political landscape in every developed country.

By 2030 at the latest, the age at which full retirement benefits start will have risen to the mid-70's in all developed countries, and benefits for healthy pensioners will be substantially lower than they are today. Indeed, fixed retirement ages for people in reasonable physical and mental condition may have been abolished to prevent the pensions burden on the working population from becoming unbearable. Already young and middle-aged people at work suspect that there will not be enough pension money to go round when they themselves reach traditional retirement age. But politicians everywhere continue to pretend that they can save the current pensions system.

(426 words)

57. In Germany, _____.
   A) birth rate has gone up to 1.3 per woman
   B) people over 65 now constitutes about half the adult population
   C) its population of under-35s is twice as large as that of over-65s
   D) by 2030 its working force may have shrunk by 25%

58. The problem that the population becomes aging _____.
   A) is exceptional to Germany
   B) has become universal
   C) can be relieved in Japan with the shrinkage of its population to around 95 m
   D) makes the economic outlook in the developed countries even more gloomy

59. A new tendency is demographic change is that _____.
   A) life expectancy has been going up steadily
   B) there is a decline of the young population
   C) in America the birth rate has gone above replacement level
   D) the old population has risen sharply in USA

60. What is the political implication of the demographic change in the developed countries?
   A) Winning the support of older people will become crucial in politics.
   B) Pension policy will become a key issue in elections.
   C) Immigration should be banned to maintain the workforce.
   D) The demographic change will change the political landscape greatly.

61. By 2030 the governments in developed countries may put an end to fixed retirement ages _____.
   A) to save the current pension system
   B) to ensure the benefits for healthy pensioners
   C) to realize full retirement benefits substantially
   D) to relieve the pensions burden on the working population

Part V Cloze (15 minutes)

Directions: *There are 20 blanks in the following passage. For each blank there are four choices marked A), B), C) and D) on the right side of the paper. You should choose the ONE that best fits into the passage. Then mark the corresponding letter on **Answer Sheer 2** with a single line through the center.*

Rising bright and early on a Saturday used to be a matter of survival in Germany. __62__ the 1990s most shops closed for the weekend at 2 pm. Today you can __63__ into the wee hours every day except Sunday. In most German states

62. A) After   B) Until
    B) When   D) While

63. A) work   B) sleep
    C) shop   D) read

shophours are, or about to be, fully __64__.

That should lay to rest the __65__ that Germany

is anti-consumer. But it also __66__ a change in attitudes to time.

Germans have long fretted over time. Wasting it is forbidden; __67__ is required. The country's austere Protestantism helps to explain this, but __68__ may a culture of industrial might. The efficient division of labor requires a __69__ schedule. And the family

__70__ of a lone male breadwinner set a broad daily framework. With few mothers working, shop opening hours could be short, schools could open for only half the day and child care assistance was __71__.

Yet with the economy __72__ driven by services, this time corset (紧身衣) is gradually loosening. More than half of employees now __73__

their own working hours. __74__ two-thirds of all women work, up from half in the 1970s. Then there is digital technology: __75__ arriving on the dot, you can send a text message apologizing for being late. __76__, many Germans seem to have trouble adjusting to their new flexibility. There are objective reasons, such as the continuing __77__ of child-care facilities, which makes it harder for mothers to combine jobs and children.

__78__, this is all an outcome of rising wealth and ever more distractions. Yet there are also __79__ barriers that keep Germans from

using their time better. One is a bias __80__ hiring help, which many see as akin to slavery. Germans spend much time toiling at home unpaid; __81__ other countries have so many home-improvement stores.

64. A) scheduled   B) fixed
    C) liberalized   D) controlled
65. A) legend   B) mystery
    C) myth   D) fantasy
66. A) reveals   B) exposes
    C) incurs   D) entails
67. A) proficiency   B) prompt
    C) perseverance   D) punctuality
68. A) so   B) also
    C) hence   D) nevertheless
69. A) loose   B) tight
    C) close   D) effective
70. A) mode   B) model
    C) module   D) mould

71. A) indispensable   B) superficial
    C) superfluous   D) significant
72. A) urgently   B) cautiously
    C) efficiently   D) increasingly
73. A) make   B) set
    C) fix   D) spend
74. A) As long as   B) As many as
    C) As few as   D) As far as
75. A) regardless of   B) as of
    C) instead of   D) in spite of
76. A) Even if   B) Even though
    C) Even as   D) Even so
77. A) development   B) lack
    C) construction   D) loss

78. A) In part   B) In short
    C) In all   D) In that
79. A) cultural   B) economic
    C) historic   D) language
80. A) for   B) with
    C) toward   D) against
81. A) few   B) many
    C) some   D) little

Part Ⅵ Translation（5 minutes）

Directions: *Complete the sentences by translating into English the Chinese given in brackets.*
  *Please write your translation on **Answer Sheet 2**.*

82. His speech was so welcome that it was _____ （不断被掌声所打断）.
83. If I had _____ （早问一下方向，就不会迷路了）.
84. She cooked the meat for a long time _____ （以使它吃起来很嫩）.
85. Young people sometimes complain of _____ （无法与父母沟通思想）.
86. The Stock Exchange _____ （对可能出现的政局变化很敏感）.

Test 7

Part Ⅰ　Writing（30 minutes）

Directions：*For this part，you are allowed 30 minutes to write a composition based on the following line graph that shows the changes of the attendance in the reading room. You should write at least 150 words following the outline given below in Chinese with the title **College Reading Room Phenomenon**.*

College Reading Room Phenomenon

1. 描述图表中的两个循环（cycle）所反映的问题
2. 分析引起该变化的原因
3. 你的结论

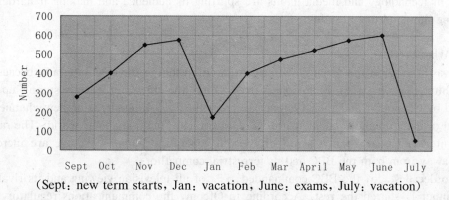

（Sept：new term starts，Jan：vacation，June：exams，July：vacation）

Part Ⅱ　Reading Comprehension（Skimming and Scanning）（15 minutes）

Directions：*In this part，you will have 15 minutes to go over the passage quickly and answer the questions on **Answer Sheet 1**. For questions 1～7，choose the best answer from the four choices marked A），B），C）and D）. For questions 8～10 complete the sentences with the information given in the passage.*

The Future of the BBC

As a boy growing up in the 1930s in the Midlands，Norman Painting，the son of a railwayman，listened to a new radio service from the British Broadcasting Corporation. His mother hoped he would get a job as a manager at the mine，but listening to the voices from London talking about world affairs，culture and music gave him other ideas. "The radio opened a door to the world," says Mr. Painting，who went on to Oxford University on a scholarship and became an academic before later working for the BBC's Radio 4 in its long-running soap, "The Archers".

Mr. Painting's story helps to explain Britain's devotion to what it calls "public-service broadcasting"，and why the state has been standing by the BBC in the financing issue. The debate had raged for years over whether the BBC should still be publicly financed，especially by a license fee paid by all those with TV sets. The BBC hates the idea of losing its license fee. Rather than go commercial，its bosses plan to keep fighting for public financing for decades. In

2006, after a heated debate, the government renewed its financing for the next ten years through a compulsory "TV license" on all households with TV sets. But when the current charter runs out in 2016, will the government take away its public subsides and leave the BBC to fend for itself?

According to recent reports, the BBC will have to make do with annual increases below retail-price inflation, less than it asked for. Even so, it is fortunate to be handed a guaranteed income over several years. Among developed countries, only Germany's government spends more than Britain's on broadcasting as a share of GDP. America's dispenses next to nothing, preferring to leave it to the market.

For the next ten years, the BBC's position looks secure. Yet it's getting increasingly harder to argue that the government should make the public pay for it. The BBC's purpose, according to its first director-general, John Reith, was to "inform, educate and entertain". But now the BBC can't have anything like the educative role it used to play. Though it remains Britain's dominant source of in-depth news and most reliable provider of high-quality programming, changes in technology and media habits are splitting its audience and making it harder to tag improving shows on to entertaining ones.

Serving What Public?

It was easy to get the teenaged Mr. Painting interested in the BBC programs because there was nothing else on. That is no longer true. First the other terrestrials sprang up: ITV, followed by Channel 4 and then Channel 5, from the 1990s, hundreds of new channels were launched on satellite and cable platforms, creating a new "multi-channel" world. The rapid rise of the Internet has also taken a toll of the old generalist channels. People are increasingly turning away from both the BBC and its terrestrial competitors.

Two decades ago, the BBC commanded 47% of all television viewing and its rivals, ITV and Channel 4, shared the rest. According to Ofcom, the communications regulator, today, BBC1 and BBC2, its terrestrial channels, account for just 33% of all viewing, multi-channel services (which include BBC3 and BBC4, both digital channels) win 30%. In homes with satellite or cable television, the corporation's share has fallen further: BBC1 and BBC2 together have just 23% of the former and 22% of the latter.

Young people especially are abandoning public-service programmers. According to Ofcom, in 2001, people between 16 and 24 spent 74% of their viewing time watching channels such as the BBC and Channel 4, but in 2005 only 58% of their time. Poorer, less educated viewers seem to be turning away, too. Serious material suffers most when people move to multi-channel television.

The result, says a BBC executive, is that "we are over-serving" middle-class 55-year-olds. The BBC is trying to widen its audience. In 2002, for example, realizing that it was hardly reaching young black people, it launched a digital radio station called 1Xtra, modeled p pirate radio.

Some say the BBC fails to attract younger viewers because it takes too few risks. Channel 4, another public-service broadcaster, has a bit more youth appeal: The average age of its viewers is 45. Kevin Lygo, its director of television, says that whereas many BBC programs are "full of integrity and truthfulness but also safe, respectful, back-looking and all about heritage". Many of the BBC's new programming offerings are "all exhumed (挖掘) from the distant past".

The BBC's Efforts

But good, innovative ideas have not entirely departed. Popular programs such as "The Office", a bone-dry comedy about a paper supply company, has been copied by broadcasters in America, France, Canada and Germany.

The BBC has long tried to tack between high-minded and populist programming in an effort to get people to watch improving stuff that they would not have encountered otherwise. But technology, which increases consumer choice, is complicating the task. "Hammocking" scheduling worthy material between smash hits is a familiar BBC technique. A recent adaptation of "Bleak House"(荒凉山庄), for example, was scheduled straight after "Eastenders", a popular soap opera. But remote controls and video recorders have made hammocking less effective.

The BBC is trying harder to conceal public service themes beneath entertainment. Its approach to ethnic minorities used to be a boring talk-show about discrimination late at night, now it's cleverer, with programs such as "Apprentice". Aspiring entrepreneurs in this reality show get knocked out week after week; many of the most successful contestants are from ethnic minorities.

The People's Telly

Many households, now watch and listen to little of the BBC's output, but almost all pay 131.5 pounds a year for it. The rapid shift to digital TV makes the debate whether the BBC should be publicly funded especially pressing. Set-top boxes (机顶盒) can tell whether a household has paid for a channel or not. Soon it will be practical and easy for everyone to choose whether or not subscribe to the BBC, or bits of it.

Toward the end of the digital switch-over, which will happen between 2008 and 2012, the government will examine other ways to finance the BBC after 2016. The likeliest change is that the television service would become partly or wholly subscription-financed. Radio would take longer to wean off public money because most radio sets now in use do not have the technology.

(1,069 words)

1. The author tells the story of Norman Painting to illustrate _____.
   A) the BBC's educative role for the working class
   B) the popularity of the BBC in the 1930s
   C) BBC's influence on ordinary people's career development
   D) the British's love for the BBC and its justification for governmental support
2. How has the BBC been financed?
   A) It's publicly financed.
   B) It's commercially financed.
   C) It's financed through private donations.
   D) It's financed through viewer subscriptions.
3. Among developed countries, _____ spends the greatest share of GDP on the public broadcasting.
   A) US government   B) British government
   C) German government   D) French government
4. What has happened to the BBC with the changes in technology and media habits?
   A) The BBC is no longer the dominant source of in-depth news.
   B) The BBC is losing its audience.
   C) The BBC programming is rapidly deteriorating in its quality.

D) The BBC is replaced by the multi-channel services.

5. According to the figures released by Ofcom, which of the following currently poses the greatest threat to the BBC?
   A) The BBC's terrestrial competitors
   B) The Internet
   C) The multi-channel services including digital channels, BBC3 and BBC4.
   D) Newspapers and magazines.

6. According to Kevin Lygo, the BBC fails to attract younger viewers because its programs are _____.
   A) too rebellious   B) a bit conservative and outdated
   C) lacking in integrity   D) too high-minded

7. The BBC adopts "hammocking" technique in order to _____.
   A) widen its audience
   B) add youth appeal to its programs
   C) conceal public service themes beneath entertainment
   D) get people to watch worthy stuff

8. The BBC used to present themes of ethnic minorities in a boring _____.

9. With increasing popularity of digital TV and set-top boxes, the debate on public funding for the BBC is _____.

10. After 2016, the BBC television service is most likely to obtain its entire, or part of, funding through _____.

Part Ⅲ Listening Comprehension (35 minutes)

Section A

Directions: *In this section, you will hear 8 short conversations and 2 long conversations. At the end of each conversation, one or more questions will be asked about what was said. Both the conversation and questions will be spoken only once. After each question there will be a pause. During the pause you must read the four choices marked A), B), C) and D), and decide which is the best answer. Then mark the corresponding letter on* **Answer Sheet 2** *with a single line through the center.*

11. A) He is a policeman.   B) He is a school runner.
    C) He is a librarian.   D) He is a teacher.

12. A) In a concert.   B) In a classroom.
    C) At a sports meeting.   D) On the school campus.

13. A) Give him the ring.
    B) Leave the ring in the locker room.
    C) Take the ring to the security office.
    D) Take the ring to the administration building.

14. A) Looking for an apartment to buy.
    B) Looking for a job.
    C) Asking the woman for her opinion on house furnishings.
    D) Taking a suburban excursion to get away from city noise.

15. A) They should definitely do it.   B) They can't find the means to do it.
    C) It should be a meaningless act.   D) She had meant to do it earlier.

16. A) It has come to a halt.   B) It will probably continue.
    C) It will end before long.   D) It will last for two weeks.
17. A) It wrecked on a rock.
    B) It turned over in the storm.
    C) It was caught in fog.
    D) Its anchor couldn't work because of the fog.
18. A) They had a better time than the other guests of the party.
    B) They didn't enjoy the party because they didn't like the food and drinks provided by the
       hostess.
    C) They enjoyed the party very much because the hostess was very friendly.
    D) They didn't enjoy the party very much because they didn't know the other guests.

Questions 19 to 22 are based on the conversation you have just heard.
19. A) Confident.   B) Pessimistic.   C) Well-loved.   D) Controversial.
20. A) Non-Indians can never truly understand Indians.
    B) Non-Indians should stop writing about Indian issues.
    C) Only Indians should practice Indian religion.
    D) Indians should have absolute sovereignty over their reservations.
21. A) Because he is not an Indian.
    B) Because he sells his spirituality.
    C) Because he has never written about his spirituality.
    D) Because he doesn't care about the market.
22. A) Because he is a public Indian figure.   B) Because he is a shaman.
    C) Because he is a writer.   D) Because he is a healer.

Questions 23 to 25 are based on the conversation you have just heard.
23. A) It may be painful.
    B) It may be a good thing.
    C) It may lead to true divorce.
    D) It may lead you to choose the wrong person.
24. A) It lies in not paying attention.
    B) It lies in asking for what they need.
    C) It lies in choosing the wrong person.
    D) It lies in pretending the marriage was fine when actually it wasn't.
25. A) Because they took you by surprise.   B) Because you were both pretending.
    C) Because you weren't paying attention.   D) Because your marriage wasn't perfect.

Section B
Directions: *In this section, you will hear 3 short passages. At the end of each passage, you will
    hear some questions. Both the passage and questions will be spoken only once. After you hear a
    question, you must choose the best answer from the four choices marked A), B), C) and D).
    Then mark the corresponding letter on **Answer Sheet 2** with a single line through the center.*

Passage One
Questions 26 to 29 are based on the passage you have just heard.
26. A) Eat with them.   B) Travel with them.

C) Dress them in costumes.   D) Sleep with them.

27. A) If their caretaker abuses them.
    B) If their caretaker scratches their bellies.
    C) If their caretaker does not come across as a leader.
    D) If their caretaker ignores them.

28. A) Attention.   B) Food.
    C) A laugh.   D) Love.

29. A) If you don't forget to feed it.
    B) If you don't get bored easily.
    C) If you don't trade it for something.
    D) If you don't expect it to be anything but a pig.

Passage Two

Questions 30 to 32 are based on the passage you have just heard.

30. A) They could have bad table manners.
    B) They are good cooks.
    C) They like the atmosphere at the office.
    D) They worry that so much could go wrong at a business lunch.

31. A) Bad table manners.   B) Arriving late.
    C) Rudeness to restaurant employees.   D) Dressing too casually.

32. A) Rudeness.   B) Nervousness.
    C) Ignorance.   D) Convention.

Passage Three

Questions 33 to 35 are based on the passage you have just heard.

33. A) In order to re-live their high school.
    B) In order to succeed.
    C) In order to follow one's dreams.
    D) For the immature demands of a startup.

34. A) Friends have ambition.   B) Friends are affordable.
    C) Friends have similar values. D) Friends can be trusted.

35. A) Enthusiastic.   B) Cautious.
    C) Ambivalent.   D) Opposed.

Section C

Directions: *In this section, you will hear a passage three times. When the passage is read for the first time, you should listen carefully for its general idea. When the passage is read for the second time, you are required to fill in the blanks numbered from 36 to 43 with the exact words you have just heard. For blanks numbered from 44 to 46 you are required to fill in the missing information. For these blanks, you can either use the exact words you have just heard or write down the main points in your own words. Finally, when the passage is read for the third time, you should check what you have written.*

Most Impressionists were born in the bourgeoisie class, and this was the world they painted. For subject matter, Impressionists looked to (36) _____ people at work and play. They are interested in the (37) _____ such as the steam engine, streetlights, camera and ready-made

fashions. They painted people hurrying through busy streets and enjoying their (38) _____ time on the in concerts and parks. It was not just city bustle that (39) _____ the Impressionists, though. Country (40) _____ appealed to them, too. Railroads gave people a new (41) _____, and they could hop on a train and be in the countryside in an hour. (42) _____ escaped the crowded city to the suburbs around Paris. The Seine River and parks provided (43) _____ for weekend picnickers, swimmers, and boat parties, which the Impressionists recorded.

One key to Impressionism's popularity is that the artist often put the viewer in the position of someone on holiday enjoying a beautiful scene. (44) _____ _____ a real landscape. The home offered other real-life subjects. Since it was unacceptable for women painters to set up an easel (画架) in public places, (45) _____ _____.

The garden was central to late 19th-century life.

Impressionist landscapes often contained people. (46) _____ _____.

It is as if the artist and we, the viewers, are watching a private, contemplative moment.

Part Ⅳ Reading Comprehension (Reading in Depth) (25 minutes)

Section A

Directions: *In this section, there is a short passage with 5 questions or incomplete statements. Read the passage carefully. Then answer the questions or complete the statements in the fewest possible words. Please write your answers on **Answer Sheet 2**.*

Today, more and more people are using credit cards instead of money to buy the things they need. Almost anyone who has a steady income and a good work record can apply for a credit card. There are many credit cards available: *American Express*, *Master Chare*, *VISA*, and *Diner's Club* are the names of some of the most popular.

If you have a credit card, you can buy a car, eat a dinner, take a trip, and even get a haircut by charging the cost to your account. In this way you can pay for purchases a month later without any extra charge. Or you may choose to spread out your payment over several months and pay only part of the total amount each month. If you do this, the credit card company, or the bank that sponsors the credit card, will add a small service charge to your total bill. This is very convenient for the customer. With the credit card in your wallet or purse, you don't have to carry much cash. This saves your trips to the bank to cash checks or withdraw cash. Also, if you carry credit cards instead of a lot of cash, you don't have to be concerned about losing your money through carelessness or theft. The card user only has to worry about paying the final bill. This, of course, can be a problem, if you charge more than you can pay for.

Credit cards are big business. Many banks sponsor their own credit card companies and issue cards free to their customers. Other credit card companies charge their members annual dues. The stores that accept credit cards must pay a small fee to the credit card company — a percentage of the purchase price of the merchandise or service. In turn, the credit card company promptly pays the store for the merchandise or service. Credit card companies make a profit from the fees they charge the store and also from the fees collected from customers who pay for their charges in monthly installments. However, credit card companies sometimes have problems collecting overdue payments from unreliable customers. Also, the use of stolen, lost, or counterfeit credit cards by criminal has become a big headache for the credit card company that's responsible for the goods and services illegally charged to its customers' accounts.

(382 words)

47. People use credit cards on condition that they have _____.

48. How long can the payment be put off without being charged?

_____

49. According to the passage, payments can be done in monthly _____ with a small service charge.

50. According to the passage, credit cards are big business because credit card companies make a big profit from both _____.

51. To deal with the cases of _____ makes the credit card companies worry most.

Section B

Directions: *There are 2 passages in this section. Each passage is followed by some questions or unfinished statements. For each of them there are four choices marked A), B), C) and D). You should decide on the best choice and mark the corresponding letter on **Answer Sheet 2** with a single line through the centre.*

Passage One

Questions 52 to 56 are based on the following passage.

Do you want to live forever? By the year 2050, you might actually get your wish — providing you are willing to leave your biological body and take up residence in silicon circuits. But long before then, perhaps as early as 2008, less radical measures will begin offering a semblance (外表,伪装) of immortality.

Researchers are confident that technology will soon be able to track every waking moment of your life. Whatever you see and hear, plus all that you say and write, can be recorded analyzed and automatically indexed, and added to your personal chronicles. By the 2030s, it may be possible to capture your nervous system's electrical activities, which would also preserve your thoughts and emotions. Researchers at the Laboratories of British Telecommunications have defined this concept as Soul Catcher.

Small electronic equipment will pave the way for Soul Catcher. It would use a wearable supercomputer, perhaps in a wristwatch, with wireless links to micro—sensors under your scalp and in the nerves that carry all five sensory signals. So wearing a video camera would no longer be required.

At first, the Soul Catcher's companion system — the Soul Reader — might have trouble copying your thought in complete details. Even in 2030, we may still be struggling to understand the brain's internal workings, so reading your thoughts and interpreting your emotions might not be possible. But these signals could be conserved for the day when they can be transferred to silicon circuits to rejuvenate minds as everlasting entities. Researchers can only wonder what it will be like to wake up one day and find yourself alive inside a machine.

For people who chose not to live in silicon, virtual immortality could still ease the sense of futility (无用) that now haunts many people. Individuals would know their lives would not be forgotten, but would be preserved as a thread in a multimedia quilt that keeps a permanent record of the human race. And future generations would have a much fuller understanding of the past. History would not be dominated by just the rich and powerful, Hollywood stars, and a few

52. The main idea of this passage is that _____.
    A) human beings long for an immortal life
    B) people can live immortally as technology develops
    C) there are many difficulties in making the Soul Catcher
    D) the invention of Soul Catcher has great significance
53. According to this passage, a Soul Catcher will be _____.
    A) a new invention in order to capture and preserve human thoughts
    B) made by British scientists to offer a semblance of immortality
    C) made of silicon circuits which can index people's nervous activity
    D) a new machine on which radical research measures have already made
54. We can infer from the text that the appearance of "immortal" life is _____.
    A) a fading hope   B) far from certain
    C) just an illusion   D) only a matter of time
55. We learned from the passage that _____.
    A) even in 2030, obstacles still exist in reading and interpreting human thought
    B) nowadays people feel angry with the domination of the history by elites
    C) by the year 2050, human beings can lead an everlasting life biologically
    D) people can only "live in" silicon to get an immortal life
56. The meaning of the word "rejuvenate" in Paragraph 4 is close to _____.
    A) change   B) activate   C) predict   D) leave

Passage Two
Questions 57 to 61 are based on the following passage.

Everyone has heard the phrase "a picture is worth a thousand words". Videoconferencing provides that picture, bringing decision makers together for face-to-face meetings regardless of their location. Merely hearing words spoken in a phone conversation limits total communication. Adding a visual link to see the face and the body language enhances communication. Seeing the picture allows the participants to comprehend the intended meaning, not just the perceived meaning of conversation.

"Researchers have suggested that when there is an incongruity between the verbal and the nonverbal message, we tend to believe the nonverbal one," according to Patton and Giffin, authors of *Decision Making Group Interaction*. In videoconferencing, hand and arm movement as well as other gestures can illustrate an idea or express an emotional state. More important, facial expression and eye movement can communicate valuable information that is lost in a mere telephone conversation. According to Goss and O'Hair, authors of *Communicating in Interpersonal Relationships*, Seven research projects in nonverbal communication have indicated that the face may be the most important body area through which nonverbal cues are conveyed. More accurate communication is achieved by facial expression and nonverbal cues.

"Today's business professionals spend more than 50 percent of the time in meetings, and nearly half of that time they feel is unproductive. Can you imagine as a resource manager spending money on travel for meetings that professionals feel are unproductive?" said Francine Savage, New Business Development Manager of 3M visual System Division. Savage suggests that money invested in videoconferencing equipment will eventually be recouped via the saving from not sending employees to meetings.

Some organizations will have to invest significant capital to take advantage of this powerful technology. Such is not the case in the Office of the ASARDA. Its information management office has been building a dynamic videoconferencing program for the past 4 years. There are now more than 60 desktop videoconferencing units installed on individual workstation and 12 conference room systems. At heart of the program is a multipoint control unit equipped with the latest software and options. This allows us full control and flexibility to support ASARDA's multipoint conferencing needs.

(356 words)

57. The power of videoconferencing lies in that it can _____.
    A) enhance the communication
    B) increase productivity
    C) understand the real meaning of the other party
    D) all of the above

58. What is the proper meaning of the word "cue" in the second paragraph?
    A) Communication.   B) Hint.
    C) Explanation.   D) Production.

59. According to Savage, the manager of 3M, videoconferencing is _____.
    A) expensive in installing the system
    B) efficient in saving employees for meetings
    C) worthwhile by not sending employees for meetings
    D) useful in changing boring meeting into exiting ones

60. The characteristic of ASARDA in using videoconferencing is that _____.
    A) it takes them 4 years to build the dynamic program
    B) they spend significant money in installing the equipment
    C) the desktop units make them have full control of multipoint needs
    D) they have the latest software developed by other companies

61. What is the attitude of the author towards the videoconferencing?
    A) Negative.   B) Indifferent.   C) Enthusiastic.   D) Neutral.

Part Ⅴ Cloze (15 minutes)

Directions: *There are 20 blanks in the following passage. For each blank there are four choices marked A), B), C) and D) on the right side fo the paper. You should choose the ONE that best fits into the passage. Then mark the corresponding letter on **Answer Sheert 2** with a single line through the center.*

Any good mystery must eventually uncover a villain, and in a recent documentary, "Who Killed the Electric Car?", the filmmakers duly pointed the finger at General Motors. The __62__ is not so simple, but there is little doubt that when GM pulled the plug on its EV1 battery-powered car a decade ago, other __63__ followed the Giant carmaker's lead.
    Yet GM has now __64__ its enthusiasm for

62. A) information   B) reality
      C) plot   D) story

63. A) manufacturers B) mechanics
      C) consumers   D) filmmakers

64. A) reviewed   B) recharged

electric vehicles — or at least for their close cousins, hybrid cars (混合动力汽车). At the upcoming auto show, the company is expected to __65__ a prototype that overtakes existing hybrids,

__66__ Toyota's Pruis.

Today's hybrids capture energy normally __67__ during braking and coasting and use it to power an electric motor that can provide extra bursts of __68__ when needed. The Pruis and other hybrids can also run __69__ battery power alone at low speeds over short distances, such as in stop-start traffic.

But GM's new car is expected to be a "plug-in" hybrid, which, as its name implied, can be recharged by __70__ it into the mains (干线). Together with a big battery pack, this provides a much larger range in all-electric __71__, after which the petrol engine kicks in. GM's car is expected to go around 50 miles (80 km) in all-electric mode, __72__ enough for American commuters, who would need to use the __73__ engine on longer trips only. The __74__ is that plug-in hybrids need a much larger and more costly battery pack. __75__ a Pirus to operate as a plug-in hybrid, as some enthusiasts have done, costs around $12,000.

GM bosses have hinted that his company planned to put a plug-in into mass __76__. It is an indication of how the pace is __77__ in the race to develop more eco-friendly cars.

Others are more __78__. Carlos Ghson, the boss of Renault and Nissan, who is __79__ for his skepticism towards hybrids, said he still had doubts that hybrid technology is __80__ for the mass market, stressing that plug-in hybrids will have to wait until battery technology improves. Toyota has also been __81__ about plug-ins, insisting the Pirus' approach is more convenient.

C) revised   D) retrieved

65. A) uncover   B) unveil
    C) identify   D) expose
66. A) such as   B) as to
    B) if any   D) as for
67. A) missed   B) employed
    C) lost   D) gone
68. A) friction   B) energy
    C) power   D) acceleration
69. A) with   B) at
    C) for   D) on

70. A) erecting   B) pulling
    C) thrusting   D) plugging
71. A) form   B) occasion
    C) mode   D) situation

72. A) more than   B) other than
    C) rather than   D) less than
73. A) electric   B) petrol
    C) battery   D) solar
74. A) advantage   B) effect
    C) drawback   D) defect
75. A) Modifying   B) Manifesting
    C) Correcting   D) Remedying

76. A) operation   B) production
    C) inspection   D) escalation
77. A) picking up   B) taking up
    C) making up   D) putting up
78. A) optimistic   B) excited
    C) confident   D) cautious
79. A) known   B) reported
    C) taken   D) noticed
80. A) equipped   B) essential
    C) ready   D) appropriate
81. A) enthusiastic   B) committed
    C) skeptical   D) faithful

Part Ⅵ   Translation（5 minutes）

Directions： *Complete the sentences by translating into English the Chinese given in brackets.*
Please write your translation on Answer Sheet 2 .

82. She preferred that we ＿＿＿＿＿＿（讲座结束后马上进行讨论）.

83. She was complaining that the doctor ＿＿＿＿＿＿（收费超过了正常费用）for the treatment.

84. Under no circumstances ＿＿＿＿＿＿（会给你退钱）.

85. It seems that he is never bothered about ＿＿＿＿＿＿（别人是如何看待他的行为的）.

86. What he wanted to emphasize was the impact of these findings ＿＿＿＿＿＿（而不是导致这些发现的过程）.

Test 8

Part Ⅰ Writing (30 minutes)

Directions: *For this part, you are allowed 30 minutes to write a composition on the title*: **Should Class Attendance Be Optional**? *You should write at least 150 words following the outline given below in Chinese.*

Should Class Attendance Be Optional

1. 描述现在大学课堂及讲座上常见的现象：态度不认真，睡觉，发短信及出勤率低……因此提出大学课堂是否应该采取自愿而非强制
2. 列举原因
3. 我的看法

Part Ⅱ Reading Comprehension (Skimming and Scanning) (15 minutes)

Directions: *In this part, you will have 15 minutes to go over the passage quickly and answer the questions on **Answer Sheet 1**. For questions 1 – 7, choose the best answer from the four choices marked A), B), C) and D). For questions 8 – 10 complete the sentences with the information given in the passage.*

End Your Back Pain

Like an expensive but temperamental sports car, the human spin is beautifully designed and maddeningly unreliable. If you are a living, breathing human being, you have probably suffered the agony of back pain. And as long as people continue to lead overweight, sedentary and stressful lives, the number of sufferers is unlikely to go anywhere other than up.

As it does, armies of new back-pain sufferers, many desperate and even disabled, will seek relief. When they do, they'll quickly discover just how complicated their problem really is, with its mystifying mix of physical symptoms and psychological underpinnings. The reality is that the agony will often go away on its own — impossible as that may seem when you are writhing (痛苦扭曲) on the kitchen floor.

The Great Pain Mystery

Back pain can originate anywhere in the elaborate spinal architecture. Degenerated discs (椎间盘), which many lead to herniation (突出) and compressed nerves, are a common problem. Then there those wrenching pain provoked by muscle injuries, which can drop grown men to the floor. What's most mysterious about back problems is the frequent disconnect between anatomical defects and pain. Unlike blood pressure and cholesterol (胆固醇), which could be measured with arm cuffs and blood tests, lower-back pain has no objective way — the volume of tears? the intensity of a grimace? — to be gauged.

Many times, the precise cause of pain remains unknown. Imaging tests found that two people with herniated discs can lead radically different lives: One spends his days popping painkillers, the other waltzes through life. In a well-known study, researchers checked 98 healthy people: Two-thirds had abnormal discs even though none complained of pain. The real issue is why some people have a mild backache and some have really crippling pain. In another research, experts compared a group of patients who reported back pain with a control group who did not. Close to two-thirds if the pain patients had cracks in their discs, so-called high-intensity zones, or HIZs. But so did 24 percent of the non-complainers.

The answer has as much to do with the mind as with the body. In the HIZ study, the best predictor of pain was not how bad the defect looked, but the patient's psychological distress. Depression and anxiety have long been linked to pain; a recent Canadian study found that people who suffer from severe depression are four times more likely to develop intense or disabling neck or low-back pain. At New York's Hospital for Special Surgery, psychiatrist Gregory Lutz says he often sees men who have two things in common: crippling sciatica（坐骨神经痛）and an upcoming wedding date. The problem in their back, possibly a degenerated or herniated disc, likely already existed, says Dr. Lutz, but was intensified by the pre-marriage jitters.

Spine Surgery Breakthrough

Pain is pain, and many want a quick fix and that means surgery. Spinal-fusion surgery, one of the most invasive and costly forms of therapy（about $42,000）has more than doubled in the US since 1993, to about 350,000 in 2003. Discectomy, which is done less invasively, has also spiked to 342,000 surgeries per year. But these procedures don't work for everyone.

The increase in all spinal surgery has been promoted in part by technical advances promising better outcomes. Perhaps the most intriguing new development is the artificial cobalt-chrome disc. In October 2004, the US Food and Drug Administration（FDA）approved the first such disc, the Charite, for patients with degenerative disc disease. The three-piece device has a sliding medical-grade plastic core sandwiched between two metal plates, which allows the spine to move. It is believed that, such discs, like knee replacements, will give patients more mobility than traditional fusion surgery. And they will get out of bed a lot sooner too. The key is to be very specific and very careful about patient selection. Not everyone who has disc degeneration should have an operation.

Alternative Treatments

Doctors, worried that too many patients seem willing to go under the knife, are now looking for simpler, more effective ways to treat one of the most vexing problems in medicine. For more and more people with back pain, alternative therapies are the way to go.

Chiropractic care（指压疗法）, the most popular nonsurgical back therapy, is booming, with 60, 000 chiropractors practising in the US today. Some happy clients visit their chiropractors more often than their hair stylists. Experts generally agree that the treatment, which involves manipulation of the joints and tissues of the spine, is safe for the lower back. It provides modest benefits equivalent to those of conventional treatments.

Massage has an increasing number of proponents, and research shows it can help knead out （揉掉）persistent pain. Steven Smith, a physical therapist at the Schuldt Performance uses massage on back-pain sufferers to loosen up muscles and increase blood flow. It's not exactly a spa-like experience, though. "You've got to get in there deep to break the pain."

Acupuncture（针灸）is also popular. The first large trial of the practice is now conducted at New York's Integrative Care Center, where therapist push the tiny needles into the patients. Acupuncture seems to stimulate the release of feel-good endorphins, has a cumulative effect. Patients describe a lingering euphoria, a nice happy state whether you've got a back problem or not.

An Integrative Approach

Jordan, a long-term back-pain sufferer, tried every wacky thing out there. "Faith healing, hanging from the ceiling, clicking my heels together and wishing I was home, you name it, I've done it." Last year, feeling especially distressed, he tried biofeedback, a technique that trains him to distance himself from the pain. "I never get rid of the pain, but these treatments provide some relief." says Jordan.

If patients' attitudes can help the pain, can more creative thinking among the experts improve the odds of beating it? Dr. Eisenberg, head of Harvard Medical School's Osher Institute, is spearheading an National Institutes of Health-funded pilot program to find out. A diverse group of 25 specialists meet regularly to educate one another on how they diagnose and treat back pain. They intend to see if there is a more efficient, multi-disciplinary way to attack the problem, and to make it cost-effective too.

No wonder there's a flood of interest in alternative medicine. Even New York's Hospital for Special Surgery opened a complementary-medicine center four years ago. Now about 13,000 patients a year, many with bad back, see its rehab specialists, massage therapists and chiropractors, as well as taking yoga and tai chi classes any noninvasive approach they can find to relieve the pain.

Can Rage Ruin Your Back?

Dr. Sarno, a professor at New York University School of Medicine, believes almost all back pain is rooted in bottled-up feelings. Sarno explains how repressed rage and anxiety can stress the body, eventually manifesting itself as muscle spasm (抽搐), nerve dysfunction, numbness and pain. Recovery begins with recognition the connection between the body and the mind. "Pain is created by the brain to make sure the rage doesn't come out." says Sarno. But skeptics say Sarno is offering a placebo (安慰剂), which could miss the true cause of the pain.

After centuries of agony, humanity could certainly use some relief. But more important than the success of any treatment is the good news that back-pain sufferers and doctors are embracing bold new ways to think about the most exquisite and frustrating work of art: the spine.

(1,270 words)

1. What accounts for the increasing number of back pain sufferers in modern life is a number of factors such as overweight, lack of exercise and _____.
   A) plain ageing   B) spine defects   C) surgical failures   D) mental stress
2. What's so mysterious about back problems?
   A) The impossibility to measure the intensity of the pain.
   B) The unknown origin of the pain.
   C) The disconnect between spine defects and pain.
   D) The low percentage of people with abnormal discs among the healthy.
3. The phenomenon of men having two things sciatica and upcoming wedding in common indicates that _____.
   A) pre-marriage anxiety is inevitable for most men
   B) psychological distress may contribute to low-back pain
   C) almost all bridegrooms have a degenerated or herniated disc
   D) back pain may intensify pre-marriage jitters
4. _____, artificial disc operation is considered a better option than the traditional fusion

surgery.

A) Giving patients greater mobility and quicker recovery

B) Suitable for every back-pain sufferers

C) Being less invasive and costly

D) With fewer post-operation side effects

5. People who want their back pain to be fixed quickly often resort to _____.

A) surgery   B) chiropractic care   C) massage   D) acupuncture

6. Besides relieving back pain, acupuncture also seems to give patients _____.

A) a spa-like experience   B) a lingering happy feeling

C) modest benefits in skin care   D) increased blood circulation

7. What's the purpose of the National Institutes of Health-funded pilot program?

A) To find out whether the patients' attitude help the pain.

B) To experiment with advanced surgical treatments.

C) To search for a cost-effective, integrative treatment.

D) To investigate experts' opinions on various treatments.

8. The great number of patients visiting the complementary-medicine center at New York's Hospital for Special Surgery reflects _____ in the US.

9. According to Dr. Sarno, almost all kinds of back pain could be attributed to _____.

10. The author feels _____ about humanity's final victory in the century-old battle against back-pain.

Part III   Listening Comprehension (35 minutes)

Section A

Directions: *In this section, you will hear 8 short conversations and 2 long conversations. At the end of each conversation, one or more questions will be asked about what was said. Both the conversation and questions will be spoken only once. After each question there will be a pause. During the pause you must read the four choices marked A), B), C) and D), and decide which is the best answer. Then mark the corresponding letter on **Answer Sheet 2** with a single line through the center.*

11. A) None.   B) One baby.
    C) Three women.   D) Three women and one baby.

12. A) A school master.   B) A computer operator.
    C) A computer engineer.   D) A career advisory officer.

13. A) An agent.   B) A tenant.
    C) A secretary.   D) A landlord.

14. A) Quietly.   B) With surprise.
    C) With hostility.   D) Enthusiastically.

15. A) Geology.   B) Ecology.
    C) Medicine.   D) Geography.

16. A) John should not talk to Bill any more.

    B) John should take Bill's remark seriously.

    C) John should tell Bill not to think negatively.

    D) John should pay little attention to what Bill says.

17. A) His mother told him to become a teacher.

B) His father told him to become a good manager.

C) His father told him to try to be a teacher and his life will be assured.

D) His teacher told him to get his teaching degree.

18. A) Five contestants won cars.   B) The woman missed the show.

    C) The man ate during the show.   D) Four contestants failed to win prizes.

Questions 19 to 22 are based on the conversation you have just heard.

19. A) He watches too much television.

    B) He won't listen to her.

    C) He is too naughty to be controlled.

    D) He spends all of his time on the Internet.

20. A) Impatient.   B) Angry.

    C) Anxious.   D) Unsatisfied.

21. A) Limit the amount of television her son watches.

    B) Forbid her son to watch television.

    C) Be firm when setting limits.

    D) Help her son gain self-control.

22. A) They are very cute.   B) They are disciplined.

    C) They are self-controlling.   D) They are impulsive.

Questions 23 to 25 are based on the conversation you have just heard.

23. A) Skier.   B) Kidnapper.

    C) Author.   D) Private Investigator.

24. A) To ski.   B) To attend a wedding.

    C) To escape kidnappers.   D) To see an art show.

25. A) Brutal.   B) Depressive.

    C) Humorous.   D) Conservative.

Section B

Directions: *In this section, you will hear 3 short passages. At the end of each passage, you will hear some questions. Both the passage and questions will be spoken only once. After you hear a question, you must choose the best answer from the four choices marked A), B), C) and D). Then mark the corresponding letter on **Answer Sheet 2** with a single line through the center.*

Passage One

Questions 26 to 29 are based on the passage you have just heard.

26. A) Because it is very new.

    B) Because it is very popular.

    C) Because it is spreading very quickly.

    D) Because it is able to hold a lot of things.

27. A) Reduced perspiration.   B) Reduced heart rate.

    C) Reduced stress.   D) Improved immunity.

28. A) At least 20 minutes a day.   B) Less than 20 minutes a day.

    C) Exactly 20 minutes a day.   D) More than 20 minutes a day.

29. A) Cautious.   B) Enthusiastic.

    C) Longing.   D) Suspicious.

Passage Two

Questions 30 to 32 are based on the passage you have just heard.

30. A) The pilot's concentration.
    B) The efficiency of the local mobile phone network.
    C) How long it takes passengers to get seated.
    D) The navigational equipment of the plane.
31. A) Absolve (赦免) them from any guilt.
    B) Help increase their profits.
    C) Frighten passengers into following the rules.
    D) Encourage pilots to use mobile phones.
32. A) They don't care.
    B) They have varied opinions on the issue.
    C) They feel that mobile phone use on planes is extremely dangerous.
    D) They feel that mobile phone use on planes is not dangerous.

Passage Three

Questions 33 to 35 are based on the passage you have just heard.

33. A) Modifying their genes.
    B) Trying to force it.
    C) Trying to buy it.
    D) Seeking it through pleasurable activities.
34. A) They will probably have a genetic defect.
    B) They will feel dazzling.
    C) They will lose their appetite.
    D) They are more likely to be in positive moods.
35. A) Habits.   B) Cholesterol.
    C) Genes.   D) Attitudes.

Section C

Directions: *In this section, you will hear a passage three times. When the passage is read for the first time, you should listen carefully for its general idea. When the passage is read for the second time, you are required to fill in the blanks numbered from 36 to 43 with the exact words you have just heard. For blanks numbered from 44 to 46 you are required to fill in the missing information. For these blanks, you can either use the exact words you have just heard or write down the main points in your own words. Finally, when the passage is read for the third time, you should check what you have written.*

   A hundred years ago it was scientifically "proved" by economists that the laws of society made it necessary to have a vast army of poor and jobless people in order to keep the economy going. Today, hardly anybody would dare to voice the (36) _____. It is generally accepted that nobody should be (37) _____ from the wealth of the nation. The opinions, that the poor owed their conditions to their (38) _____, are outdated. In all Western (39) _____ countries, a system of insurance has been introduced which (40) _____ everyone a minimum of subsistence (生活维持费) in case of unemployment, sickness and old age. I would go one step further and argue that, even if these conditions are not (41) _____, everyone has the right

to receive the means to (42) _____, in other words, he can claim this minimum life (43) _____ without having to have any "reason". (44) _____

_____ .

This may sound like a fantastic proposal, but I think our insurance system would have sounded to people a hundred years ago. (45) _____

_____ . This assumption rests on the fallacy (谬论) of the inherent haziness in human nature. (46) _____

_____ .

Part Ⅳ   Reading Comprehension (Reading in Depth) (25 minutes)

Section A

Directions: *In this section, there is a short passage with 5 questions or incomplete statements. Read the passage carefully. Then answer the questions or complete the statements in the fewest possible words. Please write your answers on Answer Sheet 2.*

Did you know that all human beings have a "comfort zone" regulating the distances they stand from someone when they talk? This distance varies in interesting ways among people of different cultures.

Greeks, others of the Eastern Mediterranean, and many of those from South America normally stand quite close together when they talk, often moving their faces even closer as they warm up in a conversation. North Americans find this awkward and often back away a few inches. Studies have found that they tend to feel most comfortable at about 21 inches apart. In much of Asia and Africa, there is even more space between two speakers in conversation. This greater space subtly lends an air of dignity and respect. This matter of space is nearly always unconscious, but it is interesting to observe.

This difference applies also to the closeness with which people sit together, the extent to which they lean over one another in conversation, how they move as they argue or make an emphatic point. In the United States, for example, people try to keep their bodies apart even in a crowded elevator; in Paris they take it as it comes!

Although North Americans have a relatively wide "comfort zone" for talking, they communicate a great deal with their hands — not only with gesture but also with touch. They put a sympathetic hand on a person's shoulder to demonstrate warmth of feeling or an arm around him in sympathy; they nudge a man in the ribs to emphasize a funny story; they pat an arm in reassurance or stroke a childhood in affection; they readily take someone's arm to help him across a street or direct him along an unfamiliar route. To many people — especially those from Asia or the Moslem countries — such bodily contact is unwelcome, especially if inadvertently (无心地) done with the left hand. (The left hand carries no special significance in the U. S. Many Americans are simply left handed and use that hand more.)

(334 words)

47. In terms of bodily distance, North Americans feel ill at ease when _____ .
48. For Asians, the comfortable zone would do something to show _____ .
49. It can be inferred from the passage that in a crowded elevator, a Frenchman could make no particular effort to _____ .
50. When Americans tell a joke, they often _____ .

51. To be specific, what does the passage mainly discuss about?

_____

Section B

Directions: *There are 2 passages in this section. Each passage is followed by some questions or unfinished statements. For each of them there are four choices marked A), B), C) and D). You should decide on the best choice and mark the corresponding letter on **Answer Sheet 2** with a single line through the centre.*

Passage One

Questions 52 to 56 are based on the following passage.

In general, our society is becoming one of giant enterprises directed by a bureaucratic management in which man becomes a small well-oiled cog(齿轮) in the machinery. The oiling is done with higher wages, well-ventilated factories and piped music, and by psychologists and "human-relations" experts; yet all this oiling does not alter the fact that man has become powerless, that he is bored with it. In fact, the blue- and the white-collar workers have become economic puppets（傀儡）who dance to the tune of automated machines and bureaucratic management.

The worker and employee are anxious not only because they might find themselves out of a job; they are anxious also because they are unable to acquire any real satisfaction of interest in life. They live and die without ever having confronted the fundamental realities of human existence as emotionally and intellectually independent and productive human beings.

Those higher up on the social ladder are no less anxious. Their lives are no less empty than those of their subordinates. They are even more insecure in some respects. They are in a highly competitive race. To be promoted or to fall behind is not a matter of salary but even more a matter of self-respect. When they apply for their first job, they are tested for intelligence as well as for the right mixture of submissiveness and independence. From that moment on they are tested again and again — by the psychologists, for whom testing is a big business, and by their superiors, who judge their behavior, sociability, capacity to get along, etc. This constant need to prove that one is as good as or better than one's fellow-competitor creates constant anxiety and stress, the very causes of unhappiness and illness.

Am I suggesting that we should return to the pre-industrial mode of production or to nineteenth-century "free enterprise" capitalism? Certainly not. Problems are never solved by returning to a stage which one has already outgrown. I suggest transforming our social system from a bureaucratically managed industrialism in which maximal production and consumption are ends in themselves into a humanist industrialism in which man and full development of his potentialities — those of all love and of reason — are the aims of social arrangements. Production and consumption should serve only as means to this end, and should be prevented from ruling man.

(395 words)

52. By "a well-oiled cog in the machinery" the author intends to render the idea that man is _____.

A) working in complete harmony with the rest of the society

B) a humble component of the society, especially when working smoothly

C) a necessary part of the society though each individual's function is negligible

D) an unimportant part in comparison with the rest of the society, though functioning smoothly

53. The real cause of the anxiety of the workers and employees is that _____.
    A) they are likely to lose their jobs
    B) they have no genuine satisfaction or interest in life
    C) they are deprived of their individuality and independence
    D) they are faced with the fundamental realities of human existence

54. From the passage we can infer that real happiness of life belongs to those _____.
    A) who are at the bottom of the society
    B) who are higher up in their social status
    C) who prove better than their fellow-competitors
    D) who could keep far away from this competitive world

55. To solve the present social problems the author suggests that we should _____.
    A) enable man to fully develop his potentialities
    B) offer higher wages to the workers and employees
    C) resort to the production mode of our ancestors
    D) take the fundamental realities for granted

56. The author's attitude towards industrialism might best be summarized as one of _____.
    A) approval   B) dissatisfaction
    C) suspicion   D) tolerance

Passage Two
Questions 57 to 61 are based on the following passage.

Admittedly, minor accidents and slip-ups continue to shake public confidence in nuclear power. Given the unquantifiable risks that nuclear power carries, it is only right that the industry be subjected to the test of public opinion and due political process. However, this argues for exceptional alerts, regulatory scrutiny and accountability — and not for bans or shut-downs. Those nuclear operators with a good safety record deserve to have their licenses renewed, so that existing plants may run to the end of their useful lives.

The Bush administration's enthusiastic support goes a lot further than this, however. It also wants to see new plants. Proponents of new nuclear power stations make three arguments in their favor. They will enhance energy security by lessening dependence on fossil fuels; far from being environmentally harmful, they will be beneficial because they will reduce the output of greenhouse gases; and, most crucially, the economics of nuclear power has improved from the days when it was wholly dependent on bail-out (紧急财政支持) and subsidy.

Yet these arguments do not stand up to investigation. The claim that governments should support nuclear power to reduce their vulnerability (致命弱点) to the OPEC oil cartel (联合企业) is doubly absurd. Little oil is used in power generation: What nuclear power displaces is mostly natural gas and coal, which are not only more plentiful than oil but also geographically better distributed. Security is enhanced not by seeking energy self-sufficiency but through diversification of supplies. Creating lots of fissile material that might be pinched by terrorists is an odd way to look for security anyway.

What about the argument that climate change might be the great savior of nuclear power? Global warming is indeed a risk that should be taken more seriously than the Bush administration has so far done. Nuclear plants do not produce any carbon dioxide, which is the principal greenhouse gas. However, rushing in response to build dozens of new nuclear plants would be both needlessly expensive and environmentally unsound.

It would make far more sense to adopt a carbon tax, which would put clean energy sources such as solar and wind on an equal footing with nuclear, whose waste poses an undeniable (if remote) environmental threat of its own for aeons to come. Governments should also dismantle (拆除) all subsidies on fossil fuels — especially for coal, the dirtiest of all. They should adopt reforms that send proper price signals to those who use power, and so reduce emissions. Global warming certainly provides one argument in favor of nuclear power, but it is not sufficient on its own to justify a nuclear renaissance.

(427 words)

57. What's the public's opinion about nuclear industry?
    A) People have little confidence in nuclear power for the potential disaster of nuclear accidents.
    B) People think it important to exercise strict monitoring and effective management of the existing plants.
    C) People believe the best way to avoid nuclear disaster is to shut down all the nuclear power stations.
    D) People agree to prohibit the existing nuclear plants from running to the end of their useful lives.
58. The most important reason why the Bush administration support more new nuclear-power plants is that _____.
    A) they need little government financial support
    B) they will increase energy security
    C) they help lessen dependence on fossil fuels
    D) they are environmentally friendly
59. According to the author, energy security can only be achieved by _____.
    A) using less oil in power generation
    B) replacing fossil fuels with more nuclear power
    C) seeking energy self sufficiency
    D) expanding the sources of power supply
60. According to the passage, which of the following measures is the least helpful in protecting the environment?
    A) Cutting off subsidies on all fossil fuels.
    B) Encouraging the use of clean energy sources.
    C) Promoting the resurgence of nuclear power.
    D) Adopting price reform to reduce emission.
61. It's implied that _____.
    A) nuclear power stations may become the targets of terrorist attack
    B) carbon dioxide is the principal source of greenhouse gas
    C) the Bush administration doesn't give due weight to environment protection
    D) nuclear waste will turn to be an environmental threat in the long-run term

Part Ⅴ   Error Correction (15 minutes)
Directions: *This part consists of a short passage. In this passage, there are altogether 10 mistakes, one in each numbered line. You may have to change a word, add a word or delete a word. Mark out the mistakes and put the corrections in the blanks provided. If you change a word, cross it out and write the correct word in the corresponding blank. If you add a word, put an insertion mark (∧) in the right place and write the missing word in the blank. If you delete a*

word, *cross it out and put a slash* (/) *in the blank*.

The result of automation may well be an increase in
employment, since it is expected that vast industries will grow
up around manufacturing, maintaining, and repairing automation
equipment. The interest of labor lies in bringing about the transition
with a minimum of convenience and distress to the workers   62. _____
involved. Also, union spokesmen emphasize that the benefit of
the increased production and lower costs made possible by
automation should be shared by workers in the form of higher
wages, more leisure, and improved living standards.

To protect the interests of its members in the era of   63. _____
automation, unions have adopted a number of new policies. One
of these is the promotion of supplementary employment benefit   64. _____
plans. It is emphasized that since the employer involved with such   65. _____
a plan has a direct financial interest in preventing unemployment,
he would have a strong drive for planning new installments so as to   66. _____
cause the less possible problems in jobs and job assignment. Such   67. _____
unions are working for dismissal pay agreements, required that   68. _____
permanently dismissed workers are paid a sum of money based   69. _____
on length of service. Another approach is the idea of the
"improvement factor", that calls for wage increases based   70. _____
on increases in productivity. It is possible, however, that labor
will rely mainly on reduction in working hour in order to gain   71. _____
a full share in the fruits of automation.

Part Ⅵ   Translation (5 minutes)

Directions: *Complete the sentences by translating into English the Chinese given in brackets.*
*Please write your translation on **Answer Sheet 2**.*

72. He was in such a hurry that he _____ (吞了几口面包和牛奶就上班了).
73. He hurried to the house _____ (结果房内空空如也).
74. _____ (当初要不是你的帮助), I really don't know what I'd have done.
75. No sooner _____ (我一出门,就认识到错了).
76. To my disappointment, the manager's plan of _____ (新产品促销
    计划根本行不通).

附录一 答案与解析

Test 1

Part Ⅰ

Sample Writing

Is Beauty an Advantage?

Recently, especially in winter holidays, plastic surgery hospitals in many large cities have received a growing number of young clients. Most of them are forth-year college students, who are hunting for their first job in society. They want their eyes enlarged or nose raised, believing that a prettier face will bring about better opportunities in the job market.

Is beauty really an advantage? Does it make a beautiful individual a more powerful candidate for the position? It seems so, at least in the eyes of the society. Nowadays, televisions, newspapers, magazines and bill-boards are beauty-obsessed as ever. Thanks to the media, we're accustomed to see pretty cover girls, gorgeous TV anchors, and handsome executives in TV series. All these are spreading a misleading message — the survival of the prettiest. As the job market grows increasingly tight, many students become convinced that good looks are of overwhelming importance. They resort to plastic surgeries and expensive clothes and make-up to build up their confidence. They package their appearance before going to an interview, in the hope that an attractive appearance will impress the interviewer and make them stand out among numerous applicants.

It's true that beauty is a marketing tool that can open doors occasionally, but it doesn't follow that an attractive appearance will take you all the way to success. In my opinion, beauty is skin-deep, and true beauty lies in the soul. After all, what the boss really needs is committed, competent employees that produce profits. If you really want to get on in today's highly competitive world, it's important to understand the myth of beauty. Our society should place more value on intelligence and character. Both the mass media and educators should help make the misguided students realize that the richness of mind is ultimately more valuable than good looks.

Part Ⅱ

1. [A] 根据第三段可知："interruption/work distractions"是高科技办公不可或缺的一部分,虽打断了手里正在进行的工作,却也可能带来积极利益。
2. [D] 参见"The Birth of Multitasking"部分第二段第一、二、三句。
3. [B] "The Birth of Multitasking"部分第一段最后两句提到:心理学家认为,对于需要密切监控数据的工作,数据的呈现(presentation)至关重要。因此,战斗机驾驶舱都是精心设计的,所有仪表数据可一目了然。第二段最后两句继续提到:办公室工作人员如今也需要盯着信息极其复杂的电脑屏幕,同时处理来信、文本文件、PowerPoint 演示、网络浏览等工作。在这一点上,现代办公室人员就如同战斗机飞行员。
4. [A] 参见"Effect of Multitasking..."部分第二段:如果持续不断的电子邮件铃声是我们感到自己有价值被需要,multitasking(多项工作同时进行)可能让我们产生积极的感受;但如果

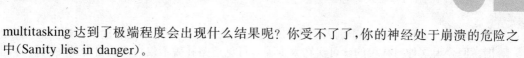

multitasking 达到了极端程度会出现什么结果呢？你受不了了，你的神经处于崩溃的危险之中(Sanity lies in danger)。

5. [A] 参见"Effect of Multitasking..."部分的第三段最后两句：On average, they juggled eight windows at the same time... they would spend barely 20 seconds looking at one window before flipping to another.

6. [B] 参见"Ways to Cope with Interruptions"部分第一段第一、二句：When Mark and Czerwinski, working separately... they each notice the same thing：Post-it notes. Workers would write brief reminders of the task they were supposed to be working on.

7. [C] 参见"Ways to Cope with Interruptions"部分第二段：These piecemeal efforts pointed out ways that our high-tech tools could be engineered to be less distracting. They (Microsoft workers) placed their applications on different screens so that each application was read at a glance.

8. a bigger, clearer screen/on the bigger screen 参见"Ways to Cope with Interruptions"小节部分第四段：On the bigger screen, some people completed the tasks as much as 44% more quickly... Czerwinski had never seen a single change to a computer system so significantly improve a user's productivity. The clearer your screen, the calmer your mind.

9. work at different places and interact online 参见"Looking for Better Interruptions"小节部分第一段第一、二句：Mark compared the way people work when sitting in cubicles with how they work when they're at different locations and interact online. She discovered people working in cubicles suffer more interruptions, but they have better interruptions because...

10. the best/the most appropriate moment to interrupt him 参见全文最后一段最后一句：He has been building automated reasoning systems equipped with artificial intelligence that observes a computer user's behavior and tries to predict the moment the user will be mentally free and ready to be interrupted.

Part Ⅲ

11. D	12. B	13. B	14. C	15. D	16. A	17. C	18. A	19. C
20. B	21. D	22. A	23. B	24. C	25. A	26. A	27. D	28. C
29. B	30. A	31. C	32. C	33. B	34. B	35. D		

36. flock 37. delivery 38. escaping 39. excitable
40. adventurous 41. incredible 42. profile 43. exclusive

44. licenses other firms to produce goods using Harry Potter characters or images, from which Ms. Rowling gets a big cut

45. each book sets the stage for a film, which boosts book sales, which lifts sales of Potter products

46. a stunning success by any measure, especially as Ms. Rowling has long demanded that Harry Potter should not be over-merchandised

Part Ⅳ

47. the rude behavior/the bad manners of the driver 参见第一段第一句：(当前路况恶劣，)我们尽可以责怪交通阻塞、油价上涨与快节奏的现代生活，然而公路上司机的行为也确实变得越来越糟糕。下文也主要谈及司机的不文明行为引发交通事故的问题。

48. The majority of motorists/Most drivers are impolite.

49. understand and react reasonably to 参见第二段：道路礼貌不仅要有良好的行为举止，还要有理智(good sense)。只有头脑冷静、脾气温和的司机在遭遇不文明行为时，才能抵制报复的诱

感。而另一方面，……对于别人的礼貌行为友好地点头或挥手示意有助于营造友好宽容的氛围。但今天这种对礼貌的认可实在太少了。可见道路礼貌不仅指司机自身的文明行为，也指司机对他人行为的正确处理态度（good sense）。

50. dangerous misplaced politeness 参见第三段：然而，不恰当的过度礼貌也会很危险。典型的例子有……同样的情况还有鼓励老太太们随时随地乱穿马路。马路上居然没有铺满这些老奶奶们的尸体，倒是一直令我称奇的一件事。

51. yield to each other/tolerate each other 参见最后一段倒数第二句：... give-and-take on the part of all road users ，指所有道路使用者之间互让互惠行为。

52. [A] 细节题。参见第一段第二句：... but few people（几乎没人）are even moderately proficient（中等程度地擅长）at pronouncing foreign language，故选 A（作者对语言发音的看法是没有多少人的外语发音算得上还不错），fairly = to some degree，一定程度上。注意：fairly good 比 quite good 程度都弱。本题考察词汇理解准确性。

53. [B] 细节题。参见第一段第三句：人们外语说得不是很好，根本原因在于他们没能掌握学习发音问题之本质，因而没有采取正确的方法来处理这个问题。故选 B（作者认为错误地处理发音问题是由于未能正确地理解这一问题）。

54. [C] 句意推断题。参见第一段倒数第二、三句：So the first point to make...close attention. 所以第一点要说明的是，英语发音必须要教；教师要为此花费一定课堂时间。只有通过教师本人对该问题的（重视）态度，才能使学生感到发音是值得密切关注的问题。故可推断选项 C 正确（学生对正确发音习惯的重视取决于教师对发音问题的处理态度/方式）。

55. [D] 句意推断题。参见第三段最后一句：如果教师头脑里对不同语言的发音习惯没有明确的概念（a clear mental picture），那么他对学生发音的评论也将不大可能起到多少作用，花在发音教学方面的课堂时间也可能是种浪费。故选 D（由于教师自己发音知识了解不多，对学生发音的评论也是不全面的，因而浪费了课堂时间）。

56. [B] 句意推断题。参见最后一段第三句：语言教师第一项也是最重要的一项技巧是他自己的表现，即他表现自己口语水平的能力，这样学生的潜在模仿力才能得到最大限度的发挥与促进。由此可推断 B 是正确的（作者认为学生模仿力的培养，主要取决于教师表现发音模式的技巧），"teacher's technique present speech models"就相当于文中的"ability to demonstrate spoken language"。本题干扰性最大的是 C 项，本段最后两句提到，教师应尽可能使自己的发音成为完美的模仿模式，但也可借助录音、收音机等手段提供外国人语音作为补充。所以并未要求教师本人一定要发音完美。

57. [D] 事实判断归纳题。选项 A（形成糖分）在第一段第六句得以体现：空气中的二氧化碳作为气体进入叶片，与叶片中所含水分溶解后，才与其中一部分水结合，形成单糖。再根据第二段第四句：叶片表层有大量微孔可供二氧化碳进入。由此推知，植物无需水就能直接从空气中摄取二氧化碳，故选 D。而选项 C（吸收矿物成分）在第一段第四句得以体现：土壤中有用的矿物质只有在土壤水分中溶解后才能进入根系。选项 B（维持植物的快速生长部分以及枝干部）在第一段最后两句也得以体现。

58. [D] 句意理解题。根据第二段第二句：在光合作用过程中，二氧化碳与水在叶绿素和光能的作用下相互结合以形成糖分。这就要求空气中的二氧化碳进入植物。可见，就植物生长需要而言，光合作用的基本功能是为了产生糖分，而不是为了使二氧化碳与水结合，也不是为了摄取光能，故选 D。

59. [A] 段落主旨大意归纳题。第二段第一句是本段的 topic sentence：植物在任何特定时期的含水量都只是其生长过程中总需量的一小部分，由此推出 A 正确（第二段采用事实以说明植物所需水分比实际含水量多得多）。

60. [B] 是非判断型细节题。参见全文最后一句：并非所有进入叶子的二氧化碳都会合成碳水化合物。此句意与选项 B 一致（植物中的二氧化碳只有一部分被合成）。

61. [B] 全文主旨题。参见文章开头两句（即全文的 topic sentences）：大多数生长中的植物，其含水量比其他所有物质的总合还要多。达尼斯指出,把植物叫做水造结构是恰当的,正如把主要由砖建造的房屋称做砖房一样。由此点明全文主旨:水在植物生长中作用巨大。故选B。其余选项只是细节性事实。

Part Ⅴ

62. the computer ∧ used to → is　电脑被用于……根据上下文应用被动语态。语态错误。

63. animal → animals　plants and animals,动植物,泛指用名词复数。名词数的错误。

64. extended → extend　genetic therapies to produce healthier babies, eliminate suffering and extend human lifespan 优生更健康的婴儿,消除痛苦,延长人类寿命的基因疗法。to produce...eliminate...extend 为三个并列不定式结构。非谓语用法错误。

65. any ∧ economic → other　这种新的基因商业所提出的问题比历史上任何其他的经济变革都更令人困惑。比较级结构错误。

66. and ∧ substitution of → the　定冠词遗漏。

67. reversible → irreversible　cause catastrophic pollution and irreversible damage 造成灾难性污染与不可挽回的破坏。irreversible 与 catastrophic 相呼应。逻辑语义相悖。

68. become → becoming　the consequences of the world's gene pool becoming patented intellectual property 世界基因库成为专利知识产权的后果。becoming 作介词 of 的动名词宾语。非谓语结构错误。

69. that → where　live in a world where babies..., and where people are... 两个均由 where 引导的并列定语从句,先行词为 world。引导定语从句的关系副词使用错误。

70. them → it　it 指代 gene science。指代错误。

71. broad → narrow　尽管生物技术革命影响着我们每个人,但这场辩论目前只涉及了生物学家、政府决策人等狭窄范围的人群。该问题的讨论应有全社会参与。逻辑语义相悖。

Part Ⅵ

72. that all flights were cancelled due to/because of bad weather

73. If only I were not so nervous!

74. unable to fall asleep again unless they eat something/without eating something

75. wasn't until last year that

76. to be subjected to receive an inferior education

Test 2

Part Ⅰ
Sample Writing

The Pleasure of Learning

Learning is one of the essential pleasures of the human race. Those who avoid learning often find life boring and meaningless, for they deprive themselves of the excitement and fulfillment in learning something new.

The pleasure of learning is universal, everywhere to be found. Many of us have tasted the joy of learning by reading interesting books. Books are no lumps of lifeless paper, but a voice far distant in time and space, talking to readers, mind to mind, heart to heart. Beyond books, we

can also enjoy the fruits of traveling, provided that we travel with an open mind to understand other people and other places, and an alert eye for all kinds of novel experiences. Finally, learning also means learning to practise, or at least, to appreciate an art. Every new art we learn blesses us with a new sense, by which we may enjoy the wonders of the world more intensely.

If the pleasure of learning is universal, why are there so many dull, unhappy students in school? It is because they were made dull by bad teaching, by isolation, by surrender to routine and by their own laziness. The students who "suffer from" learning should break away from the bonds of textbooks and tests, and embrace various other fields of knowledge with renewed energy.

Part Ⅱ

1. [D] 根据第一段可知:Woods 是澳大利亚职业橄榄球队员。新年除夕夜他给母亲打电话说又与球队签了合同,可第二天却将管子插在汽车排气管上并连接到车窗内,废气中毒自杀。

2. [A] 参见第二段:But the sun, the beaches and the sporting culture are the cheery <u>backdrop</u> (灿烂的背景) for <u>a disturbing trend: young Australian men are now killing themselves</u> at the rate of one a day....

3. [B] 根据"Causes for Suicide"部分第一段第一 、三句可知:澳大利亚向来把坚强寡言、任劳任怨的银幕硬汉作为教育男孩的榜样。近年来,学校和社会机构由主要致力于为女孩提供更多的机会,而要求困惑中的男孩自立自强。

4. [C] 参见"Causes for Suicide"部分第二段第四句:The Haywards sent Mark to various counselors, none of whom warned that he had <u>suicidal tendencies</u>.

5. [B] 参见"Causes for Suicide"部分第三段第三句:Suicide is especially high among the most marginal: young Aboriginal men, isolated by <u>poverty, alcoholism and racism.</u>

6. [C] 参见"Causes for Suicide"部分最后一段第一、二句:The deeper mystery is why the <u>universal anguish</u>(痛苦)<u>of growing up</u> should have such particularly <u>devastating effects</u> in Australia. One answer is that the country allows <u>easier access to guns</u> than most other developed Asian countries.

7. [A] 参见"Efforts to Tackle Suicide Problem"部分第一段第一、二句:...That is no easy task in a <u>society that generally avoids introspection</u>.

8. a shock advertising campaign 参见 "Efforts to Tackle Suicide Problem"小节部分第二段第一句:To get Australia's attention, psychiatrist Tiller wants the government to <u>sponsor a shock advertising campaign</u>...

9. The creation of a National Office for Yong People 参见 "Efforts to Tackle Suicide Problem"小节部分第三段第一、三句:The rising death toll has just begun to force suicide onto the nation's <u>political agenda</u>(政治日程)... Brendan Nelson, a physician and backbencher in Parliament(国会普通议员), recently called for <u>the creation of a National Office for Young People</u> to report to the prime minister on youth concerns.

10. are taught to express themselves/learn to seek help for themselves 参见全文最后一段最后几句 Tony Woods 的感言:"We need to tell them:You're worthwhile. <u>Seek help</u>...We need to <u>teach boys to express themselves</u>. "

Part Ⅲ

| 11. B | 12. A | 13. B | 14. C | 15. C | 16. D | 17. D | 18. A | 19. B |
| 20. B | 21. D | 22. C | 23. C | 24. B | 25. B | 26. D | 27. B | 28. D |

29. C   30. C   31. A   32. D   33. A   34. B   35. C

36. priorities   37. fundamental   38. connections   39. intuition

40. separation   41. intelligence   42. evolution   43. programs

44. to see what's happening around the house, to spot an approaching danger, to notice changes in the children's behavior and appearance.

45. which explains their narrow range of vision, while women's brains are able to interpret a wider range of information.

46. while women pay attention to the guests' faces to find out who they are and how they feel.

Part Ⅳ

47. foot, head and eyes 根据第一段可知,Hans 会用前足点地、点头摇头进行交流;根据第三段可知,Hans 还能"看"懂题板上写的数字,说明 Hans 也能用眼睛交流。

48. his ability to reason and talk 参见第二段最后一句:他们对测试结果印象深刻,并发表声明说没有证据表明提问者对 Hans 进行了有意识的影响或帮助。

49. his questioner could not see the numbers on the cards 参见第三段最后一句:当 Pfungst(提问者)不看题板(不知上面写的什么数字)时,Hans 只能答对 8%。

50. observing/reading his questioners 参见倒数第二段。

51. the appropriate use of research procedures 参见最后一段:专家也可能出错,有时表面看上去正确的东西只不过是一种假象。如果没有采用适当的研究步骤来检测观察结果,即使专家也会上当。

52. [D] 全文主旨题。根据第一段第一句(即全文主题句):住房状况是一个由社会因素决定的变量(socially determinant variable),可推断 D 正确,即作者主要论证住房状况随社会因素而变化。B、C 项的内容文中虽有所提到,但不是主旨。

53. [A] 句意理解型细节题。参见第一段最后一句:过去,在很长一段时间里,主要问题是住房的短缺,但近几年来,住房条件的恶化引起了人们更大的关注。故选 A(近年来,住房状况的恶化成为主要住房问题)。

54. [D] 细节归纳题。参见第三段第一句:近几十年来,住房问题的处理政策已从促进建筑的宏观经济策略转向(政府)房贴。本段后半部分还提到,由于政府停止投资兴建住房,那些因为各种理由无法廉价租房的低收入家庭别无选择只能选择买房,由于政府出台的购房贷款条件宽松,低收入家庭购房不但没受到限制反而受到鼓励。由此可推断 D 正确(政府近来采取的解决住房问题的措施是政府津贴与较容易的贷款)。

55. [C] 是非判断型细节题。参见第三段第四句:许多地位低下的贫困家庭由于对租户的挑选、现有住房饱和、破产等原因被排除在廉租房之外,别无选择只好自己购房。故选项 C(低收入家庭只能住租金低廉的房子)与本文内容不相符。选项 A、B、D 分别在第三段最后一句、第二段第一句、最后一段第二句得以体现。

56. [B] 参见最后一段的第二、三句:随着国家与地方政府紧缩政策的实施,廉租房项目遭到削减,低收入家庭发现住房难觅,无家可归者的数量激增。

57. [A] 词汇理解型细节题。参见第一段第一句:我们长久以来一直寻找着由来已久的体重问题的答案,新一代的减肥药似乎提供了这一答案。chronic weight problem = the problem of overweight that has long since troubled people.

58. [B] 词义理解型细节题。第一段第二句提到:Hundreds of thousands of pound-conscious Americans had discovered...成千上万的体重意识强烈的美国人就是本段最后一句所提及的"hundreds of thousands of new pill poppers","pill poppers"指服用减肥药的那些美国人。

59. [D] 句意理解型细节题。参见第二段最后一句:新泽西州一位医生 Sheldon Levine 曾在电视上和自己的书里大肆宣扬 Redux,而现在也已停止给重度肥胖者以外的病人开此减肥药。

选项 D 与"the diet-drug revolution is facing a setback"意义相悖。

60. [B] 句意理解型细节题。第三段提到 82 个服用 fen-phen 和 7 个服用 Redux 的病人都患了心脏病。紧接着第四段第一句说,"可这一切好像还不够糟糕,医生们报告一位服用 fen-phen 不足一个月的妇女死于高血压。"故选 B(揭示减肥药致命副作用的最糟病例是一位服用 fen-phen 的妇女死于高血压)。

61. [C] 推论题。参见全文最后一句:减肥药当前的这种回落是一种本不该出现的过山车现象。roller coaster(过山车)指大起大落、急转突变。故可推知 C(先把减肥药当做灵丹妙药大加推崇,而后又作为危险药品弃之一旁,这样的事本不该发生)。而选项 A、B、D 的内容是最后一段明确提及的事实。

Part Ⅴ

62. six → sixth　a sixth of the population 六分之一的人口,分母应用序数词。

63. elder → elderly　the elderly and the poor 老年人与穷人,the 后需用形容词 elderly。

64. estimating → estimated　an estimated 47 million people 约 4,700 万人。过去分词 estimated 表示"据估计"。

65. Because → That　that 引导主语从句。That so many people....country is a disgrace. 名词性从句引导词错误。

66. not ∧ their → just 或者 only　not just/only their jobs but their healthcare benefits as well,不仅担心他们的工作还害怕失去保健福利。固定搭配错误。

67. arrived → arrives　根据上下文应用一般现在时。时态错误。

68. with → without　由于那些没有保险的病人通常付不起医疗费,账单被分摊给了每个人。与逻辑语义相悖。

69. by → in　in turn 反过来。介词搭配错误。

70. get → take　And it is one that politicians at last seem ready to take. 在这个句子中,one 指代前文所提的 step,take the step(采取的行动)为习惯搭配。

71. with → and　between conservatives, who think... and those on the left, who think... 在保守派与左翼分子之间。

Part Ⅵ

72. it doesn't mean/it doesn't follow that you won't be good at it

73. a summer program designed/aimed to make girls interested in engineering

74. If the whether were not so wet

75. lest she (should) disrupt the court order

76. considering/and consider this (to be) a sign of respect

Test 3

Part Ⅰ

Sample Writing

Evaluation by Students

Nowadays, a growing number of universities have launched the "Student Evaluation Project", in which students are invited to evaluate the job performance of their teachers. In most cases, students get evaluation forms at the end of a semester and are asked to fill them out anonymously.

There are varied opinions among teachers and university authorities about this educational reform program. University administrators consider student evaluation to be an effective means to discipline teachers and help enhance the teaching quality. However, many teachers feel uncomfortable, even resentful about it, because different students may have different standards by which to judge their teachers. In their opinion, the evaluation results may be influenced by individual student's personal feelings and therefore can't be counted on as an objective reflection of the teaching performance. As for students, their attitudes are also varied: some like to be given a voice to express their views, some don't understand it, while some simply don't care.

As a whole, Student Evaluation Project took a bold step in the university education reform process, which encourages students to get more actively involved in the class teaching, thus positively creating an interactive academic atmosphere. Nevertheless, many other problems may arise correspondingly. For instance, some students may be too critical about a certain professor just because the professor is not fun or he is too strict, which might have a negative impact on the impartiality of evaluation itself, misleading the reform orientation.

Part Ⅱ

1. [B] 参见第 1 段。
2. [C] 参见第四段第一句：*Nano* 一词源于希腊语，表示"侏儒"。纳米技术就是对小于 100 纳米以下物质的研究与应用，这些物质就相当于分子、病毒的大小。
3. [D] 参见"Stunning Uses of Nanotechnology"部分第三段：But a nanotube is tough…It's thin sheet graphite that's formed into a tube（将石墨片卷成管状）. These tiny straw-like cylinders（稻草状微型圆柱体）…are <u>among the world's best conductors of heat and electricity</u>.
4. [B] 参见"Stunning Uses of Nanotechnology"部分第三段最后一句。
5. [A] 参见"Stunning Uses of Nanotechnology"部分第四段第二句。
6. [D] 参见"Stunning Uses of Nanotechnology"部分第四段最后一句。
7. [A] 参见"Stunning Uses of Nanotechnology"部分最后一段最后一句：One idea, therefore, is to put these sheets in windshields of the car and <u>run current</u> through them <u>to defrost car windows</u>.
8. combining modern nanoscience with old-fashioned cure 参见"Medicine and Nanotechnology"小节部分第一段第三句：Nucryst Pharmaceuticals has come up with a winning formula that <u>combines nanoscience with old-fashioned folk wisdom.</u> 下文主要列举了应用纳米技术改良用银子抗感染的古希腊烫伤疗法。
9. copying lotus leaf with nanotechology 参见"Copy Nature with Nanotechnology"小节部分第一段。
10. a nanotube coating 参见最后一段：…Fenniri has made <u>a nanotube coating for the artificial joint.</u> It's a very good imitation of collagen, a natural protein that is part of bone. As a result, the coating attracts bone cells. This is important because bone growth helps integrate an artificial joint into the body.

Part Ⅲ

11. B	12. C	13. C	14. D	15. B	16. D	17. A	18. B	19. D
20. D	21. B	22. B	24. C	25. D	26. A	26. B	27. D	28. B
29. C	30. D	31. C	32. A	33. C	34. A	35. B		

36. toll 　　　　37. irony 　　　　38. artificial 　　　　39. dwellers

40. roar 　　　　41. philosopher 　　　42. essence 　　　43. spaciousness

44. next to impossible to find these things externally in the big city, which makes it all the more imperative to look within

45. There is, of course, a certain amount of stressful activity that city people must put up with to make a living

46. So why do people fill the empty spaces with more loud noise and near manic imagery

Part Ⅳ

47. constantly create new ideas 参见第一段最后两句:事实上,你应不断创新才能避免亏损。对未来没有创新思想的企业可能无法生存。固定搭配"keep out of water"意为"使自己免遭困境"。

48. Because no technology company has a guaranteed future. 参见第二段倒数第二、三、四句:微软是一个十分强大的机构,短期内不可替代。但两三年以后,没有人能肯定地说任何高科技公司都能保持稳固的地位。

49. Colec Industries 参见第三段:Colec 公司 1985 年的"Cabbage Patch Kids"系列洋娃娃十分畅销,但在推出一系列轰动一时的洋娃娃后开始暗自满足,再也没创造出值得一提的新产品,结果 1988 年 Colec 公司破产。

50. its 15% rule 参见倒数第二段第一、二句。

51. companies may go bankrupt without realizing it 参见最后一段。

52. [A] 全文主旨题。congestion(拥堵、阻塞)是文中多次出现的核心词。

53. [B] 推论题。参见第一段第一句:现代城市对人类造成的悲惨影响扼杀了人类的审美意识。由此可推断,过去人们拥有较强的审美意识。故选 B。

54. [D] 作者态度推论题。参见第三段倒数第二句:这种投机方式以及人口增长的压力造成城市的高空纵向发展,结果是人们被迫去适应拥挤,以维持这些人为提升的土地价值。该句中"speculative""forced to""artificial"等词体现了作者对地价增值的否定态度,故选 D(城市地价的剧增是人为的、无意义的恼人现象)。选项 A 中的"desirable"与 C 中的"efficient""positive"都不符合作者的态度。选项 B 可能有道理,但文中未提及。

55. [D] 句意理解型细节题。参见第三段最后一句:从传统的市中心地带向外大规模发展,这种部分分散方式只是将(拥挤)问题转移到了城市周边地区。

56. [C] 作者在最后两段里表达了自己关于城市重塑的一些建议。根据第四段的第二、三句:我们必须对城市彻底重新规划,以形成合理的人口密度,必须为人们提供所谓的"心理上可自由活动的空间"。可见,作者建议通过控制人口密度来避免城市居民心理上的过分拥挤,而非满足地产商心理需求。故选项 C 没有提及。而选项 B、D、A 分别在第四段的第四句、最后一段的第一句与最后一句有所提及。

57. [C] 段落主旨题。根据标记词"but"可知,第一段的主题句是该段最后一句:……教学与研究互相矛盾,研究在学术晋升中所起的作用太大了,而教学则大打折扣。这些话都有一定道理,但同时却忽视了(教学与科研二者间)更深层、更重要的联系。可见,作者认为,教学与科研间的关系不能过于简单化。故选 C。

58. [B] 句意理解型细节题。参见第三段第一、二句:多数研究性大学奖励优秀教学,但更看重的还是学术研究方面的成就。部分原因是教学质量难以评价。故选 B(研究性高校在学术晋升中仍强调科研的分量,部分原因在于教学质量的客观评估很难进行)。

59. [B] 推论题。参见第四段第二、三、四句:培养新的科学家需要优秀的教学,文科院校与研究性高校都需要。尽管科学家的造就要从小学开始,但大学或研究生阶段的拙劣教学却可能使科学家被埋没。解决办法不是割裂教学与科研,而是要认识到二者的结合虽困难重重,却

至关重要。由此可推论选项 B 正确(将教学与科研割裂会影响未来科学家的素质)。

60. [B] 词义猜测题。参见第四段最后两句:大学应该把教授这一头衔授予那些愿意"profess",愿意真正成为学者团体一分子的人。那些不愿意从事教学的教授可以称做为"知名研究员"或者别的什么称号。由此可推知,profess ＝ teach。

61. [D] 上下文理解题。最后一段提到:由于现代科学飞速发展,要同时成为一名出色的教师与出色的科研人员越来越难了,然而许多人却被授予如此大名。那些认为可以分裂教学与科研的人显然不了解教育体制,而那些认为问题会自行消失的人则实在没履行自身的职责。联系上下文可知,"the problem"指"做到教研双优的困难",故选 D(教研相结合)。

Part V

62. increasing → increasingly   increasingly widespread acceptance 日益普遍的认可,副词 increasingly 修饰形容词 widespread。形容词与副词混淆错误。

63. which → that   that 引导同位语从句,修饰 principle。名词性从句引导词使用错误。

64. has → is   he is allowed to...他获准去……根据上下文,本句应用被动语态。语态错误。

65. by → of   require sth of sb 为动词固定搭配。在"requiring of them the necessary self-discipline and hard work"结构中,宾语较长而后置。

66. Fortunately → Unfortunately   逻辑语义相悖。

67. demanded → demanding   demanding,形容词,意为"高要求的"。

68. but → so   just as...so...为固定搭配,表"正如……同样也……"。

69. speaks∧intense → of   speaks of intense mental exertion as...将高强度的脑力劳动说成是……

70. exposing → exposed   have sth done 结构。

71. a → the   the joy is the result of... joy 第二次出现表特指,用定冠词。冠词错误。

Part VI

72. When I found myself in difficult situations over the years

73. may have dominated the headlines three years ago

74. all urgent matters had been attended to/taken care of

75. (should) be abolished as soon as possible

76. that you are buying more than just metal and rubber

Test 4

Part I

Sample Writing

Post-graduate Craze Cools Off

The post-graduate craze has long since been a hot issue on most campuses around the country. According to the statistics released by Shanghai Educational Test Institute, 79,299 students in Shanghai sat in for the post-graduate entrance exams in 2003, a dramatic rise of 32.6% over the previous year. The year of 2003 is the tenth year since the number of post-graduate test takers began to grow rapidly and steadily. However, since then, the rising line has gradually plateaued year by year, with a modest rise of 6.7%, 1.8%, 2.1% respectively in

2004，2005，2006. In 2007, the number of test takers even dropped by 6.5% in comparison with 2006. All these statistics point to an interesting phenomenon — the post-graduate test, after a ten-year craze, is starting to cool off.

Three major factors account for the cooling off of the post-graduate craze. One is the post-graduate education reform. Post-graduate students used to enjoy a modest government subsidy for their three－year studies. But according to the new graduate program, they have to pay for all their living and learning expenses. Faced with the rising education costs, some students hesitate to apply for the test. Another factor is the pressure from the increasingly competitive job market. Many students used to believe that the more education they received, the better job opportunities they would have. With the expanded enrollment for both undergraduates and post-graduates, job hunt becomes more and more difficult. Many students fear that when they finish their post-graduate studies, the positions will have been already occupied. Moreover, many companies prefer experienced employees to new graduates who tend to know nothing but impractical book knowledge. As a result, some students decide to start work early so as to accumulate more work experiences.

In my opinion, before we make the choice, we need to think twice. What kind of job do I really want to do? Does the job require practical work experience or theoretical knowledge? Can the graduate program offer what I want to learn? Our final decision should be based on our personal situations.

Part Ⅱ

1. [B] 参见第一段倒数第二句：... a growing land-hungry population killed off the last of Germany's wolves.

2. [A] 根据第二段可知,最近欧洲农村人口锐减主要由于低出生率与农村人口迁往城市(the region's low birth rate and rural flight)。

3. [D] 参见"Environmental Changes"部分第一、二段。

4. [C] 参见"Environmental Changes"部分第三段最后两句：农田因无人照料而荒芜,雨水导致水土流失,果园与牧场为干燥的灌木所覆盖,夏季常自燃引起火灾。

5. [B] 参见"Varied Pictures of Rural Depopulation"部分第一段最后一句：Once they die out, many of their farms will join the 6 million hectares — one third of Italy's farmland — that has already been abandoned.

6. [D] 参见"Varied Pictures of Rural Depopulation"部分第二段第一句：Rising economic pressures, especially from reduced government subsidies, will amplify the trend.

7. [A] 参见"Big Challenges"部分第一段第三句：Already, attractive areas within driving distance of prosperous cities are seeing robust revivals, driven by urban flight and an in-flooding of childless retirees.

8. baby boomers start dying out around 2020 参见"Big Challenges"小节部分第三段：But once baby boomers start dying out around 2020, populations will start to decline so sharply that there simply won't be enough people to reinvent itself. It's simply unclear how long current government policies can put off the inevitable.

9. Public taxi-on-demand service and videoconferencing and Internet for remote medical examination 参见"Big Challenges"小节部分第四段。

10. attract foreign immigrants 参见全文倒数第二段第二句：... Mayor Manznanares began offering free air-fares and housing for foreign families to settle in Aguvivia.

Part Ⅲ

11. A	12. B	13. D	14. C	15. C	16. B	17. D	18. A.	19. B
20. B	21. A	22. D	23. A	24. C	25. B	26. B	27. D	28. C
29. C	30. C	31. D	32. D	33. B	34. C	35. A		

36. manifest 37. calculations 38. minimal 39. visual

40. disturbance 41. triggered 42. infection 43. oxygen

44. Generally, males are more likely than females to have both severe and mild learning disabilities

45. 25 - 40 per cent of people with learning disabilities also have mental health problems as well as a high level of unrecognized illness

46. 23 per cent of adults with learning disabilities have experienced physical abuse and 47 percent of them verbal abuse and bullying

Part Ⅳ

47. expect protection from law/from the legal system 参见第一段最后两句：幸运的是，如果门垫或炉子没有标有关于可能发生的灾难的警示标签，一个成功的法律诉讼可帮你挽回损失——至少自 20 世纪 80 年代早期以来，人们一直持有这样的看法，当时陪审团开始判定厂商要为顾客的不幸负责。

48. avoid legal liability 参见第二段第一句：日益增多的赔偿案令生产商备感威胁，他们便把商品标签上的警告写得很长，预计可能发生的任何一种意外，以逃避法律责任。

49. are no longer supported by law 最后一段前两句提到，目前局势有所扭转。虽然人身伤害造成的赔偿案仍在增长，但一些法庭开始站在被告一边，尤其当商品的警示标签无论怎样写都于事无补的情况下。

50. the benefit of customers 参见最后一段后半部分，the American Law Institute 发布新指令，建议厂家不必写过多的警告，因为这样一来，真正重要警示信息反而被淹没忽略了。商品警示信息本来应用于保护顾客的利益而非逃避法律责任。

51. Objective. 作者客观叙述了关于产品潜在危险的警示问题及相关赔偿案的审理，既没偏袒厂家，也没偏袒顾客。

52. [D] 段落大意推论题。第一、二段作者主要提出了电脑的一些局限性。尤其是第二段最后一句提出，电脑无法使人们与自己必须面对的问题产生链接，"the possibilities of creative growth in himself; the memory of the race and the rights of the next generation"等问题都是人们必须应当注意的"real problems in human society"。故选 D（根据第一、二段可推知，如果电脑能使人们关注真正的社会问题，作者就不会对电脑如此不满。）

53. [B] 细节性推论题。根据第三段，在电脑时代，人们倾向于将 data（事实数据）误当做 wisdom（智慧），而只有当人们想要并有能力找到这些数据的意义与导向时，这种毫无障碍地获取事实数据（data or facts）的方式才能带来无尽的益处。由此可推知，在电脑时代，必须优先注重 wisdom（即发现数据意义的能力）。故选 B。

54. [C] 推论题。段首句"Facts are terrible things if left spreading and unattended"为第四段的主题句，本段主要说明数据泛滥又无人管理时的危害性。最后一句特别指出，电脑只能提供一个正确的数字（number or fact），在没有作出分析判断之前，这个数字是无关紧要的。由此可推知：在电脑时代，人类判断力的运用十分重要。故选 C。

55. [D] 段落大意推论题。倒数第二段指出，如果人们无法区分人工智能的中介作用与人类判断力的最终责任性，电脑则只能证明不相关的事物。电脑有一定的误导性，使人们误以为自己提出的功能性问题就是本质性问题，也使人们误以为电脑就是人类智力的替代品（substitute），而事实上电脑只是人类智力的延伸（extension），由此可见，作者认为电脑只具

有次要辅助功能(subsidiary function)。

56. [C] 作者态度判断题。本文指出了电脑的一系列局限性,可见作者对电脑持批评态度。

57. [C] 论点与论据区分题。在第一段,作者将鸟儿和鱼儿同人类作类比,指出鸟儿和鱼儿对其赖以生存的天空和海洋的影响力毫无所知,正如人类对自己所沉浸其中的文化模式(cultural norms or codes)也是在不知不觉中受其影响的。

58. [B] 词汇语境意义推测题。第三段第二句提到对广泛的事物与不同民族的敏感性需要克服"such cultural parochialism",parochialism 即第二段最后一句提到的"the blindness that limits what can be experienced and what can be learnt from others",由此推知 parochialism 指地方狭隘主义(provincialism)。

59. [A] 细节题。根据第二段最后一句可知,"both individual mentality and collective mentality"都可能"keep people out of contact with neighbors"或者"separate neighbors from different cultures"。

60. [C] 推论性细节题。最后一段提到,人们在童年时代形成自己的个性与文化,当时他们对此都还没有理解能力……但一旦有了自己的个性与文化,便很难对自身的文化进程作出客观评价,因为用于评价的工具也正是有待评价的文化机制。

61. [D] 全文主旨题。第一段第一句一般是全文主题句,该句提到"cultural norms"的普遍性,下文主要讲"cultural norms"为何难以突破,这就是所谓的"根深蒂固的文化无远见现象"。

Part V

62. greatly → great   caused...great damage to property 造成巨大的财产损失。形容词与副词混淆。

63. with → as   连词 as 引导状语从句。

64. its → their   their 指代复数名词 earthquakes。指代错误。

65. many → few   上文提到"地震学是一门比较新兴的科学研究",因为"直到 18 世纪有关地震的真实描述几乎还没有什么(few)记载"。逻辑语义相悖错误。

66. believe → believed   当时人们相信……,根据上下文应用一般过去时。时态错误。

67. rushed → rushing   caused by air rushing out the caves...由冲出地球内部深处的空气引起,动名词 rushing 作介词 by 的宾语。非谓语动词错误。

68. had → were   ...were felt in many parts of the world(震动)在世界许多地方都被感觉到了。根据上下文,应用被动态。语态错误。

69. system → systematic   ...the first systematic attempt to document the effects of an earthquake 记录地震影响的首次系统尝试。词性错误。

70. to → of   keep a record of...作记录,为固定搭配。

71. are → is   the ability to...is very limited ……的能力十分有限。主谓语单复数不一致。

Part VI

72. was the president's hasty decision in investment issues that

73. on hearing (that) he had won the first prize in the speech contest

74. whether to confess or not

75. that today's vehicles are far/much more advanced than those produced 5 years ago

76. nothing (for us) to do but pray

Test 5

Part Ⅰ

Sample Writing

Is Long Holiday Necessary?

As competition in today's society becomes fiercer, some people regard long holiday as something unaffordable because work will be piled up during their absence. But still a lot of career pursuers go on enjoying their vacation time. They think that having a good rest during the holiday provides them with renewed energy and fresh outlook of their job.

Personally I agree with the latter view. Holiday is beneficial to our work in many ways and work should not prevent us from enjoying our life and spending quality time with friends and family. First, after months of working under pressure, one needs to relax his mind and body to get prepared for the next round of work. We human beings, like a clock, should periodically relax ourselves. Second, time away from work may give one a chance to look at his work with new ideas and fresh outlook when back to it again. Overwork may not only reduce work efficiency, but also hamper one's original thinking. Moreover, after a long period of work, one may feel bored with the daily routines and lose interest in the job. When one no longer appreciates his own work, how can he come up with good ideas and produce good results? With regard to its effects on our family relationship and friendship, holiday plays a big role in providing us sufficient time and good opportunity for family members and friends to share precious time together. If we go on letting work robbing us of the quality time spent with our beloved, if we let work completely take control of us, we will lose too many things essential in our life.

All in all, we should not fall victims to the rat race. In order to survive the competition, in order to live a complete life, we have to strike a balance between work and leisure.

Part Ⅱ

1. [C] 参见文章第一段第一、二句：low-income shoppers must consider... when selecting food products. Food-purchase decisions... often entail balances among ... to meet spending constraints.

2. [D] 参见"The Correlation between the Location and the Price"部分最后一句：…the poor face higher prices due to their greater representation in urban and rural areas, where food prices tend to be higher.

3. [C] 参见"The Main Economizing Practices"部分前三句。

4. [C] 参见"The Main Economizing Practices"部分最后一句话：Although quality differences... often contribute to prices differences, differences in nutritional quality also are evident...（食品营养含量的不同对价格的影响还是很明显的。）

5. [B] "More Spending on Promotional Items"部分主要强调了随意称重的商品和固定重量商品的促销手段对三个不同收入层的消费者的影响，参见本部分第一段第二句及第二段第一句。

6. [C] 参见"More Spending on Promotional Items"部分第二段倒数第二句。

7. [A] 参见"Choice of Package Size"部分第一、二句：虽然大包装商品比小包装的价格便宜，理论上可以帮助那些低收入家庭节约开支，但是从实际的一些大包装的商品销售情况看却比以往

少。正如本题所述，原文的 however 也突出了理论和现实的差异。

8. private-label 参见"More Spending on Promotional Items"小节第二段第四句：Low-income households spent 11.5% of their RTE cereal expenditures on private-label cereals, while the higher-income households spent lower shares...

9. budget and storage 题干提示有三点解释，因此还需要填写另外两点，要用两个名词概括原文的两句话，即倒数第二段第二句："they cannot afford to store staple products, and they perceive that the cost of storing large packages in higher than the savings from the volume discount."

10. savings 参见本文最后一句："This implies that these house holds are choosing less expensive fruits and vegetables, which saves a lot for them."

Part Ⅲ

11. D　12. B　13. C　14. C　15. B　16. B　17. D　18. A　19. C
20. B　21. A　22. D　23. C　24. A　25. C　26. B　27. B　28. A
29. A　30. A　31. C　32. A　33. A　34. C　35. B
36. purchase　37. differentiate　38. attractive　39. significance
40. competitive　41. phenomenon　42. deceptive　43. decline

44. The manufacturer has increased the unit price of his product by changing his package size to lower the quantity actually delivered

45. The producers of packaged products argue strongly against changing sizes of packages to contain even weights and volumes

46. Packaging has become a very expensive luxury and one-third of American garbage is packaging materials

Part Ⅳ

47. for nicotine 本文一开始就说人们一旦停止吸烟，极可能感到紧张、焦躁不安、易激动、甚至吃得更多。人们可能认为这是纯粹的心理现象，然而这也是生理反应。这些现象或反应均是由于戒烟者的身体渴望尼古丁的缘故。

48. burden 第一段大意为戒烟使人产生一些令人难受的症状，第二段讲到难以忍受的戒烟症状往往使人又重新抽起烟来，而戒烟剂只能起到减轻这些症状的作用，并不能使吸烟者彻底戒烟。可见戒烟对戒烟者确实是个负担，同时第三段第一句 burdensome 也是一个很好的提示。

49. To help lessen the symptoms of withdrawing nicotine. 第二段第一句指出：Habitrol 是一种尼古丁药膏，有助于减轻人们戒烟的反应。

50. in the first 3 months 参见文中第二段第三句：经临床证明，在戒烟最关键的前三个月期间，Habitrol 能增大戒烟的可能性。

51. give up smoking before using it 参见最后一段第一句话：在使用 Habitrol 之前必须完全戒烟。

52. [B] 细节性理解题。由第一段第四句可知，法国人对理想的追求是要对整个人类文化有全面的了解，他们不赞成只注重某个方面的培养。故选 B。

53. [D] 细节性推断题。由第一段倒数第二句可知，比较英法两国不同的教育制度时，作者指出两种教育制度在培养目标、组织方式以及教学目标等方面均有所不同，言外之意是差异不仅仅在教学方法上。故选 D。

54. [C] 细节性推断题。根据第二段中的"This precocity is encouraged by his upbringing among adults"（法国儿童的早熟是家里大人的教育方式促成的）以及"They have little patience with childish ideas"（父母不大容忍孩子的天真想法），故选 C。本文阐述了英法两国教育体制的

差别,法国人追求全面教育,教育孩子时注重理性,所以法国孩子早熟。而英国人喜欢处处替孩子着想,因而更易于同孩子沟通。

55. [A] 细节性推论题。文中第二段提到,以孩子们理解的语言同他们进行交谈,这样的谈话方式是英国方式,所以法国儿童喜欢读从英文翻译过来的书。这从另一个侧面说明法国父母不同于英国父母。他们不去适应孩子,不用孩子们理解的语言和孩子交流,他们不把孩子看成是未成年的儿童。因此文章关于书籍的谈论前后并不矛盾。故选 A。

56. [B] 细节题。从第二段可知,法国父母注重理性,他们通过理智教育孩子变得聪明,而不是靠情感去打动孩子的心灵。词组"identify with"意为"认同",故选 B(他们把智慧同理性等同起来)。

57. [D] 段落大意推断题。第二段第二句,作者指出行为主义的基本原则是"正激励"(positive reinforcement),这一原则在美国人的生活中无处不在。并且本段最后一句指出"虽然行为主义理论已经失去了它的统治地位,但是刺激与奖励已经成为美国人生活的一部分,很难想象没有这一点生活会是什么样的,故选 D。

58. [C] 细节性归纳题。参见文中第二段前三句中提供的信息可知,著名的行为主义心理学派(以斯金纳为代表)的核心是正激励(positive reinforcement),故选 C。而且第二句的 Although 也是一个很好的提示,后半句可能正是考点所在。

59. [D] 细节性推断题。根据第二段第二句有关行为主义对美国人生活方式的影响的描述。可知正确答案为 D(美国人对奖励非常痴迷)。而由第三段可知奖励在美国并不是非常有效的,反而有负面影响,所以可排除 B。

60. [A] 细节性理解题。文章第四段集中讨论了奖励(rewards)或正激励(positive reinforcement)对人们的动力和工作效率的影响。提出了与行为主义截然不同的看法,即奖励不但不利于提高人的工作效率和动机,反而扼杀人们工作的兴趣,降低工作效率,故选 A。

61. [C] 细节性归纳题。文章最后一段首句指出:在一种庆祝糟蹋成功的文化中是很难进行辩论的。而后深入讨论了奖励所造成的负面影响——工作不努力、轻易放弃目标,很快失去对工作的兴趣等。孩子的行为方式一例旨在说明这一点。故选 C。

Part Ⅴ

62. [C] So say many nutritionists, who object to the demonization of some foods as junk. 许多营养学家也这么说,他们反对将某些食物贬为垃圾食品。(句中 so 指代前文"There are... only bad diets")。argue for 辩解支持;stand for 代表;stick to 坚持(原则等)。

63. [A] A recent nationwide weigh-in of 11-year-olds reveals that... 最近一次全国范围内 11 岁儿童体重测量揭示……demonstrate 演示,证明;illustrate 举例说明;appreciate 欣赏,理解。

64. [C] ...larger children were less likely to step on the scales 较胖的儿童不太会走上磅秤量体重。possible, probable(很可能)一般用形式主语 it。potential 潜在的。

65. [B] So Ofcom...has decided that... 于是 Ofcom 得出结论,认为应该对一些食品进行妖魔化(宣传其害处)。decide that... = conclude that...; determine 决定。

66. [D] a ban on... 对……的禁令。固定介词搭配。

67. [D] appeal particularly to children 尤其吸引孩子;attract (sb) vt. 吸引;reply to (sb)回答;attribute...to...将……归因于……

68. [A] brand advertising...will be exempt 品牌广告将得以豁免(不受禁令)。exempt adj. 豁免的;immune adj. 有免疫力的;impair vt. 损坏。

69. [C] There are also worries about the specific foods targeted. 关于被选定的特定食品存在担忧。target vt. 以……为目标。

70. [B] ...foods are awarded points for good qualities 食物因其自身优点被授予积分点。

award sb sth 授予某人某物；reward sb with... 以……奖赏某人；allow sb to do 允许某人做某事；ascribe...to... 将……归因于……

71. [B] the calculations are based on a 100g-portion of the food 营养成分的计算是以每 100 克食品为单位计算的。be based on... 以……为基础；rely on 依赖；focus on 注意力集中于……

72. [D] consume vt. 消费，吃掉；resume vt. 恢复；presume vt. 假定；assume vt. 主观臆断认为，承担。

73. [B] while conj. 而（表前后对照关系）。根据上下文逻辑关系判定。

74. [A] Were breast milk for sale，it would be banned. 若人乳可以出售，也会（因脂肪、糖分过高）而被禁止。虚拟语气，相当于 if breast milk were for sale...

75. [B] for it is too high in fat and sugar 因脂肪、糖分过高，for 补充说明原因。

76. [C] have...enthusiasm for... 对……充满热情。

77. [C] get round the definitional difficulties by... 通过（……手段）绕过定义困难问题。

78. [B] The immediate impact...will anyway be limited，as...（因为这些新定的垃圾食品本来就没有做过大量广告），对英国食品业的直接冲击还是有限的。

79. [A] be at stake 处于危险之中，利害攸关。

80. [A] suffer vitamin and mineral deficiencies 患上维生素与矿物质缺乏症。deficiency（体内营养成分）不足；shortage n.（物质供应）不足，匮乏；poisoning n. 中毒；efficiency n. 效率。

81. [B] starve themselves 让自己挨饿。

Part Ⅶ

82. for an extended visit to Oxford

83. As might be expected

84. being a useful tool in serving the people

85. now all that is left is poverty

86. plans to get an M. A. degree within one year

Test 6

Part Ⅰ

Sample Writing

How to Treat Our Aging Population?

China has already stepped into an aging society according to international standards. Those beyond 65 made up more than 7 per cent of the national population. According to experts' prediction，this phenomenon is going to continue for decades. Now the society is faced up with the issue of tackling the old people's problems.

First，the society should foster a social environment that champions respect and care for the old. This is prerequisite in tackling the various problems the elderly face. Without love and respect for the old，any welfare measure could not be implemented fully and for the benefit of the old. Though in most area，the traditional idea of loving and respecting the old still prevails，there are some young people who consider old people as economic and mental burden and are eager to get rid of them. Therefore，changing this kind of attitude towards old people is uppermost in ensuring that our Grandma and Grandpa lead a happy life. Second, based on the fact that the tradition of home care for the elderly faces big challenge due to the shrinking family size, a combination of family care, community-based services and social welfare necessary to help our old population in helping and supporting their lives. In this way, old people can enjoy the help and love from both the society and their families, thus relieving the pressure on their younger children. Third, old people not only need help, they can also give a hand in raising their grandchildren. If we treat them as precious assets, they may not only live a fuller life, but also make further contributions to our social and economic developments.

At present, both the proportion of the old in the Chinese population and the number of retired people are increasing. How to respond to this phenomenon affects everybody now and in the future. We should combine community help with family care and offer help to them in every way.

Part Ⅱ

1. [A] 参见第一段...spent much of the early 20th century looking for ways to improve... making shelter more comfortable and efficient, and more economically available to a greater number of people(更舒适有效,使更多的人有能力支付).

2. [B] 参见第三段 ...Fuller had developed a prototype of family dwelling which could be produced rapidly, using the same equipment which had previously built war-time airplanes.

3. [D] 参见第四段倒数第二句:...the main obstruction was obtaining the financing for the tooling costs... No bank would finance the project...

4. [B] 参见第五段:...focused on the problem of how to build a shelter which is so lightweight that it can be delivered by air...follow nature's design as seen by the spider's web which can float in a hurricane because of its high strength-to-weight ratio. New shelter would have to be designed that assimilates these principles(吸纳这些原则)...这里 principles 指"high strength-to-weight ratio",既结实又轻便。

5. [D] 参见第六段倒数第二句:...directed his studies toward creating a new architectural design, the geodesic dome, based also upon his idea of "doing more with less"(以较小成本获取较大收益).

6. [C] 参见倒数第五段:More specifically, the dome is energy efficient for many reasons...

7. [C] 参见倒数第四段第一句:The net annual energy savings for a dome owner is 30% more than normal rectilinear homes...(圆顶房屋的主人每年能源开支节约额要比常规的直线房屋的主人多 30%。)

8. air circulation 参见本文第八段第一句:"The spherical(球形的)structure of a dome is...efficient interior atmospheres...because air and energy are allowed to circulate without obstruction.

9. the most efficient 参见本文第八段最后一句:Geodesic shelters have been built...and still they have proven to be the most efficient human shelter one can find.

10. the Grand Premio 参见本文最后一句:The 42-foot paper board Geodesic was installed...and came away with the highest award, the Grand Premio.

Part Ⅲ

11. B	12. C	13. D	14. A	15. B	16. A	17. D	18. C	19. D
20. B	21. C	22. B	23. C	24. A	25. A	26. D	27. A	28. C
29. B	30. C	31. D	32. B	33. D	34. C	35. B		

36. insignificant   37. dedicated   38. nurture   39. flourish
40. quality   41. extinct   42. desperately   43. guidance

44. Some couples feel that by giving their children one-on-one attention they are able to give them a better, more rounded education

45. Learning from Mom or Dad can secure the child with an atmosphere of faith and a moral environment thatfosters character and discipline

46. Still others are concerned about the physical safety of their sons and daughters in increasingly violent school settings

Part Ⅳ

47. journalistic interviewing 文章第一段后半部分提到,在新闻界,如同在其他领域一样,通过对专业实践进行系统的研究可以学到许多东西。这种研究可积累证据,人们可以从中形成广泛的具有概括性的原理。可见,本段中心思想应为:重视对新闻采访进行系统性的研究。

48. been neglected 参见本文第二段第一句:但对新闻采访本身的研究并未受到重视。第四句又指出:不幸的是,这些大量有关采访的论著几乎忽略了新闻采访。由此可见,作为一个特殊领域,新闻采访被人们忽视了。

49. interviewed in person/interviewed personally 参见本文第二段倒数第三句:然而,我们当中很少有人真正地亲自受过大众媒体的采访,尤其是电视采访。由此可见,西方人虽然对新闻采访很熟悉,但是大多数人都未被采访过。

50. The patient. 参见本文第二段后半部分:在临床采访中,采访者,即专业人士只想得到必要的信息以对寻求帮助的人进行诊断和治疗。由此可推断出在临床采访中被采访者应该是患者。

51. preface 参见本文最后一句:正如本书中所陈述的。由此可推断出这篇文章摘自一本书的前言。

52. [C] 细节性归纳题。本文第一段详细阐述了与暴力有关的因素。过去许多人认为暴力与缺乏自尊有关,但最近三位学者提出了相反的结论——暴力与过分自尊有着密切的联系。第二段第二句,作者又进一步引述相关的研究结果,指出暴力经常与那些具有不切实际的过分自尊的人有关,他们会因别人质疑他们的自我形象而去攻击他们。故选 C。

53. [C] 细节题。根据第二段第一句可知,C 项正确(传统观念认为,缺乏自尊的人会通过伤害别人的方式来获取自尊)。

54. [B] 主旨归纳题。本题问及最新研究的结果和启示。作者在第三、第四段中详细阐述了这些方面,并在第四段第二句中引述 Baumeister 的话指出自控比自尊对国家更有利。故选 B。

55. [A] 细节性推断题。本题问及目前学校教育中自尊心教育对学生的影响。文章最后一段明确指出,目前学校教育应将自尊心的培养作为终极目标(as an end in itself),而非随成功而至的"副产品"。教育者竭力培养学生自尊心的传统至今仍然根深蒂固,由此可排除 B、C 项。作者认为学校的这种做法只不过制造出一种虚假的平等(the disguised equality),由此可排除 D。故选 A。

56. [D] 细节题。本题要求考生在理解全文的基础上,准确地概括出作者的观点。与 A 项相关的陈述可在第三段段末找到;B 项的内容可在最后一段中找到;与 C 项相关的信息可在第四段中找到。文中未涉及 D 项的相关内容。故选 D。

57. [D] 细节性归纳题。文章第一段介绍了德国的人口老龄化问题。根据最后一句可知,到2030 年德国的劳动人口将减少四分之一(a full quarter),即 25%,所以正确答案为 D。而该段第一句指出:与现在年龄超过 65 岁的人口占老年人口的 1/5 相比,到 2030 年,在世界上第三大经济体的德国,年龄超过 65 岁的人口将占老年人口的一半。因此可知 B 项错误。

58. [B] 段落归纳题。文章第二段第一句话提出,德国的人口统计(即老龄化问题)绝非特例,言

外之意即目前人口老龄化问题已经成为世界性问题,后文的实例也证明了这一点。故选 B。

59. [B] 细节题。文章第三段谈到世界人口变化的新趋势:青年人数的减少(But the decline in the number of young people is something new)。故选 B。

60. [A] 细节性归纳题。本题问及人口构成模式的变化的政治意义,这正是文章第四段讨论的内容。作者认为,在发达国家,能否赢得老年选民的支持对于各派政党将是至关重要的问题。故选 A。同时最后一句指出,这两个问题使每个发达国家的政坛局势都发生了巨大变化。

61. [D] 细节性归纳题。文章最后一段谈及有关退休年龄的各种问题。作者预测,到 2030 年,发达国家或许已经取消了对退休年龄的规定,甚至将退休年龄推迟到 75 岁左右,以便减轻工薪族必须缴付的津贴负担。故选 D。

Part Ⅴ

62. [B] Until the 1990s... 到 20 世纪 90 年代为止(根据下文可知 20 世纪 90 年代后德国商店营业时间大大延长了)。

63. [C] Today you can shop into the wee hours... 如今你可以购物直到深夜。

64. [C] shop hours are... fully liberalized 购物时间完全灵活自由化了。

65. [C] the myth that Germany is anti-consumer 关于德国反顾客的缪传。myth 传说,无根据的观念或说法;legend 民间传说故事;fantasy 幻想;mystery 谜。

66. [C] reveals a change in attitude to time 揭示了时间观念的变化。expose 暴露,揭露;incur 招致(灾祸);entail 导致。

67. [D] Wasting it (time) is forbidden; punctuality is required. 禁止浪费时间;要求准时。punctuality n. 准时;prompt adj. 迅速的,及时的;proficiency n. 水平,熟练;perseverance n. 坚持不懈。

68. [A] The country's austere Protestantism helps to explain this, but so may a culture of industrial might. 德国新教的冷峻造就了这种高度的时间观念,同样,工业强国的文化加强了德国人的时间观。(this 指 punctuality;"but so may..."是部分倒装结构,so 替代前面的"help to explain this")。hence 因此;nevertheless 然而。

69. [B] The efficient division of labor requires a tight schedule. 高效的劳动分工要求紧凑的时间安排。

70. [B] the family model of a lone male breadwinner 男子汉一人养家糊口的典范。model n. 典范,榜样;mode n. (操作/行为)方式,模式;module n. 模块;mould n. (铸造)模子。

71. [C] ...child care assistance was superfluous 无须他人帮助照料孩子。superfluous 多余的;superficial 表面的;significant 具有重要意义的;indispensable 必不可少的。

72. [D] ...with the economy increasingly driven by services 随着经济越来越受到服务业的驱动。

73. [B] set one's own working hours 制订自己的工作时间安排。

74. [B] As many as two-thirds of all women 大约三分之二的妇女。

75. [C] instead of 替代;regardless of 不顾;in spite of 尽管;as of 自……起。

76. [D] even so 即便如此;even if/ though...(十从句)即使;even as...(十从句)恰当……时候。

77. [B] ...the continuing lack of child-care facilities, which makes it harder for mothers to combine jobs and children. 儿童看护设施的持续缺乏使母亲更难一边工作一边照料孩子。

78. [A] in part 部分而言,一定程度上;in all 总共;in short 简而言之;in that 因为。

79. [A] cultural barriers 文化障碍(下文举例提到德国人对雇家佣持有偏见)。

80. [D] a bias against... 对……的偏见。

81. [A] few other countries have so many home-improvement stores. 德国人花费大量时间自己干家务，不计报酬，包揽下装修、园艺、洗刷等各类杂活，故没有几个国家拥有像德国那样多的出售住房修缮工具的商店。

Part Ⅵ

82. constantly interrupted by applause
83. asked for directions, I wouldn't have gotten lost
84. so as to make it tender enough to eat
85. not being able to communicate with their parents
86. is sensitive to likely political changes

Test 7

Part Ⅰ

Sample Writing

College Reading Room Phenomenon

As is shown in the graph of the college reading room attendance, there are roughly two cycles with great rise and fall. When the new term starts in September, there are about 275 students who go to the reading room. The number increases rapidly with each passing month till November and still increases at a much lower rate, reaching the peak just before the exams in early December. During the winter vacation, most students go home, so the number of students using the reading room drops to almost 175. The second cycle in the spring semester is similar to the first. After three months the number goes up greatly. It is only after April, with the approaching final exams in mind that most students start seriously using the facilities of the reading room. During the summer vacation, students are rarely seen in it.

The attendance figures reflect the students' life at college. The graph indicates that exams are the driving force for many students. In the first two months of each semester, quite a few students relax since exams are still far away. They only study hard in reading room a few weeks before the exams because there they can easily get hold of all the references they need for their term papers or the exams. In fact, students should not study for the sake of exams because it is just one effective way of testing the knowledge they have absorbed. Therefore, if they studied not for the exams but for acquiring knowledge, their lives would be much easier.

As I see it, the key to real success in study lies in one's willingness to acquire knowledge and get good command of modern science and technology. So if one wants to be a talented student, he should attend every lecture and eagerly absorb new knowledge in the reading room. Thus the graph above would have a smoother or steadier curve.

Part Ⅱ

1. [D] 参见第二段第一句：Mr. Painting's story helps to explain Britain's devotion to what it calls "public-service broadcasting", and why the state has spent increasing sums of money on the BBC.

2. [A] 第二段提到，在英国，就 BBC 是否仍应获得公众资助（public financing / subsidies）产生争议，政府决定在 2006 决定今后 10 年里继续通过电视用户义务交纳执照费的形式赞助 BBC

(the government renewed its financing for the next ten years through a compulsory "TV license" on all households with TV sets)。

3〔C〕参见第三段最倒数第二句：... only Germany's government spends more than Britain's on broadcasting as a share of GDP.

4.〔B〕参见第四段最后一句：... changes in technology and media habits are splitting its audience（观众/听众分流）...

5.〔C〕根据"Serving What Public?"部分第一段最后一句可知，BBC 在拥有卫星或有线电视的家庭，丧失的收视率最严重，而根据前文"hundreds of new channels were launched on satellite and cable platforms，creating a new 'multi-channel' world"与"multi-channel services（which include BBC3 and BBC4，both digital channels）win 30%"可知，"multi-channel services including BBC3 and BBC4"主要建立于卫星与有线技术平台。故可推知，包括数字频道 BBC3 与 BBC4 在内的"multi-channel services"对 BBC 构成最大收视率竞争威胁。

6.〔B〕参见"Serving What Public?"部分最后一段：... because it takes too few risks... backward-looking and all about heritage（文化遗产）... all exhumed from the distant past（从遥远的过去发掘出）.

7.〔D〕根据"The BBC's Efforts"部分第二段可知"Hammocking"是将有深刻思想、有价值的节目穿插在大众流行剧之间（scheduling worthy material between smash hits），BBC 这样安排的目的是让观众有机会观看高质量的节目（in an effort to get people to watch improving stuff）。

8. talk show 参见"The BBC's Efforts"部分第三段第二句：Its approach to ethnic minorities used to be a boring talk-show about discrimination late at night...

9. getting especially pressing 参见"The People's Telly"部分第一段第二句：The rapid shift to digital TV makes the debate over whether the BBC should be publicly funded especially pressing.

10. subscription 参见"The People's Telly"部分第一段第二句：The likeliest change is that the television service would become partly or wholly subscription-financed（其资助部分或全部来源于观众的订购费）。

Part Ⅲ

11. D   12. B   13. C   14. A   15. A   16. B   17. C   18. D   19. D
20. B   21. C   22. A   23. B   24. D   25. C   26. A   27. C   28. B
29. D   30. D   31. C   32. B   33. A   34. A   35. D
36. contemporary   37. inventions   38. leisure   39. intrigued
40. themes   41. mobility   42. commuters   43. recreation
44. Most Impressionists worked directly and spontaneously from nature, submitting to the first impression of what they saw
45. they relied on domestic scenes of women holding babies, playing with their children, dressing in their bedrooms, or tending their gardens
46. We see men, women, and children floating in a rowboat, strolling under the trees, or just watching the river flow.

Part Ⅳ

47. a steady/fixed income and a good work record 本文第一段指出：只有具有稳定收入和良好工作履历的人才能申办信用卡。

48. One month. 参见文章第二段第二句：你买东西的钱可以晚一个月付清，而且在这期间不必支付额外的费用。

49. <u>installments</u> 参见文章第二段第三、四句：你也可以选择把支付的款项分几个月付清，每月只付总款的一部分（即 installments），若以这种方式还款，信用卡公司或者发行信用卡的银行要收取一定的服务费。

50. <u>the stores and customers</u> 参见文章第三段第六句：信用卡之所以是一桩大买卖，主要在于信用卡公司从商店收的费用以及从分期付款的客户收取的费用中赚钱，即从商店和顾客双方赚钱。

51. <u>using stolen and lost credit cards</u> 文章最后一句指出：罪犯使用偷来的、丢失的或伪造的信用卡，是信用卡公司非常头疼的问题。

52. [B] 全文主旨题。总结各段的主题句即可得出本文主题：随着科技的发展，人类可以实现"永生"。

53. [A] 细节题。文中第二段第三、四句给出了 Soul Catcher 的定义：...It may be possible to capture your nervous system's electrical activities, which would also preserve your thoughts and emotions. 由 which 引导的非限制性定语从句可知，它（Soul Catcher）是用来获取和保存人类思想的。

54. [D] 推断题。文中第二段第一句指出：Researchers are confident that technology will soon be able to track every waking moment of your life. 科研工作者有信心随着科技发展实现人类的"永生"。

55. [A] 细节题。文中第四段第二句指出：Even in 2030, we may still be struggling to understand the brain's internal workings, so reading your thoughts and interpreting your emotions might not be possible. 到 2030 年，障碍是依然存在的，所以 A 项是正确的。B 项在文中没有提及，所以排除 B。C 项不是"肉体上"的"永生"，而是一种保存"人类思想"的方式。D 项与最后一段第一句不符。

56. [B] 词义理解题。文中出现 rejuvenate 的地方是在"to rejuvenate minds as everlasting entities"中。因为 everlasting 是"永恒的"意思，所以，要使思想成为永恒，可推断 rejuvenate 是"使活跃，激活"的意思。

57. [D] 细节性综合题。纵观全文后，可总结出文章前三段分别指出了电视会议的优势，即加强交流、提高效率、增强理解。此题看似一个细节题，实际上却是一个综合题。

58. [B] 词义判断题。"nonverbal cues"中的 nonverbal 是"非语言的"，也就是不能直接用言语表达的，即一种暗示。另外，从第二次出现该词的地方"facial expression and nonverbal cues"也可以猜出该词的意思。

59. [C] 细节题。这一点从文中的"Savage suggests that money... will eventually be recouped via the saving from not sending employees to meetings"得到答案。他认为投资在电视会议设备上的钱最终会从不用派人参加会议而节省下来的差旅费中得到补偿，因此从这点上看，电视会议是值得的。而 B 项中电视会议应该是提高了员工的<u>工作</u>效率，而且节省了员工的能量。故选 C。

60. [A] 推理判断题。排除法。本文最后一段第二句"Such is not the case..."已指出该公司并没有投入大量的资金，所以 B 项是错的。文章最后一句的 This 指代的是前一句的"multipoint control unit"，而非"desktop units"，所以 C 项也是错误的。至于备选答案 D 项，由于文章并没有提及软件的来源，所以属于臆断。从本段第三句话不难看出选项 A 是正确的。

61. [C] 观点态度题。纵观全文，可以看出作者对电视会议的态度是积极肯定的。

Part Ⅴ

62. [B] The <u>reality</u> is not so simple（与纪录片中的描述相比，）现实没有那么简单。

63. [A] other <u>manufacturers</u> follow the Giant carmaker's lead 其他汽车制造商也仿效汽车制造业巨头 GM 的做法（取消电力汽车）。

64. ［B］　recharged its enthusiasm for... 重燃对……的热情。recharge *vt.* 给……再充电；review *v.* 复习；retrieve *v.* 收回，重获(失物)。

65. ［B］　unveil a prototype 推出(新型汽车)原型。unveil *vt.* 揭开……面纱，首次展示；uncover *vt.* 揭露；expose *vt.* 使暴露。

66. ［A］　exiting hybrids, such as Toyota's Pruis 现有的混合动力汽车，比如丰田的 Pruis。as to (sth)至于；as for (sb)至于；if any 如果有的话(插入语)。

67. ［C］　Today's hybrids capture energy normally lost during braking... 今天的混合动力汽车可以捕捉利用通常刹车中损失的能源。

68. ［D］　provide extra bursts of acceleration when needed 在需要得时候可迅速提速。acceleration *n.* 加速；friction *n.* 摩擦。

69. ［D］　run on battery power alone 仅靠电池动力行驶

70. ［D］　plugging it into the mains 将其插入总电源。erect *vt.* 使树立；thrust *vt.* 猛推；pull *v.* 拉，拔；plug *v.* 插入(电源)。

71. ［C］　in an all-electric mode 在全电能动力模式下。mode *n.* (机器)操作模式。

72. ［A］　more than enough 绰绰有余；other than 非，除了；rather than 而不是；less than 少于。

73. ［B］　use the petrol engine on longer trips only 只有在行驶较长距离时才使用汽油引擎；solar *adj.* 太阳能的。

74. ［C］　The drawback is that... 缺点是充电式混合动力车需要较大、较昂贵的电池板。defect *n.* 缺陷。

75. ［A］　modify *vt.* 改良；manifest *vt.* 证明；correct *vt.* 改正；remedy *vt.* 补救，纠正。

76. ［B］　put...into mass production 投入批量生产。

77. ［A］　...the pace is picking up in the race... 在……比赛中加快步伐。

78. ［D］　Others are more cautious. 其他厂商则更为谨慎。(下文提到 Nissan、Toyota 老总对 plug-in hybrid cars 的怀疑态度。)

79. ［A］　is known for his skepticism... 以其怀疑态度而闻名。

80. ［C］　be ready for the mass market (混合动力技术)是否作做好了大量投入市场的准备。

81. ［C］　be skeptical about... 对……持怀疑态度。committed *adj.* 敬业的；faithful *adj.* 忠实的。

Part Ⅵ

82. should have the discussion right after the lecture
83. charged/was charging more than the regular fee
84. will your money be refunded
85. what people would think about his behavior
86. rather than the process that led to these findings

Test 8

Part Ⅰ
Sample Writing

Should Class Attendance Be Optional?

Those who have been to college lectures will find the following situation a common sight: The classroom is half empty; those attending classes are not always listening to the teacher;

some are texting their friends while others have fallen asleep. Such situation poses a question to us: Should class attendance be compulsory or optional? To answer the question, we should consider the nature and quality of courses and also the needs of the students.

First of all, we should consider what courses are put in the school curriculum. If they are well designed and suit the levels and needs of the students, they should be made compulsory courses. Of course, the teachers' professional and academic standards are also important in implementing course goals and ensuring desired outcome. Unnecessary courses and poor quality teaching can only lead to wasting time if students are forced to attend such courses. Secondly, those students at the top of the class and most competitive in their learning and also capable of studying independantly do not have to attend all the courses offered by the school curriculum. They should be encouraged to learn more under the tutor's individual guidance, instead of studying what they already know. In many world famous universities like Harvard and Cambridge, students spend much less time attending lectures. They gain their knowledge and skills by reading and doing research work.

In conclusion, colleges should not force students to attend all courses without carefully considering the two factors discussed above. As a matter of fact, to bring up students who can meet the demands of our new era, our education needs reforming and traditional views on teaching and learning should be challenged. Only in this way can we hope to motivate more talented students to learn well and aim high in school and in their future jobs.

Part Ⅱ

1. [D] 参见第一段最后一句：... as long as people continue to lead overweight, sedentary and stressful lives, the number of sufferers is unlikely to go anywhere other than up. 只要人们继续过着身体超重、久坐不动、充满压力的生活，背痛患者的人数将有增无减。

2. [C] 参见"The Great Pain Mystery"部分第一段第四句：What's most mysterious about back problems is the frequent disconnection between anatomical defects and pain.

3. [B] 参见"The Great Pain Mystery"部分第三段：通过许多男人们婚前精神紧张加剧坐骨神经痛一例说明，背痛程度与心理及身体状况均有关（has as much to do with the mind as with the body），背痛的最佳预示不是脊柱缺陷程度而是病人的心理焦虑。

4. [A] 参见"Spine Surgery Breakthrough"部分第二段倒数三、四句"It is believed that, such discs, like knee replacements, will give patients more mobility than traditional fusion surgery. And they will get out of bed a lot sooner too.

5. [A] 参见"Spine Surgery Breakthrough"部分第一段第一句：... many want a quick fix and that means surgery.

6. [B] 参见"Alternative Treatments"部分第四段最后两句。

7. [C] 参见"An Integrative Approach"部分第二段最后一句：... see if there is a more efficient, multi-disciplinary（多学科）way to attack the problem, and to make it cost-effective too. "multi-disciplinary way"意味着"complementary（互补的）, integrative（综合的）approach"。

8. a growing interest in/popularity of alternative/nonsurgical treatments 参见"An Integrative Approach"部分第三段第一句与最后一句。

9. bottled-up emotions/repressed anxieties 参见"Can Rage Ruin Your Back?"部分第一段第一句：... believes almost all back pain is rooted in bottled-up feelings.

10. optimistic 参见最后一段：... the good news... embracing bold new ways to think about...

Part Ⅲ

11. A	12. D	13. A	14. C	15. B	16. D	17. C	18. B	19. A

20. C   21. B   22. D   23. D   24. A   25. C   26. B   27. C   28. A

29. B   30. D   31. C   32. B   33. A   34. D   35. B

36. principle   37. excluded   38. ignorance   39. industrialized

40. guarantees   41. present   42. survive   43. expenditure

44. I would suggest that it should be limited to a definite period of time so as to avoid the encouraging of an abnormal attitude which refuses any kind of social obligation

45. The main objection to such a scheme would be that if each person were entitled to receive minimum support, people would not work

46. However, the suspicions against this system are not groundless for those who want to use ownership of capital to force others to accept the work conditions they offer

Part Ⅳ

47. staying too close 参见本文第二段:北美人认为南美人说话时与对方挨得很近,很令人尴尬。他们经常要退后几步说话。因此站得太近令美国人感到不安(feel ill at ease)。

48. dignity and respect/esteem 参见文中第二段倒数第二句:亚洲人之间谈话时,较大的间距微妙地造成一种高贵、尊敬的氛围。因此对亚洲人而言,令人感觉舒服的间距对表示尊敬起了一定的作用。

49. distance himself/keep his bodies apart 参见文中第三段末句:甚至在一个拥挤的电梯里,美国人也设法使他们的身体之间保持一定的距离。而在巴黎,当发生这种事情时,他们顺其自然(随它去:they take it as it comes)。因此,不必刻意保持一定的距离。

50. dig people in the ribs/nudge people in the ribs. 参见本文最后一段,作者分别告诉我们美国人表示同情、热情和使人放心的手势。讲笑话时的手势是用肘碰别人的肋骨。

51. Distance and bodily contact. 全文是围绕具有不同文化背景的人谈话之间的距离展开论述的。讲美国人的手势和接触时,是从身体接触的角度谈的。所以全文的主题是"距离和身体接触"。

52. 〔D〕细节性理解题。文章第一段指出:人成为了社会大机器中一个小小的、润滑良好的齿轮(well-oiled cog),高工资、通风良好的厂房等因素便是这润滑油。尽管如此,事实上人是无能为力的(powerless)。无论蓝领工人还是白领阶层皆是毫无自主权的傀儡(puppets)。这就说明了人的工作生活条件虽然不错(functioning smoothly),但他们在社会中是无足轻重的。

53. 〔C〕细节性归纳题。参见文章第二段的最后一句话。真正的原因是作为"情感与理智上独立的,富有创造性的"个人被忽视。选项 A、B 只是部分原因,不是真正的原因;D 的意思与文章内容相悖,故选 C。

54. 〔D〕段落主旨推断题。从文中第二、三段可知:选项 A"社会底层者"B"社会上层者"C"竞争中的胜利者"都摆脱不了充满各种竞争的生存环境,因而都生活在各式各样的 anxiety 与 stress 之中,所以都无幸福可言。只有选项 D(远离这个充满竞争的社会的人可推断为幸福之人)切题。

55. 〔A〕推断题。依据是文章倒数第二句,改革现实社会和解决社会问题,要重视人和充分发挥人的潜能,故 A 项正确。B 项只是维持社会正常运转的手段之一,而不是解决社会问题的建议;C 项是作者在最后一段中所不同意的观点;D 项不合原文意思。

56. 〔B〕作者态度题。从文章最后一段中的句子"I suggest transforming our social system..."可以看出作者的态度是"不满的"。

57. 〔B〕段落主旨题。文章第一段着重描述了大众对核电技术的种种忧虑和看法。然而这一段理解的重点应该在转折连词 however 之后。群众所要求的并非禁止或关闭所有核电站,而

强调"高度警惕""定期检查评估",对于运行安全的核反应堆可以续发执照,以便于充分利用现有的核电资源,因此 A、C、D 三项都与本段内容不符,故选 B。

58. [A] 细节性理解题。文章第二段列举了布什政府支持建设更多核电站的三个主要原因,这三个原因有主次之分。文中在提到第三个原因的时候,用了"most crucially"(最关键的是)这样的字句,表明现任政府支持核电发展的最主要的原因是核电站的建设和运营已不再完全依赖政府的财政援助(wholly dependent on bail-out),故选 A。

59. [D] 细节性归纳题。本题要求考生理解作者的意图和观点。文章第三段探讨了核电的发展是否有助于实现能源安全的问题,在这里作者提出异议。由此可以判断正确答案为 D。

60. [C] 细节性归纳题。文章最后一段中作者提出了几点有助于环保的建议,并且在文章的最后作者再次重申全球气候变暖不足以成为大规模发展核电的理由。

61. [C] 全文主旨推断题。要求考生认真理解细节,并区别作者明确陈述的观点和间接含蓄的观点。在文章中作者都直截了当地阐述了选项 A、B、D 中涉及的内容。但在第三段中作者只是含蓄地批评了布什政府的环境政策。(Global warming is indeed a risk that should be taken more seriously than the Bush administration has so far done.)故选 C。

Part V

62. convenience → inconvenience minimum of inconvenience and distress 最少的不便和烦恼,minimum 修饰的应该是不便,另外由 distress 推知与其并列的意思应为 inconvenience。逻辑语义相悖。

63. its → their their 指代后文的复数名词 unions。代词指代错误。

64. employment → unemployment the promotion of supplementary unemployment benefit plans 对失业补助津贴计划的提倡。逻辑语义相悖。

65. with → in employer involved in such a plan 涉及这个计划的雇主。动词词组固定搭配错误。

66. would → will will have a strong drive for planning new installments 将会有更强的动力来安排……结合上下文可知此处表示将来而不是虚拟。时态错误。

67. less → least to cause the least possible problems 尽可能少地产生问题。形容词比较级与最高级混淆。

68. required → requiring requiring that permanently dismissed workers... 要求被永久性解雇的工人可根据其服务期的长短领一笔钱。因此 require 表示主动而非被动。

69. are → be require 引导从句,从句中应用虚拟语气,即"(should)+动词原形"。虚拟语气用法错误。

70. that → which which 在此引导非限制性定语从句。定语从句关系代词错误。

71. hour → hours reduction in working hours 减少工作时间。名词单复数错误。

Part VI

72. swallowed some bread and milk and went to work

73. only to find that it was empty

74. If it hadn't been for your help

75. had I left home than I realized my mistake

76. promoting the new products doesn't work at all

附录二 真卷题库

2006年12月大学英语六级(新题型)考试试题

Part Ⅰ **Writing** (30 minutes)

Directions: *For this part，you are allowed 30 minutes to write a short essay commenting on the importance of reading classics．You should write at least 150 words following the outline given below in Chinese．*

The Importance of Reading Classics

1. 阅读经典著作对人的成长至关重要
2. 现在人们越来越少阅读经典著作，原因是……
3. 作为大学生，你应该怎么做

Part Ⅱ **Reading Comprehension** (Skimming and Scanning) (15 minutes)

Directions: *In this part，you will have 15 minutes to go over the passage quickly and answer the questions on **Answer Sheet 1**．*

For questions 1 - 4，mark

    Y (*for YES*)   *if the statement agrees with the information given in the passage*；

    N (*for NO*)   *if the statement contradicts the information given in the passage*；

    NG (*for NOT GIVEN*) *if the information is not given in the passage*．

For questions 5 - 10，complete the sentences with the information given in the passage．

Space Tourism

Make your reservations now. The space tourism industry is officially open for business, and tickets are going for a mere $20 million for a one-week stay in space. Despite reluctance from National Air and Space Administration (NASA), Russia made American businessman Dennis Tito the world's first space tourist. Tito flew into space aboard a Russian Soyuz rocket that arrived at the International Space Station (ISS) on April 30, 2001. The second space tourist, South African businessman Mark Shuttleworth, took off aboard the Russian Soyuz on April 25, 2002, also bound for the ISS.

Lance Bass of N Sync was supposed to be the third to make the $20 million trip, but he did not join the three-man crew as they blasted off on October 30, 2002, due to lack of payment. Probably the most incredible aspect of this proposed space tour was that NASA approved of it.

These trips are the beginning of what could be a profitable 21st century industry. There are already several space tourism companies planning to build suborbital vehicles and orbital cities within the next two decades. These companies have invested millions, believing that the space tourism industry is on the verge of taking off.

In 1997, NASA published a report concluding that selling trips into space to private citizens could be worth billions of dollars. A Japanese report supports these findings, and projects that space tourism could be a $10 billion per year industry within the next two decades. The only

obstacles to opening up space to tourists are the space agencies, who are concerned with safety and the development of a reliable, reusable launch vehicle.

Space Accommodations

Russia's Mir space station was supposed to be the first destination for space tourists. But in March 2001, the Russian Aerospace Agency brought Mir down into the Pacific Ocean. As it turned out, bringing down Mir only temporarily delayed the first tourist trip into space.

The Mir crash did cancel plans for a new reality-based game show from NBC, which was going to be called Destination Mir. The *Survivor*-like TV show was scheduled to air in fall 2001. Participants on the show were to go through training at Russia's cosmonaut（宇航员）training center, Star City. Each week, one of the participants would be eliminated from the show, with the winner receiving a trip to the Mir space station. The Mir crash has ruled out NBC's space plans for now. NASA is against beginning space tourism until the International Space Station is completed in 2006.

Russia is not alone in its interest in space tourism. There are several projects underway to commercialize space travel. Here are a few of the groups that might take tourists to space：

Space Island Group is going to build a ring-shaped, rotating "commercial space infrastructure（基础结构）" that will resemble the Discovery spacecraft in the movie "2001：A Space Odyssey." Space Island says it will build its space city out of empty NASA space-shuttle fuel tanks（to start, it should take around 12 or so）, and place it about 400 miles above Earth. The space city will rotate once per minute to create a gravitational pull one third as strong as Earth's.

According to their vision statement, Space Adventures plans to "fly tens of thousands of people in space over the next 10 – 15 years and beyond, around the moon, and back, from spaceports both on Earth and in space, to and from private space stations, and abroad dozens of different vehicles..."

Even Hilton Hotels has shown interest in the space tourism industry and the possibility of building or co-funding a space hotel. However, the company did say that it believes such a space hotel is 15 to 20 years away.

Initially, space tourism will offer simple accommodations at best. For instance, if the International Space Station is used as a tourist attraction, guests won't find the luxurious surroundings of a hotel room on Earth. It has been designed for conducting research, not entertainment. However, the first generation of space hotels should offer tourists a much more comfortable experience.

In regard to a concept for a space hotel initially planned by Space Island, such a hotel could offer guests every convenience they might find at a hotel on Earth, and some they might not. The small gravitational pull created by rotating space city would allow space-tourists and residents to walk around and function normally within the structure. Everything from running water to a recycling plant to medical facilities would be possible. Additionally, space tourists would even be able to take space walks.

Many of these companies believe that they have to offer an extremely enjoyable experience in order for passengers to pay thousands, if not millions, of dollars to ride into space. So will space create another separation between the haves and have-nots?

The Most Expensive Vacation

Will space be an exotic retreat reserved for only the wealthy? Or will middle-class folks have a chance to take their families to space? Make no mistake about it, going to space will be the most expensive vacation you ever take. Prices right now are in the tens of millions of dollars. Currently, the only vehicles that can take you into space are the space shuttle and the Russian Soyuz, both of which are terribly inefficient. Each spacecraft requires millions of pounds of fuel to take off into space, which makes them expensive to launch. One pound of payload（有效载重）costs about $10,000 to put into Earth's orbit.

NASA and Lockhead Martin are currently developing a single-stage-to-orbit launch space plane, called the VentureStar, that could be launched for about a tenth of what the space shuttle costs to launch. If the VentureStar takes off, the number of people who could afford to take a trip into space would move into the millions.

In 1998, a joint project from NASA and the Space Transportation Association stated that improvements in technology could push fares to space as low as $55,000, and possibly down to $20,000 or $10,000 a decade later. The report concluded that at a ticket price of $50,000, there could be 500,000 passengers flying into space each year. While still leaving out many people, these prices would open up space to a tremendous amount of traffic.

Since the beginning of the space race, the general public has said, "Isn't that great — when do I get to go?" Well, our chance might be closer than ever. Within the next 20 years, space planes could be taking off for the moon at the same frequency as airplanes flying between New York and Los Angeles.

1. Lance Bass wasn't able to go on a tour of space because of health problems.
2. Several tourism companies believe space travel is going to be a new profitable industry.
3. The space agencies are reluctant to open up space to tourists.
4. Two Australian billionaires have been placed on the waiting list for entering space as private passengers.
5. The prize for the winner in the fall 2001 NBC TV game show would have been _____.
6. Hilton Hotels believes it won't be long before it is possible to build a _____.
7. In order for space tourists to walk around and function normally, it is necessary for the space city to create a _____.
8. What makes going to space the most expensive vacation is the enormous cost involved in ____ _____.
9. Each year 500,000 space tourists could be flying into space if ticket prices could be lowered to _____.
10. Within the next two decades, _____ could be as common as intercity air travel.

Part Ⅲ Listening Comprehension（35 minutes）

Section A

Directions: *In this section, you will hear 8 short conversations and 2 long conversations. At the end of each conversation, one or more questions will be asked about what was said. Both the conversation and questions will be spoken only once. After each question there will be a pause. During the pause you must read the four choices marked A), B), C) and D), and decide which is the best answer. Then mark the corresponding letter on* **Answer Sheet 2** *with a single line through the center.*

11. A) Dr. Smith's waiting room isn't tidy.

B) Dr. Smith enjoys reading magazines.

C) Dr. Smith has left a good impression on her.

D) Dr. Smith may not be a good choice.

12. A) The man will rent the apartment when it is available.

B) The man made a bargain with the landlady over the rent.

C) The man insists on having a look at the apartment first.

D) The man is not fully satisfied with the apartment.

13. A) Packing up to go abroad.

B) Brushing up on her English.

C) Drawing up a plan for her English course.

D) Applying for a visa to the United States.

14. A) He is anxious to find a cure for his high blood pressure.

B) He doesn't think high blood pressure is a problem for him.

C) He was not aware of his illness until diagnosed with it.

D) He did not take the symptoms of his illness seriously.

15. A) To investigate the causes of AIDS.

B) To raise money for AIDS patients.

C) To rally support for AIDS victims in Africa.

D) To draw attention to the spread of AIDS in Asia.

16. A) It has a very long history.

B) It is a private institution.

C) It was founded by Thomas Jefferson.

D) It stresses the comprehensive study of nature.

17. A) They can't fit into the machine.

B) They have not been delivered yet.

C) They were sent to the wrong address.

D) They were found to be of the wrong type.

18. A) The food served in the cafeteria usually lacks variety.

B) The cafeteria sometimes provides rare food for the students.

C) The students find the service in the cafeteria satisfactory.

D) The cafeteria tries hard to cater to the students needs.

Questions 19 to 22 are based on the conversation you have just heard.

19. A) He picked up some apples in his yard.

B) He cut some branches off the apple tree.

C) He quarreled with his neighbor over the fence.

D) He cleaned up all the garbage in the woman's yard.

20. A) Trim the apple trees in her yard.

B) Pick up the apples that fell in her yard.

C) Take the garbage to the curb for her.

D) Remove the branches from her yard.

21. A) File a lawsuit against the man.

B) Ask the man for compensation.

C) Have the man's apple tree cut down.

D) Throw garbage into the man's yard.

22. A) He was ready to make a concession.

B) He was not prepared to go to court.

C) He was not intimidated.

D) He was a bit concerned.

Questions 23 to 25 are based on the conversation you have just heard.

23. A) Bad weather.

    B) Human error.

    C) Breakdown of the engines.

    D) Failure of the communications system.

24. A) Two thousand feet.

    B) Twelve thousand feet.

    C) Twenty thousand feet.

    D) Twenty-two thousand feet.

25. A) Accurate communication is of utmost importance.

    B) Pilots should be able to speak several foreign languages.

    C) Air controllers should keep a close watch on the weather.

    D) Cooperation between pilots and air controllers is essential.

Section B

Directions: *In this section, you will hear 3 short passages. At the end of each passage, you will hear some questions. Both the passage and the questions will be spoken only once. After you hear a question, you must choose the best answer from the four choices marked A), B), C) and D). Then mark the corresponding letter on* **Answer Sheet 2** *with a single line through the center.*

Passage One

Questions 26 to 29 are based on the passage you have just heard.

26. A) His father caught a serious disease.

    B) His mother passed away.

    C) His mother left him to marry a rich businessman.

    D) His father took to drinking.

27. A) He disliked being disciplined.

    B) He was expelled by the university.

    C) He couldn't pay his gambling debts.

    D) He enjoyed working for a magazine.

28. A) His poems are heavily influenced by French writers.

    B) His stories are mainly set in the State of Virginia.

    C) His work is difficult to read.

    D) His language is not refined.

29. A) He grieved to death over the loss of his wife.

    B) He committed suicide for unknown reasons.

    C) He was shot dead at the age of 40.

    D) He died of heavy drinking.

Passage Two

Questions 30 to 32 are based on the passage you have just heard.

30. A) Women.　　　　　　　　　C) Manual workers.
　　B) Prisoners.　　　　　　　　D) School age children.

31. A) He taught his students how to pronounce the letters first.
　　B) He matched the letters with the sounds familiar to the learners.
　　C) He showed the learners how to combine the letters into simple words.
　　D) He divided the letters into groups according to the way they are written.

32. A) It can help people to become literate within a short time.
　　B) It was originally designed for teaching the English language.
　　C) It enables the learners to master a language within three months.
　　D) It is effective in teaching any alphabetical language to Brazilians.

Passage Three

Questions 33 to 35 are based on the passage you have just heard.

33. A) The crop's blooming period is delayed.
　　B) The roots of crops are cut off.
　　C) The topsoil is seriously damaged.
　　D) The growth of weeds is accelerated.

34. A) It's a new way of applying chemical fertilizer.
　　B) It's an improved method of harvesting crops.
　　C) It's a creative technique for saving labor.
　　D) It's a farming process limiting the use of ploughs.

35. A) In areas with few weeds and unwanted plants.
　　B) In areas with a severe shortage of water.
　　C) In areas lacking in chemical fertilizer.
　　D) In areas dependent on imported food.

Section C

Directions: *In this section, you will hear a passage three times. When the passage is read for the first time, you should listen carefully for its general idea. When the passage is read for the second time, you are required to fill in the blanks numbered from 36 to 43 with the exact words you have just heard. For blanks numbered from 44 to 46 you are required to fill in the missing information. For these blanks, you can either use the exact words you have just heard or write down the main points in your own words. Finally, when the passage is read for the third time, you should check what you have written.*

　　Adults are getting smarter about how smart babies are. Not long ago, researchers learned that 4-day-olds could understand (36) ＿＿＿＿＿＿＿ and subtraction. Now, British research (37) ＿＿＿＿＿＿ Graham Schafer has discovered that infants can learn words for uncommon things long before they can speak. He found that 9-month-old infants could be taught, through repeated show-and-tell, to (38) ＿＿＿＿＿＿ the names of objects that were foreign to them, a result that (39) ＿＿＿＿＿＿ in some ways the received (40) ＿＿＿＿＿＿ that, apart from learning to (41) ＿＿＿＿＿＿ things common to their daily lives, children don't begin to build vocabulary until well into their second year. It's no (42) ＿＿＿＿＿＿ that children learn words, but

the words they tend to know are words linked to (43) _____ situations in the home, explains Schafer. (44) _____

_____ with an unfamiliar voice giving instructions in an unfamiliar setting.

Figuring out how humans acquire language may shed light on why some children learn to read and write later than others, Schafer says, and could lead to better treatments for developmental problems. (45) _____

_____. Language is a test case for human cognitive development, says Schafer. But parents eager to teach their infants should take note: (46) _____

_____. "This is not about advancing development," he says. "It's just about what children can do at an earlier age than what educators have often thought."

Part Ⅳ　Reading Comprehension (Reading in Depth) (25 minutes)
Section A

Directions: *In this section, there is a short passage with 5 questions or incomplete statements. Read the passage carefully. Then answer the questions or complete the statements in the fewest possible words. Please write your answers on Answer Sheet 2.*

Questions 47 to 51 are based on the following passage.

I've heard from and talked to many people who described how Mother Nature simplified their lives for them. They'd lost their home and many or all of their possessions through fires, floods, earthquakes, or some other disasters. Losing everything you own under such circumstances can be distressing, but the people I've heard from all saw their loss, ultimately, as a blessing.

"The fire saved us the agony of deciding what to keep and what to get rid of," one woman wrote. And once all those things were no longer there, she and her husband saw how they had weighed them down and complicated their lives.

"There was so much stuff we never used and that was just taking up space. We vowed when we started over, we'd replace only what we needed, and this time we'd do it right. We've kept our promise: We don't have much now, but what we have is exactly what we want."

Though we've never had a catastrophic loss such as that, Gibbs and I did have a close call shortly before we decided to simplify. At that time we lived in a fire zone. One night a firestorm raged through and destroyed over six hundred homes in our community. That tragedy gave us the opportunity to look objectively at the goods we'd accumulated.

We saw that there was so much we could get rid of and not only never miss, but be better off without. Having almost lost it all, we found it much easier to let go of the things we knew we'd never use again.

Obviously, there's a tremendous difference between getting rid of possessions and losing them through a natural disaster without having a say in the matter. And this is not to minimize the tragedy and pain such a loss can generate.

But you might think about how you would approach the acquisition process if you had it to do all over again. Look around your home and make a list of what you would replace.

Make another list of things you wouldn't acquire again no matter what, and in fact would be happy to be rid of.

When you're ready to start unloading some of your stuff, that list will be a good place to start.

47. Many people whose possessions were destroyed in natural disasters eventually considered their loss _____.

48. Now that all their possessions were lost in the fire, the woman and her husband felt that their lives had been _____.

49. What do we know about the author's house from the sentence "Gibbs and I did have a close call" (Lines 1 - 2, Para. 4)?

_____

50. According to the author, getting rid of possessions and losing them through a natural disaster are vastly _____.

51. What does the author suggest people do with unnecessary things?

_____

Section B

Directions: *There are 2 passages in this section. Each passage is followed by some questions or unfinished statements. For each of them there are four choices marked A), B), C) and D). You should decide on the best choice and mark the corresponding letter on **Answer Sheet 2** with a single line through the centre.*

Passage One

Questions 52 to 56 are based on the following passage.

In a purely biological sense, fear begins with the body's system for reacting to things that can harm us the so-called fight-or-flight response. "An animal that can't detect danger can't stay alive," says Joseph LeDoux. Like animals, humans evolved with an elaborate mechanism for processing information about potential threats. At its core is a cluster of neurons (神经元) deep in the brain known as the amygdala (扁桃核).

LeDoux studies the way animals and humans respond to threats to understand how we form memories of significant events in our lives. The amygdala receives input from many parts of the brain, including regions responsible for retrieving memories. Using this information, the amygdala appraises a situation — *I think this charging dog wants to bite me* — and triggers a response by radiating nerve signals throughout the body. These signals produce the familiar signs of distress: trembling, perspiration and fast-moving feet, just to name three.

This fear mechanism is critical to the survival of all animals, but no one can say for sure whether beasts other than humans know they're afraid. That is, as LeDoux says, "if you put that system into a brain that has consciousness, then you get the feeling of fear."

Humans, says Edward M. Hallowell, have the ability to call up images of bad things that happened in the past and to anticipate future events. Combine these higher thought processes with our hardwired danger-detection systems, and you get a near-universal human phenomenon: worry.

That's not necessarily a bad thing, says Hallowell. "When used properly, worry is an incredible device," he says. After all, a little healthy worrying is okay if it leads to constructive action — like having a doctor look at that weird spot on your back.

Hallowell insists, though, that there's right way to worry. "Never do it alone, get the facts and then make a plan," he says. Most of us have survived a recession, so we're familiar with the belt-tightening strategies needed to survive a slump.

Unfortunately, few of us have much experience dealing with the threat of terrorism, so it's been difficult to get facts about how we should respond. That's why Hallowell believes it was okay for people to indulge some extreme worries last fall by asking doctors for Cipro (抗炭疽菌的药物) and buying gas masks.

52. The "so-called fight-or-flight response" (Line 2, Para. 1) refers to "_____".
    A) the biological process in which human beings' sense of self-defense evolves
    B) the instinctive fear human beings feel when faced with potential danger
    C) the act of evaluating a dangerous situation and making a quick decision
    D) the elaborate mechanism in the human brain for retrieving information

53. From the studies conducted by LeDoux we learn that _____.
    A) reactions of humans and animals to dangerous situations are often unpredictable
    B) memories of significant events enable people to control fear and distress
    C) people's unpleasant memories are derived from their feelings of fear
    D) the amygdala plays a vital part in human and animal responses to potential danger

54. From the passage we know that _____.
    A) a little worry will do us good if handled properly
    B) a little worry will enable us to survive a recession
    C) fear strengthens the human desire to survive danger
    D) fear helps people to anticipate certain future events

55. Which of the following is the best way to deal with your worries according to Hallowell?
    A) Ask for help from the people around you.
    B) Use the belt-tightening strategies for survival.
    C) Seek professional advice and take action.
    D) Understand the situation and be fully prepared.

56. In Hallowell's view, people's reaction to the terrorist threat last fall was _____.
    A) ridiculous   B) understandable
    C) over-cautious   D) sensible

Passage Two
Questions 57 to 61 are based on the following passage.

Amitai Etzioni is not surprised by the latest headings about scheming corporate crooks (骗子). As a visiting professor at the Harvard Business School in 1989, he ended his work there disgusted with his students' overwhelming lust for money. "They're taught that profit is all that matters," he says. Many schools don't even offer ethics (伦理学) courses at all.

Etzioni expressed his frustration about the interests of his graduate students. "By and large, I clearly had not found a way to help classes full of MBAs see that there is more to life than money, power, fame and self-interest," he wrote at the time. Today he still takes the blame for not educating these business-leaders-to-be, "I really feel like I failed them," he says. "If I was a better teacher maybe I could have reached them."

Etzioni was a respected ethics expert when he arrived at Harvard. He hoped his work at the university would give him insight into how questions of morality could be applied to places where self-interest flourished. What he found wasn't encouraging. Those would-be executives had, says Etzioni, little interest in concepts of ethics and morality in the boardroom — and their professor was met with blank stares when he urged his students to see business in new and different ways.

Etzioni sees the experience at Harvard as an eye-opening one and says there's much about

business schools that he'd like to change. "A lot of the faculty teaching businesses are bad news themselves," Etzioni says. From offering classes that teach students how to legally manipulate contracts, to reinforcing the notion of profit over community interests, Etzioni has seen a lot that's left him shaking his head. And because of what he's seen taught in business schools, he's not surprised by the latest rash of corporate scandals. "In many ways things have got a lot worse at business schools, I suspect," says Etzioni.

Etzioni is still teaching the sociology of right and wrong and still calling for ethical business leadership. "People with poor motives will always exist," he says. "Sometimes environments constrain those people and sometimes environments give those people opportunity." Etzioni says the booming economy of the last decade enabled those individuals with poor motives to get rich before getting in trouble. His hope now: that the cries for reform will provide more fertile soil for his long-standing messages about business ethics.

57. What impressed Amitai Etzioni most about Harvard MBA students?
   A) Their keen interest in business courses.
   B) Their intense desire for money.
   C) Their tactics for making profits.
   D) Their potential to become business leaders.

58. Why did Amitai Etzioni say "I really feel like I failed them" (Line 4, Para. 2)?
   A) He was unable to alert his students to corporate malpractice.
   B) He didn't teach his students to see business in new and different ways.
   C) He could not get his students to understand the importance of ethics in business.
   D) He didn't offer courses that would meet the expectations of the business-leaders-to-be.

59. Most would-be executives at the Harvard Business School believed that _____.
   A) questions of morality were of utmost importance in business affairs
   B) self-interest should not be the top priority in business dealings
   C) new and different principles should be taught at business schools
   D) there was no place for ethics and morality in business dealings

60. In Etzioni's view, the latest rash of corporate scandals could be attributed to _____.
   A) the tendency in business schools to stress self-interest over business ethics
   B) the executives lack of knowledge in legally manipulating contracts
   C) the increasingly fierce competition in the modern business world
   D) the moral corruption of business school graduates

61. We learn from the last paragraph that _____.
   A) the calls for reform will help promote business ethics
   B) businessmen with poor motives will gain the upper hand
   C) business ethics courses should be taught in all business schools
   D) reform in business management contributes to economic growth

Part V Error Correction (15 minutes)

Directions: *This part consists of a short passage. In this passage, there are altogether 10 mistakes, one in each numbered line. You may have to change a word, add a word or delete a word. Mark out the mistakes and put the corrections in the blanks provided. If you change a word, cross it out and write the correct word in the corresponding blank. If you add a word, put an insertion mark (∧) in the right place and write the missing word in the blank. If you delete a*

word, cross it out and put a slash (/) in the blank.

The National Endowment for the Arts recently released the results of its "Reading at Risk" survey, which described the movement of the American public away from books and literature and toward television and electronic media. According to the survey, "reading is on the decline on every region, within every ethnic group, and at every educational level."

62. _____

The day the NEA report released, the U.S. House, in a tie vote, upheld the government's right to obtain bookstore and library records under a provision of the USA Patriot Act. The House proposal would have barred the federal government from demand library records, reading lists, book customer lists and other material in terrorism and intelligence investigations.

63. _____

64. _____

These two events are completely unrelated to, yet they echo each other in the message they send about the place of books and reading in American culture. At the heart of the NEA survey is the belief in our democratic system depends on the leaders who can think critically, analyze texts and writing clearly. All of these are skills promoted by reading and discussing books and literature. At the same time, through a provision of the Patriot Act, the leaders of our country are unconsciously sending the message that reading may be connected to desirable activities that might undermine our system of government rather than helping democracy flourish.

65. _____

66. _____

67. _____

68. _____

Our culture's decline in reading begin well before the existence of the Patriot Act. During the 1980s' culture wars, school systems across the country pulled some books from library shelves because its content was deemed by parents and teachers to be inappropriate. Now what started in schools across the country is playing itself on a nation stage and is possibly having an impact on the reading habits of the American public.

69. _____

70. _____

71. _____

Part VI　Translation　(5 minutes)

Directions: *Complete the sentences by translating into English the Chinese given in brackets.*
　Please write your translation on Answer Sheet 2.

72. If you had _____ (听从了我的忠告,你就不会陷入麻烦).

73. With tears on her face, the lady _____ (看着她受伤的儿子被送进手术室).

74. After the terrorist attack, tourists _____ (被劝告暂时不要去该国旅游).

75. I prefer to communicate with my customers _____ (通过写电子邮件而不是打电话).

76. _____ (直到截止日他才寄出) his application form.

2006年12月大学英语六级(新题型)试题答案与解析

Part Ⅰ

Sample Writing

The Importance of Reading Classics

It is widely acknowledged that reading the classics is both important and beneficial to the character development and personal growth of the young people. For me, nothing can bring more joy and happiness than reading those masterpieces created by the great figures like Confucius and Cao Xueqin. I believe works like *The Dream in the Red Chamber* and *The Legend of Three Kingdoms* can enhance one's aesthetic taste and deepen the understanding of the glorious history of Chinese culture.

However, the modern society is full of temptations. Compared with TV soap operas, sporting events, and video games, classical literary works are old-fashioned and time-consuming. In bookstores, "fast-food" reading materials are replacing classics, and young writers with sensational and "cool" remarks win the applause of a large number of fans.

We college students should be fully aware of the important role the classics play in broadening one's vision. Therefore, we should start reading and studying the treasuries our ancestors left and absorbing the essence of those classical works. We should also advocate to the public the importance of classics so that an increasing number of people can enjoy the pleasure of reading.

Part Ⅱ

1. [N] 参见第二段第一句:Lance Bass... didn't join the three-man crew... due to lack of payment.(Lance Bass 本打算成为世界上第三个尝试耗资 2,000 万美金作太空旅行的人,但当 2002 年 10 月 30 日飞船升空时,他却由于缺乏资金未能与三位宇航员同行。)

2. [Y] 参见第三段第一、二句:These trips are the beginning... within the next two decades.(这些太空旅行开启了 21 世纪最有利可图的行业。已有数家太空旅行社计划在今后 20 年里修建亚轨道飞行器与轨道环行城市。)

3. [Y] 参见第四段最后一句:对游客开放太空游所剩下的障碍是一些宇航机构,他们担忧的是安全问题以及可靠的、可重复使用的发射器的研制问题。

4. [NG] 本文只提到美国商人 Tito 和南非商人 Shuttleworth 尝试太空飞行,并未提到"two Australian billionaires"。

5. a trip to the Mir space station 参见"Space Accommodations"小节的第二段倒数第三句:Each week, one of the participants would be eliminated from the show, with the winner receiving a trip to the Mir space station.

6. space hotel 参见"Space Accommodations"小节的第六段:Even Hilton Hotels has shown interest in the space tourism industry and the possibility of building or co-funding a space hotel.

7. small gravitational pull 参见"Space Accommodations"小节的倒数第二段的第二句:The small gravitational pull created by rotating space city would allow space-tourists and residents to walk around and function normally within the structure.

8. launching the spacecraft 参见"The Most Expensive Vacation"小节部分的第一段倒数第二句:

Each spacecraft requires millions of pounds of fuel to take off into space, <u>which makes them expensive to launch.</u>

9. $50,000 参见 "The Most Expensive Vacation" 小节部分的第三段第二句：The report concluded that <u>at a ticket price of $50,000</u>, there could be 500,000 passengers flying into space each year.

10. space travel 参见全文最后一句：Within the next 20 years, <u>space planes could be taking off</u> for the moon at the same frequency as airplanes flying between New York and Los Angeles.

Part Ⅲ

Section A

| 11. D | 12. C | 13. B | 14. C | 15. D | 16. A | 17. B | 18. A | 19. B |
| 20. D | 21. A | 22. C | 23. B | 24. C | 25. A |

Section B

| 26. B | 27. C | 28. C | 29. A | 30. A | 31. D | 32. A | 33. C | 34. D | 35. B |

Section C

| 36. addition | 37. psychologist | 38. recognize | 39. challenges |
| 40. wisdom | 41. identify | 42. secret | 43. specific |

44. This is the first demonstration that we can choose what words the children will learn and that they can respond to them

45. What's more, the study of language acquisition offers direct insight into how humans learn

46. Even without being taught new words, a control group caught up with the other infants within a few months

Part Ⅳ

47. (as) a blessing 参见第一段最后一句：在这些情况（自然灾难）下，失去所拥有的一切固然令人沮丧，但据我了解，那些人基本上都将他们的损失看做是一种福分(as a blessing)。

48. simplified 文章第一段第一句提到，许多人都曾描绘过大自然是如何帮助他们简化生活的(simplify their lives)。第二段最后一句提及，当所有的东西都不复存在，她和丈夫两人都明白了这些东西曾经是怎样拖累他们，并使他们的生活复杂化。由此可推出，那位女士和她丈夫在火灾夺取了他们所有的财物后，都感到生活被简单化了(simplified)。

49. It narrowly escaped the firestorm. Gibbs and I did have a close call shortly before we decided to simplify. 一句意为："还没等我和吉波斯决定简化我们的生活，我们就经历了一场死里逃生的劫难"。"have a close call"指"侥幸逃脱"。下文提到，夫妇二人所在的居民区曾遭遇过一次火灾，六百多户人家的房屋财产被毁。那次悲剧使他们得以客观地看待自己囤积多年的那些财物，于是他们决定进行简化生活，抛弃一些无用之物。由此可推知该夫妇二人的房屋在那次火灾中幸免于难。

50. different. 参见倒数第四段第一句：显然，主动抛弃财物与在自然灾难中无助地失去财物之间存在着极大的差异。

51. To get rid of them. 根据文章最后两段可知，作者建议人们扔掉无用之物，轻松生活。

52. [B] 细节题。参见第一段第一句：从纯粹的生物学意义上说，恐惧始于人体系统对可能伤害我们的东西作出的反应——即所谓的"迎击或逃离反应"。故选 B("so-called fight-or-flight response"是指人类面临潜在危险时感受到的本能的恐惧)。

53. [D] 语篇论证结构理解题。第二段陈述了 LeDoux 关于扁桃核功能的研究成果，以支撑第一段最后一句：(在人与动物对潜在危险反应过程中,)起着核心作用的是一组位于大脑深处的神经元，这组神经元被称为"扁桃核"。故选 D(从 LeDoux 的研究中我们了解到，扁桃核在人

与动物对潜在危险作出反应的过程中起着关键作用）。

54. [A] 段落大意理解题。参见倒数第三段：若应用得当，"担忧"是一种不可思议的工具。毕竟，少量健康的"担忧"如能导致建设性的积极行动也并无大碍，比如让医生检查一下你背上那个奇怪的斑点。故选 A（根据本文我们得知，少量的"担忧"若处理得当，还是对我们有好处的）。

55. [D] 细节题。参见倒数第二段第一句：Hollowell 坚持认为要以合理的方式对待"担忧"，"永远不要独自忧愁，弄清问题真相，作出相应计划"。故选 D（根据 Hollowell 的观点，对待 worry 的最佳方式是了解局势，作好充分准备）。

56. [B] 段落大意理解题。参见最后一段：不幸的是，我们中很少有人对恐怖主义的威胁有应对经验，所以很难弄明白我们该如何反应。因此，Hallowell 认为，去年秋天人们向医生索要抗炭疽病药物、购买防毒面具，那些沉溺于极端恐惧的行为并不离奇。故选 B（在 Hallowell 看来，人们去年秋天对恐怖主义威胁的反应是可以理解的）。

57. [B] 细节题。参见第一段第二句：1989 年 Etzioni 作为客座教授到哈佛商学院讲学，他结束那里的工作时，学生对金钱的强烈欲望令他十分反感。故选 B（哈佛大学 MBA 学员给 Etzioni 留下的最深印象是他们对金钱的强烈欲望）。

58. [C] 细节题。参见第二段第一、二句：对于那些研究生的金钱欲，Etzioni 表达了他的遗憾。他说："总的来说，我还没有找到很好的办法来帮助那些 MBA 学员看清生活不仅仅只是金钱、权力、名望与个人利益。"故选 C（Etzioni 之所以说"我自觉有负于他们"，是因为他没能使学生明白商业道德的重要性）。

59. [D] 细节题。参见第三段第四句：那些未来的经理人对董事会议室里的伦理与道德观念没有什么兴趣。故选 D（多数哈佛商学院的未来经理人都认为，伦理道德在商业交易中没有一席之地）。

60. [A] 细节题。参见第四段第二、三、四句："许多商科教师本身就是坏的影响，"Etzioni 说。他们教学生如何合法处理合同，强调利润高于社区利益……由于商学院里所教的这些，他并不奇怪为什么最近公司丑闻频繁不断。故选 A（在 Etzioni 看来，最近公司丑闻频繁不断，主要应归结于商学院教学倾向于强调个人利益而忽视商业伦理）。

61. [A] 段落大意理解题。参见全文最后一句：他现在的希望是，对改革的呼吁将为他所长期传播的关于商业道德规范重要性的思想提供肥沃的土壤。故选 A（从最后一段我们了解到，对改革的呼吁将促进商业道德规范）。

Part Ⅴ

62. on → in in every region 在每个地区。介词搭配错误。

63. the NEA report ∧ released → was The day the NEA report was released 在 NEA 报告公布于众的那天。被动语态与主动语态混淆。

64. demand → demanding … would have barred the federal government from demanding library records 会阻止联邦政府索求图书馆记录资料。动词词组固定搭配错误。

65. unrelated to → unrelated 毫不相关的，去掉 to。

66. system ∧ depends → that 依赖于……的民主体制。定语从句关系代词遗漏。

67. writing → write … the leaders who can think critically, analyze texts and write clearly，能够用批判的方式思考、分析文本、用清晰的思路写作的领导，句中 think、analyze、write 为三个并列谓语动词，均置于情态动词 can 之后，用动词原形。并列谓语动词形式错误。

68. desirable → undesirable … undesirable activities that might undermine our system of government 破坏政府体制的不良活动。逻辑语义相悖。

69. begin → began … began well before the existence of the Patriot Act 早在《爱国法案》存在前就开始了，根据上下文应用一般过去时。时态错误。

70. its → their   their 指代前文中的复数名词 books。代词指代错误。
71. nation → national   on the national stage 在全国舞台上，词性错误。

Part VI

72. followed my advice，you would not have got into trouble
73. watched her injured son taken to the operating room
74. were advised not to visit the country for the time being
75. via/by email instead of by phone
    through writing email rather than/instead of talking over the phone
76. It was not until the deadline that he sent/Not until the deadline did he send

2007 年 6 月大学英语六级(新题型)考试试题

Part Ⅰ Writing (30 minutes)

Directions：*For this part, you are allowed 30 minutes to write a short essay entitled **Should One Expect a Reward When Doing a Good Deed**? You should write at least 150 words following the outline given below.*

1. 有人做好事期望得到回报
2. 有人认为应该像雷锋那样做好事不图回报
3. 我的观点

Should One Expect a Reward When Doing a Good Deed?

Part Ⅱ Reading Comprehension (Skimming and Scanning) (15 minutes)

Directions：*In this part, you will have 15 minutes to go over the passage quickly and answer the questions on **Answer Sheet 1**.*

For questions 1 - 4, mark

Y (for YES)　　　　*if the statement agrees with the information given in the passage;*

N (for NO)　　　　*if the statement contradicts the information given in the passage;*

NG (for NOT GIVEN) *if the information is not given in the passage.*

For questions 5 - 10, complete the sentences with the information given in the passage.

Seven Steps to a More Fulfilling Job

Many people today find themselves in unfulfilling work situations. In fact, one in four workers is dissatisfied with their current job, according to the recent "Plans for 2004" survey. Their career path may be financially rewarding, but it doesn't meet their emotional, social or creative needs. They're stuck, unhappy, and have no idea what to do about it, except move to another job.

Mary Lyn Miller, veteran career consultant and founder of the Life and Career Clinic, says that when most people are unhappy about their work, their first thought is to get a different job. Instead, Miller suggests looking at the possibility of a different life. Through her book, *8 Myths of Making a Living*, as well as workshops, seminars and personal coaching and consulting, she has helped thousands of dissatisfied workers reassess life and work.

Like the way of Zen, which includes understanding of oneself as one really is, Miller encourages job seekers and those dissatisfied with work or life to examine their beliefs about work and recognize that "in many cases your beliefs are what brought you to where you are today." You may have been raised to think that women were best at nurturing and caring and, therefore, should be teachers and nurses. So that's what you did. Or, perhaps you were brought up to believe that you should do what your father did, so you have taken over the family business, or become a dentist "just like dad." If this sounds familiar, it's probably time to look at the new possibilities for your future.

Miller developed a 7-step process to help potential job seekers assess their current situation and beliefs, identify their real passion, and start on a journey that allows them to pursue their passion through work.

Step 1: Willingness to do something different.

Breaking the cycle of doing what you have always done is one of the most difficult tasks for job seekers. Many find it difficult to steer away from a career path or make a change, even if it doesn't feel right. Miller urges job seekers to open their minds to other possibilities beyond what they are currently doing.

Step 2: Commitment to being who you are, not who or what someone wants you to be.

Look at the gifts and talents you have and make a commitment to pursue those things that you love most. If you love the social aspects of your job, but are stuck inside an office or "chained to your desk" most of the time, vow to follow your instinct and investigate alternative careers and work that allow you more time to interact with others. Dawn worked as a manager for a large retail clothing store for several years. Though she had advanced within the company, she felt frustrated and longed to be involved with nature and the outdoors. She decided to go to school nights and weekends to pursue her true passion by earning her master's degree in forestry. She now works in the biotech forestry division of a major paper company.

Step 3: Self-definition.

Miller suggests that once job seekers know who they are, they need to know how to sell themselves. "In the job market, you are a product. And just like a product, you most know the features and benefits that you have to offer a potential client, or employer." Examine the skills and knowledge that you have and identify how they can apply to your desired occupation. Your qualities will exhibit to employers why they should hire you over other candidates.

Step 4: Attain a level of self-honoring.

Self-honoring or self-love may seem like an odd step for job hunters, but being able to accept yourself, without judgment, helps eliminate insecurities and will make you more self-assured. By accepting who you are — all your emotions, hopes and dreams, your personality, and your unique way of being — you'll project more confidence when networking and talking with potential employers. The power of self-honoring can help to break all the falsehoods you were programmed to believe — those that made you feel that you were not good enough, or strong enough, or intelligent enough to do what you truly desire.

Step 5: Vision.

Miller suggests that job seekers develop a vision that embraces the answer to "What do I really want to do?" One should create a solid statement in a dozen or so sentences that describe in detail how they see their life related to work. For instance, the secretary who longs to be an actress describes a life that allows her to express her love of Shakespeare on stage. A real estate agent, attracted to his current job because he loves fixing up old homes, describes buying properties that need a little tender loving care to make them more saleable.

Step 6: Appropriate risk.

Some philosophers believe that the way to enlightenment comes through facing obstacles and difficulties. Once people discover their passion, many are too scared to do anything about it. Instead, they do nothing. With this step, job seekers should assess what they are willing to give up, or risk, in pursuit of their dream. For one working mom, that meant taking night classes to learn new computer-aided design skills, while still earning a salary and keeping her day

job. For someone else, it may mean quitting his or her job, taking out loan and going back to school full time. You'll move one step closer to your ideal work life if you identify how much risk you are willing to take and the sacrifices you are willing to make.

Step 7: Action.

Some teachers of philosophy describe action in this way, "If one wants to get to the top of a mountain, just sitting at the foot thinking about it will not bring one there. It is by making the effort of climbing up the mountain, step by step, that eventually the summit is reached." All too often, it is the lack of action that ultimately holds people back from attaining their ideals. Creating a plan and taking it one step at a time can lead to new and different job opportunities. Job-hunting tasks gain added meaning as you sense their importance in your quest for a more meaningful work life. The plan can include researching industries and occupations, talking to people who are in your desired area of work, taking classes, or accepting volunteer work in your targeted field.

Each of these steps will lead you on a journey to a happier and more rewarding work life. After all, it is the journey, not the destination, that is most important.

1. According to the recent "Plans for 2004" survey, most people are unhappy with their current jobs.
2. Mary Lyn Miller's job is to advise people on their life and career.
3. Mary Lyn Miller herself was once quite dissatisfied with her own work.
4. Many people find it difficult to make up their minds whether to change their career path.
5. According to Mary Lyn Miller, people considering changing their careers should commit themselves to the pursuit of _____.
6. In the job market, job seekers need to know how to sell themselves like _____.
7. During an interview with potential employers, self-honoring or self-love may help a job seeker to show _____.
8. Mary Lyn Miller suggests that a job seeker develop a vision that answers the question "_____".
9. Many people are too scared to pursue their dreams because they are unwilling to _____.
10. What ultimately holds people back from attaining their ideals is _____.

Part III Listening Comprehension (35 minutes)
Section A
Directions: *In this section, you will hear 8 short conversations and 2 long conversations. At the end of each conversation, one or more questions will be asked about what was said. Both the conversation and the questions will be spoken only once. After each question there will be a pause. During the pause, you must read the four choices marked A), B), C) and D), and decide which is the best answer. Then mark the corresponding letter on **Answer Sheet 2** with a single line through the centre.*

11. A) Surfing the net. B) Watching a talk show.
    C) Packing a birthday gift. D) Shopping at a jewelry store.
12. A) He enjoys finding fault with exams.
    B) He is sure of his success in the exam.
    C) He doesn't know if he can do well in the exam.

D) He used to get straight A's in the exams he took.

13. A) The man is generous with his good comments on people.
    B) The woman is unsure if there will be peace in the world.
    C) The woman is doubtful about newspaper stories.
    D) The man is quite optimistic about human nature.

14. A) Study for some profession.
    C) Stay in business.
    B) Attend a medical school.
    D) Sell his shop.

15. A) More money.
    C) A college education.
    B) Fair treatment.
    D) Shorter work hours.

16. A) She was exhausted from her trip.
    C) She was impressed by Mexican food.
    B) She missed the comforts of home.
    D) She will not go to Mexico again.

17. A) Cheer herself up a bit.
    C) Seek professional advice.
    B) Find a more suitable job.
    D) Take a psychology course.

18. A) He dresses more formally now.
    B) What he wears does not match his position.
    C) He has ignored his friends since graduation.
    D) He failed to do well at college.

Questions 19 to 22 are based on the conversation you have just heard.

19. A) To go sightseeing.
    C) To promote a new champagne.
    B) To have meetings.
    D) To join in a training program.

20. A) It can reduce the number of passenger complaints.
    B) It can make air travel more entertaining.
    C) It can cut down the expenses for air travel.
    D) It can lessen the discomfort caused by air travel.

21. A) Took balanced meals with champagne.
    B) Ate vegetables and fruit only.
    C) Refrained from fish or meat.
    D) Avoided eating rich food.

22. A) Many of them found it difficult to exercise on a plane.
    B) Many of them were concerned with their well-being.
    C) Not many of them chose to do what she did.
    D) Not many of them understood the program.

Questions 23 to 25 are based on the conversation you have just heard.

23. A) At a fair.
    C) In a computer lab.
    B) At a cafeteria.
    D) In a shopping mall.

24. A) The latest computer technology.
    C) The purchasing of some equipment.
    B) The organizing of an exhibition.
    D) The dramatic changes in the job market.

25. A) Data collection.
    C) Corporate management.
    B) Training consultancy.
    D) Information processing.

Section B

Directions: *In this section, you will hear 3 short passages. At the end of each passage, you will hear some questions. Both the passage and the questions will be spoken only once. After you hear a question, you must choose the best answer from the four choice marked A), B), C) and*

D). Then mark the corresponding letter on **Answer Sheet 2** with a single line through the centre.

Passage One
Questions 26 to 28 are based on the passage you have just heard.

26. A) Improve themselves.   B) Get rid of empty dreams.
    C) Follow the cultural tradition.   D) Attempt something impossible.

27. A) By finding sufficient support for implementation.
    B) By taking into account their own ability to change.
    C) By constantly keeping in mind their ultimate goals.
    D) By making detailed plans and carrying them out.

28. A) To show people how to get their lives back to normal.
    B) To show how difficult it is for people to lose weight.
    C) To remind people to check the calories on food bags.
    D) To illustrate how easily people abandon their goals.

Passage Two
Questions 29 to 31 are based on the passage you have just heard.

29. A) Michael's parents got divorced.
    B) Karen was adopted by Ray Anderson.
    C) Karen's mother died in a car accident.
    D) A truck driver lost his life in a collision.

30. A) He ran a red light and collided with a truck.
    B) He sacrificed his life to save a baby girl.
    C) He was killed instantly in a burning car.
    D) He got married to Karen's mother.

31. A) The reported hero turned out to be his father.
    B) He did not understand his father till too late.
    C) Such misfortune should have fallen on him.
    D) It reminded him of his miserable childhood.

Passage Three
Questions 32 to 35 are based on the passage you have just heard.

32. A) Germany.   B) Japan.
    C) The U.S.   D) The U.K.

33. A) By doing odd jobs at weekends.
    B) By working long hours every day.
    C) By putting in more hours each week.
    D) By taking shorter vacations each year.

34. A) To combat competition and raise productivity.
    B) To provide them with more job opportunities.
    C) To help them maintain their living standard.
    D) To prevent them from holding a second job.

35. A) Change their jobs.   B) Earn more money.
    C) Reduce their working hours.   D) Strengthen the government's role.

Section C

Directions: *In this section, you will hear a passage three times. When the passage is read for the first time, you should listen carefully for its general idea. When the passage is read for the second time, you are required to fill in the blanks numbered from 36 to 43 with the exact words you have just heard. For blanks numbered from 44 to 46 you are required to fill in the missing information. For these blanks, you can either use the exact words you have just heard or write down the main points in your own words. Finally, when the passage is read for the third time, you should check what you have written.*

Nursing, as a typically female profession, must deal constantly with the false impression that nurses are there to wait on the physician. As nurses, we are (36) _____ to provide nursing care only. We do not have any legal or moral (37) _____ to any physician. We provide health teaching, (38) _____ physical as well as emotional problems, (39) _____ patient-related services, and make all of our nursing decisions based upon what is best or suitable for the patient. If, in any (40) _____, we feel that a physician's order is (41) _____ or unsafe, we have a legal (42) _____ to question that order or refuse to carry it out.

Nursing is not a nine-to-five job with every weekend off. All nurses are aware of that before they enter the profession. The emotional and physical stress. However, that occurs due to odd working hours is a (43) _____ reason for a lot of the career dissatisfaction. (44) ____ _____. That disturbs our personal lives, disrupts our sleeping and eating habits, and isolates us from everything except job-related friends and activities.

The quality of nursing care is being affected dramatically by these situations. (45) _____ _____. Consumers of medically related services have evidently not been affected enough yet to demand changes in our medical system. But if trends continue as predicted, (46) _____.

Part IV Reading Comprehension (Reading in Depth) (25 minutes)
Section A

Directions: *In this section, there is a short passage with 5 questions or incomplete statements. Read the passage carefully. Then answer the questions or complete statements in the fewest possible words. Please write your answers on **Answer Sheet 2**.*

Questions 47 to 51 are based on the following passage.

Google is a world-famous company, with its headquarters in Mountain View, California. It was set up in a Silicon Valley garage in 1998, and inflated (膨胀) with the Internet bubble. Even when everything around it collapsed the company kept on inflating. Google's search engine is so widespread across the world that search became Google, and *google* became a verb. The world fell in love with the effective, fascinatingly fast technology.

Google owes much of its success to the brilliance of S. Brin and L. Page, but also to a series of fortunate events. It was Page who, at Stanford in 1996, initiated the academic project that eventually became Google's search engine. Brin, who had met Page at a student orientation a year earlier, joined the project early on. They were both Ph.D. candidates when they devised the search engine which was better than the rest and, without any marketing, spread by word of mouth from early adopters to, eventually, your grandmother.

Their breakthrough, simply put, was that when their search engine crawled the Web, it did more than just look for word matches, it also tallied (统计) and ranked a host of other critical factors like how websites link to one another. That delivered far better results than anything else. Brin and Page meant to name their creation Googol (the mathematical term for the number 1 followed by 100 zeroes), but someone misspelled the word so it stuck as Google. They raised money from prescient (有先见之明的) professors and venture capitalists, and moved off campus to turn Google into business. Perhaps their biggest stroke of luck came early on when they tried to sell their technology to other search engines, but no one met their price, and they built it up on their own.

The next breakthrough came in 2000, when Google figured out how to make money with its invention. It had lots of users, but almost no one was paying. The solution turned out to be advertising, and it's not an exaggeration to say that Google is now essentially an advertising company, given that that's the source of nearly all its revenue. Today it is a giant advertising company, worth $100 billion.

47. Apart from a series of fortunate events, what is it that has made Google so successful?

48. Google's search engine originated from _____ started by L. Page.

49. How did Google's search engine spread all over the world?

    _____

50. Brin and Page decided to set up their own business because no one would _____.

51. The revenue of the Google company is largely generated from _____.

Section B

Directions: *There are 2 passages in this section. Each passage is followed by some questions or unfinished statements. For each of them there are four choices marked A), B), C), and D). You should decide on the best choice and mark the corresponding letter on **Answer Sheet 2** with a single line through the centre.*

Passage One

Questions 52 to 56 are based on the following passage.

You hear the refrain all the time: the U.S. economy looks good statistically, but it doesn't feel good. Why doesn't ever-greater wealth promote ever-greater happiness? It is a question that dates at least to the appearance in 1958 of *The Affluent* (富裕的) *Society* by John Kenneth Galbraith, who died recently at 97.

The Affluent Society is a modern classic because it helped define a new moment in the human condition. For most of history, "hunger, sickness, and cold" threatened nearly everyone, Galbraith wrote. "Poverty was found everywhere in that world. Obviously it is not of ours." After World War II, the dread of another Great Depression gave way to an economic boom. In the 1930s unemployment had averaged 18.2 percent; in the 1950s it was 4.5 percent.

To Galbraith, materialism had gone mad and would breed discontent. Through advertising, companies conditioned consumers to buy things they didn't really want or need. Because so much spending was artificial, it would be unfulfilling. Meanwhile, government spending that would make everyone better off was being cut down because people instinctively — and wrongly — labeled government only as "a necessary evil."

It's often said that only the rich are getting ahead; everyone else is standing still or falling behind. Well, there are many undeserving rich — overpaid chief executives, for instance. But over any meaningful period, most people's incomes are increasing. From 1995 to 2004, inflation-adjusted average family income rose 14.3 percent, to $43,200. People feel "squeezed" because their rising incomes often don't satisfy their rising wants — for bigger homes, more health care, more education, faster Internet connections.

The other great frustration is that it has not eliminated insecurity. People regard job stability as part of their standard of living. As corporate layoffs increased, that part has eroded. More workers fear they've become "the disposable American," as Louis Uchitelle puts it in his book by the same name.

Because so much previous suffering and social conflict stemmed from poverty, the arrival of widespread affluence suggested utopian (乌托邦式的) possibilities. Up to a point, affluence succeeds. There is much less physical misery than before. People are better off. Unfortunately, affluence also creates new complaints and contradictions.

Advanced societies need economic growth to satisfy the multiplying wants of their citizens. But the quest for growth lets loose new anxieties and economic conflicts that disturb the social order. Affluence liberates the individual, promising that everyone can choose a unique way to self-fulfillment. But the promise is so extravagant that it predestines many disappointments and sometimes inspires choices that have anti-social consequences, including family breakdown and obesity (肥胖症). Statistical indicators of happiness have not risen with incomes.

Should we be surprised? Not really. We've simply reaffirmed an old truth: the pursuit of affluence does not always end with happiness.

52. What question does John Kenneth Galbraith raise in his book *The Affluent Society*?
   A) Why statistics don't tell the truth about the economy.
   B) Why affluence doesn't guarantee happiness.
   C) How happiness can be promoted today.
   D) What lies behind an economic boom.

53. According to Galbraith, people feel discontented because _____.
   A) public spending hasn't been cut down as expected
   B) the government has proved to be a necessary evil
   C) they are in fear of another Great Depression
   D) materialism has run wild in modern society

54. Why do people feel squeezed when their average income rises considerably?
   A) Their material pursuits have gone far ahead of their earnings.
   B) Their purchasing power has dropped markedly with inflation.
   C) The distribution of wealth is uneven between the rich and the poor.
   D) Health care and educational cost have somehow gone out of control.

55. What does Louis Uchitelle mean by "the disposable American" (Line 3, Para. 5)?
   A) Those who see job stability as part of their living standard.
   B) People full of utopian ideas resulting from affluence.
   C) People who have little say in American politics.
   D) Workers who no longer have secure jobs.

56. What has affluence brought to American society?
   A) Renewed economic security.   B) A sense of self-fulfillment.
   C) New conflicts and complaints.   D) Misery and anti-social behavior.

Passage Two
Questions 57 to 61 are based on the following passage.
The use of deferential (敬重的) language is symbolic of the Confucian ideal of the woman,

185

which dominates conservative gender norms in Japan. This ideal presents a woman who withdraws quietly to the background, subordinating her life and needs to those of her family and its male head. She is a dutiful daughter, wife, and mother, master of the domestic arts. The typical refined Japanese woman excels in modesty and delicacy; she "treads softly（谨言慎行）in the world," elevating feminine beauty and grace to an art form.

Nowadays, it is commonly observed that young women are not conforming to the feminine linguistic（语言的）ideal. They are using fewer of the very deferential "women's" forms, and even using the few strong forms that are know as "men's." This, of course, attracts considerable attention and has led to an outcry in the Japanese media against the defeminization of women's language. Indeed, we didn't hear about "men's language" until people began to respond to girls' appropriation of forms normally reserved for boys and men. There is considerable sentiment about the "corruption" of women's language — which of course is viewed as part of the loss of feminine ideals and morality — and this sentiment is crystallized by nationwide opinion polls that are regularly carried out by the media.

Yoshiko Matsumoto has argued that young women probably never used as many of the highly deferential forms as older women. This highly polite style is no doubt something that young women have been expected to "grow into"— after all, it is a sign not simply of femininity, but of maturity and refinement, and its use could be taken to indicate a change in the nature of one's social relations as well. One might well imagine little girls using exceedingly polite forms when playing house or imitating older women — in a fashion analogous to little girls' use of a high-pitched voice to do "teacher talk" or "mother talk" in role play.

The fact that young Japanese women are using less deferential language is a sure sign of change — of social change and of linguistic change. But it is most certainly not a sign of the "masculization" of girls. In some instances, it may be a sign that girls are making the same claim to authority as boys and men, but that is very different from saying that they are trying to be "masculine." Katsue Reynolds has argued that girls nowadays are using more assertive language strategies in order to be able to compete with boys in schools and out. Social change also brings not simply different positions for women and girls, but different relations to life stages, and adolescent girls are participating in new subcultural forms. Thus what may, to an older speaker, seem like "masculine" speech may seem to an adolescent like "liberated" or "hip" speech.

57. The first paragraph describes in detail _____.
    A) the standards set for contemporary Japanese women
    B) the Confucian influence on gender norms in Japan
    C) the stereotyped role of women in Japanese families
    D) the norms for traditional Japanese women to follow
58. What change has been observed in today's young Japanese women?
    A) They pay less attention to their linguistic behavior.
    B) The use fewer of the deferential linguistic forms.
    C) They confuse male and female forms of language.
    D) They employ very strong linguistic expressions.
59. How do some people react to women's appropriation of men's language forms as reported in the Japanese media?
    A) They call for a campaign to stop the defeminization.
    B) They see it as an expression of women's sentiment.
    C) They accept it as a modern trend.

D) They express strong disapproval.

60. According to Yoshiko Matsumoto, the linguistic behavior observed in today's young women _____.
   A) may lead to changes in social relations
   B) has been true of all past generations
   C) is viewed as a sign of their maturity
   D) is a result of rapid social progress

61. The author believes that the use of assertive language by young Japanese women is _____.
   A) a sure sign of their defeminization and maturation
   B) an indication of their defiance against social change
   C) one of their strategies to compete in a male-dominated society
   D) an inevitable trend of linguistic development in Japan today

Part Ⅴ　Cloze (15 minutes)

Directions: *There are 20 blanks in the following passage. For each blank there are four choices marked A), B), C) and D) on the right side of the paper. You should choose the ONE that best fits into the passage. Then mark the corresponding letter on **Answer Sheet 2** with a single line through the centre.*

Historically, humans get serious about avoiding disasters only after one has just struck them. __62__ that logic, 2006 should have been a breakthrough year for rational behavior. With the memory of 9/11 still __63__ in their minds, Americans watched hurricane Katrina, the most expensive disaster in U.S. history, on __64__ TV. Anyone who didn't know it before should have learned that bad things can happen. And they are made __65__ worse by our willful blindness to risk as much as our __66__ to work together before everything goes to hell.

Granted, some amount of delusion (错觉) is probably part of the __67__ condition. In A.D. 63, Pompeii was seriously damaged by an earthquake, and the locals immediately went to work __68__, in the same spot — until they were buried altogether by a volcano eruption 16 years later. But a __69__ of the past year in disaster history suggests that modern Americans are particularly bad at __70__ themselves from guaranteed threats.

We know more than we __71__ did about the

62. A) To　　B) By
　　C) On　　D) For

63. A) fresh　　B) obvious
　　C) apparent　　D) evident

64. A) visual　　B) vivid
　　C) live　　D) lively

65. A) little　　B) less
　　C) more　　D) much

66. A) reluctance　　B) rejection
　　C) denial　　D) decline

67. A) natural　　B) world
　　C) social　　D) human

68. A) revising　　B) refining
　　C) rebuilding　　D) retrieving

69. A) review　　B) reminder
　　C) concept　　D) prospect

70. A) preparing　　B) protesting
　　C) protecting　　D) prevailing

71. A) never　　B) ever
　　C) then　　D) before

dangers we face. But it turns __72__ that in

times of crisis, our greatest enemy is __73__

the storm, the quake or the __74__ itself.
More often, it is ourselves.

So what has happened in the year that
__75__ the disaster on the Gulf Coast? In
New Orleans, the Army Corps of Engineers
has worked day and night to rebuild the flood
walls. They have got the walls to __76__ they
were before Katrina, more or less. That's
not __77__ , we can now say with confidence.

But it may be all __78__ can be expected
from one year of hustle (忙碌).

Meanwhile, New Orleans officials have
crafted a plan to use buses and trains to __79__
the sick and the disabled. The city estimates
that 15,000 people will need a __80__ out.
However, state officials have not yet
determined where these people will be taken.
The __81__ with neighboring communities are
ongoing and difficult.

72. A) up   B) down
    C) over   D) out

73. A) merely   B) rarely
    C) incidentally   D) accidentally

74. A) surge   B) spur
    C) surf   D) splash

75. A) ensued   B) traced
    C) followed   D) occurred

76. A) which   B) where
    C) what   D) when

77. A) enough   B) certain
    C) conclusive   D) final

78. A) but   B) as
    C) that   D) those

79. A) exile   B) evacuate
    C) dismiss   D) displace

80. A) ride   B) trail
    C) path   D) track

81. A) conventions   B) notifications
    C) communications D) negotiations

Part Ⅵ   Translation（5 minutes）

Directions：*Complete the sentences by translating into English the Chinese given in brackets.
Please write your translation on Answer Sheet 2.*

82. The auto manufacturers found themselves _____ （正在同外国公司竞
争市场的份额）.

83. Only in the small town _____ （他才感到安全和放松）.

84. It is absolutely unfair that these children _____ （被剥夺了受教育的权
利）.

85. Our years of hard work are all in vain, _____ （更别提我们花费的
大量金钱了）.

86. The problems of blacks and women _____ （最近几十年受到公众相当
大的关注）.

2007 年 6 月大学英语六级(新题型)试题答案与解析

Part Ⅰ
Sample Writing

Should One Expect a Reward When Doing a Good Deed?

With the development of material and spiritual civilization, our society has witnessed a steady increase in good deeds and heroic behavior. What motivates people to conduct good deeds? Do they give help out of sheer sympathy and generosity? Or do they expect something in return?

Those who expect a reward for their good deeds have sufficient reasons. Maybe they regard the reward as a form of social recognition, which makes them feel valued and honored. Maybe they feel they deserve the reward because it's only fair to get something back for their kind efforts.

However, some other people think they should act like a living Lei Feng, doing good deeds without any "selfish" expectation. They help people in need without a second thought, because their conscience and their innate kindness condition them to do so. That is, they feel genuinely happy in the act of giving. A reward, in their eyes, will only make good deeds less noble, less pure.

In my opinion, this is a matter of different perspectives. As far as the government is concerned, a good deed should be rewarded so as to honor the doer and to encourage more people to follow the example. As individuals, we shouldn't ask for a reward for our contribution. In doing a good deed, we have given out our love. Hopefully, the receiver will be touched by the true spirit of Lei Feng and pass that love along by helping others. When everyone is contributing their love, the world will certainly become a better place to live in!

Part Ⅱ

1. [N]　参见第一段第二句"In fact, one in four workers is dissatisfied with their current jobs, according to the recent 'Plans for 2004' survey",调查表明四分之一的工人对当前工作不满。而题中则说"most people are unhappy with their current jobs(大多数人目前工作不开心)"。

2. [Y]　参见第二段第一句"Mary Lyn Miller, veteran career consultant and founder of the Life and Career Clinic(资深职业咨询师、生活与职业诊所的创立人)",由此可推知 Mary Lyn Miller 的工作是"advise people on their life and career"。

3. [NG]　全文主要讲述 Mary Lyn Miller 提供的职业建议,并未提及她个人的工作满意度。

4. [Y]　参见"Step 1：Willingness to do something different."小节部分第二句"Many find it difficult to steer away from a career path or make a change (许多人觉得很难脱离职业轨道或做出改变)"。

5. things they love most/their dreams　参见"Step 2：Commitment to being who you are..."小节部分第一句"Look at the gifts and talents you have and make a commitment to pursue those things you love(下决心去追求你喜爱的事情)"。

6. products　参见"Step 3：Self-definition"小节部分第一、二句"Miller suggests that once job seekers know who they are, they need to know how to sell themselves(如何推销自己). In the job market, you are a product."

7. self-assurance/self-confidence　参见"Step 4：Attain a level of self-honoring ."小节部分第一

句"Self-honoring or self-love（自重或自爱）may seem like an odd step for job hunters，but being able to accept yourself，without judgment，helps eliminate insecurities（消除不安全感）and will make you more self-assured（更加自信）"。

8. "What do I really want to do?" 参见"Step 5：Vision"小节部分第一句"Miller suggests that job seekers develop a vision that embraces the answer to What do I really want to do?"

9. give up or risk 参见"Step 6：Appropriate risk"小节部分第二、三、四句"Once people discover their passion（激情），many were too scared to do anything about it... job seekers should assess what they are willing to give up，or risk，in pursuit of their dreams"。

10. the lack of action 参见"Step 7：Action."小节部分第三句"All too often，it is the lack of action that ultimately holds people back from attaining their ideals"。

Part Ⅲ

11. A	12. B	13. D	14. C	15. A
16. B	17. C	18. A	19. B	20. D
21. D	22. C	23. A	24. C	25. B
26. D	27. D	28. D	29. C	30. B
31. A	32. B	33. D	34. A	35. C

36. licensed   37. obligation   38. assess   39. coordinate

40. circumstance   41. inappropriate   42. responsibility   43. prime

44. It's sometimes required that we work overtime and that we change shifts four or five times a month.

45. Most hospitals are now staffed by new graduates as experienced nurses finally give up trying to change the system.

46. they will find that the most critical hospital care will be provided by new inexperienced and sometimes inadequately trained nurses.

Part Ⅳ

Section A

47. The brilliance of S. Brin and L. Page 参见第二段第一句：Google owes much of its success to the brilliance of S. Brin and L. Page，but also to a series of fortunate event.（Google 的成功很大程度上不仅归功于 S. Brin 与 L. Page 两人的聪明才智，还与一系列幸运事件有关。）

48. the academic project 参见第二段第二句：It was Page who，at Stanford in 1996，initiated the academic project that eventually became Google's search engine.（Page 于 1996 年在斯坦福大学发起了一项学术项目，该项目最后演变成 Google 搜索引擎。）

49. By word of mouth 参见第二段最后一句：They were both Ph. D candidates when they devised the search engine which was better than the rest and，without any marketing，spread by word of mouth from early adopters to，eventually，your grandmother.（他们两人在攻读博士期间设计的搜索引擎比其他引擎都优越，无须任何营销活动，该引擎通过口头传颂从早期使用者最终传到了你的老祖母那里。）

50. meet their price 参见第三段最后一句：... when they tried to sell their technology to other search engines，but no one met their price，and they built it up on their own.（……他们试图将自己的技术出售给其他搜索引擎公司，但没人能接受他们的报价，于是他们创办了自己的公司。）

51. advertising 参见最后一段倒数第二句：The solution turned out to be advertising，and it's not an exaggeration to say that Google is now essentially an advertising company，given that

that's the source of nearly all its revenue.（最后的出路就是广告,如今的 Google 本质上是一个广告公司,这样说毫不夸张,因为广告几乎是其所有收入的来源。）

Section B

52. [B] 细节理解题。参见第一段第二、三句:Why doesn't ever-greater wealth promote ever-greater happiness? It is a question that dates at least to the appearance in 1958 of *The Affluent Society* by John Kenneth Galbraith...（为什么日益增长的财富不能促进幸福感的不断增强? 这个问题的首次提出至少可以追溯到 John Kenneth Galbraith 于 1958 出版的 *The Affluent Society*。）故选 B（Galbraith 在 *The Affluent Society* 一书中提到的问题是"为什么富裕不能保证幸福"）。

53. [D] 细节理解题。参见第三段第一句:To Galbraith, materialism has gone mad and would breed discontent.（对 Galbraith 而言,物质主义已经发展到了疯狂的地步,必将滋生人心的不满足。）故选 D（在 Galbraith 看来,人们感到不满是因为物质主义在现代社会疯狂发展）。

54. [A] 细节理解题。参见第四段最后一句:People feel "squeezed" because their rising incomes often doesn't satisfy their rising wants — for bigger homes, more health care, more education, faster Internet connections.（人们感到手头紧、钱不够花,是因为日益增长的收入往往并不能满足日益增长的需要——需要更大的住房、更好的保健、更高的教育、更快的联网等。）故选 A（人们的物质需求已远远超过了所挣的收入）。

55. [D] 段落理解与推断题。第五段提到,不安全感尚未消除是另一件让人倍感受挫的事。人们将工作稳定（job security）看做是生活水准的一部分（part of their standard of living）。而那一部分（job stability）随着公司裁员已被损耗（that part has eroded）。工人们害怕自己已变成了 Louis Uchitelle 在同名书中提到的"只有一次性使用价值的美国人"（the disposable American）。由此可推论答案为 D（Uchitelle 的"the disposable American"是指不再拥有稳定工作的人）。

56. [C] 细节理解题。参见第六段最后一句:Unfortunately, affluence also creates new complaints and contradictions（不幸的是,富裕也造成了新的抱怨与矛盾）"。故选 C（conflict = contradiction）。

57. [B] 段落大意理解题。第一段第一句是主题句,提到礼貌敬语的使用象征着孔子思想中的理想女子,这一女子的言行模式主宰了日本保守的性别标准。下文对这种理想的女子言行作了细节描述。故选 B（第一段详细描述了孔子思想对日本性别模式的影响）。

58. [B] 细节理解题。参见第二段第一、二句:Nowadays, it is commonly observed that young women...even using the few strong forms that are known as men's（普遍发现当今年轻女子不再恪守理想中的女性言语标准。礼貌敬重的"女士言语"用得越来越少,甚至还用上了少数"男士"强势语言）故选 B（从当今年轻日本女子身上可观察到的变化是,她们较少使用礼貌敬语）。此题 D 项的干扰较大,D 项"employ very strong linguistic forms"错在"very strong"表达上。

59. [D] 细节综合理解题。第二段后半部分提到,年轻女子言语模式的变化导致日本媒体对女性语言男性化的公开强烈反对（outcry）,人们开始关注女孩挪用本来专属男性的语言形式（girls' appropriation of forms normally reserved for boys and men）,女性语言的"腐化"在民众中引起很大反响,被看做是理想女性标准与道德的丧失。这种感觉在媒体经常进行的民意调查中有着具体体现。故选 D（根据日本媒体报道,民众对女性挪用男士语言表示了强烈的反对）。

60. [C] 细节理解题。第三段第一、二句:... it is a sign not simply of feminity, but of maturity and refinement and its use could be taken to indicate a change in the nature of one's social relations as well.（……礼貌用语的使用不仅仅是女性化的标志,还象征着成熟和优雅,而且礼貌用语的使用还可看成是使用此语言的人的社会关系性质的变化。）故选 C。本题 A 项干

扰较大,参考译文即可看出 A 项是对第二句后半句话的曲解。

61. [C] 细节理解题。参见最后一段第四句:...girls nowadays are using more assertive language strategies in order to compete with boys in schools and out.(……女孩们使用更多的果断自信的语言策略,目的是为了在校内外与男生竞争。)故选 C(年轻日本女子使用"assertive language"是她们在男性主导社会中的竞争策略之一)。

Part Ⅴ

62. [B] that logic 根据那种逻辑。固定词组搭配。

63. [A] With the memory of 9/11 still fresh in their minds 他们脑海中关于"9·11"事件的记忆犹新。习惯搭配。fresh memory 记忆犹新。

64. [C] watched...on live TV 通过电视直播观看。习惯搭配。live broadcast 直播;lively atmosphere 活跃的气氛;vivid description 生动的描述;visual aids 视觉辅助。

65. [D] are made much worse 被弄得更糟。语法考点:much 用于形容词比较级前表强调。

66. [A] our reluctance to work together 我们不情愿合作。习惯搭配。be reluctant to do sth/ one's reluctance to do sth 不愿意做某事;a denial of the rumor/justice 否认谣言/拒绝给予公正处理;an rejection of an application 拒绝申请;the decline of an invitation 谢绝邀请。

67. [D] part of the human condition 人类状况的一部分/人性的一部分。上下文理解题。下文提到公元 63 年,庞培城遭受地震严重破坏,震后人们又在同样的震区迅速重建家园,结果 16 年后火山爆发,整个城市全部被埋没。作者以此例说明人类总是不吸取灾难教训,面对灾难人类最大的敌人不是天灾而是人类自身。所以上文提到的人的错觉(即人类对危险的盲目性)很大程度上是一种"human condition"。

68. [C] went to work rebuilding 开始重建工作。词义辨析。rebuild 重建;revise 修改,修订; refine 加工,纯炼,使精细/精美;retrieve 重新挽回。

69. [A] a review of the past year 回顾去年。词组语义搭配题。prospect 前景,展望;reminder 提醒;concept 概念。

70. [C] protecting oneself from threats 保护自己远离危险。习惯搭配。prepare(oneself) for...为……作好准备;protest against 抗议;prevail 盛行,主宰。

71. [B] (We know more than we ever did about the dangers. 关于危险我们现在比以往了解得都要多。语法考点:ever 表"曾经",常用于比较状语从句,强调语气。

72. [D] But it turns out that...结果……习惯搭配。

73. [B] our greatest enemy is rarely the storm 我们最大的敌人很少会是风暴。词义辨析。 rarely 很少,几乎不;merely 仅仅;incidentally = by the way 顺便提及;accidentally 意外地。

74. [A] the storm, the quake, or the surge 风暴、地震或潮涌。词义辨析。surge 汹涌澎湃;surf 冲浪;spur 刺激;splash 泼洒。

75. [C] So what has happened in the year that followed the disaster on the Gulf Coast? 海湾海岸灾难之后的那一年发生了什么?)词性考点:ensue 随之产生或出现;follow 跟随;occur 发生;trace...to...追溯到。

76. [B] They have got the walls to where they were before Katrina 在 Katrina 飓风来临之前他们已将防洪墙筑到了自己的家园。语法考点:where 引导地点状语从句。

77. [A] That's not enough 那还不够。上下文理解题。that 指"修筑防洪墙"。

78. [C] But it may be all that can be expected from one year of hustle. 但一年的忙碌就只能指望得到这么多。语法考点:that 引导定语从句修饰 all。

79. [B] use buses and trains evacuate the sick and the disabled 用公交车与火车疏散病人与残疾人员。词义辨析。exile 驱逐,流放;dismiss 解散,遣散,开除;displace 使离开家园/原有位置。

80. [A] need a ride out 需要乘车离开。上下文理解题。

81. [D] The <u>negotiations</u> with neighboring communities are ongoing and difficult. 与邻近社区的谈判还在艰难进行中。上下文理解题。前文提到难民疏散,由于政府尚未决定何处安置人员的问题,所以要临时与周边社区协商(negotiation)。

Part Ⅵ

82. competing with foreign firms for marketing share
83. does he feel safe and relaxed
84. are deprived of the rights to receive education
85. not to mention/let alone the large amount of money we have spent
86. have gained/caused considerable public concern in recent decades

2007 年 12 月大学英语六级(新题型)考试试题

Part Ⅰ　Writing　(30 minutes)

Directions: *For this part, you are allowed 30 minutes to write a short essay entitled* **The digital age** *You should write at least 150 words following the outline given below.*

The digital age

1. 如今,数字化产品越来越多,如……
2. 使用数字化产品对于人们学习工作和生活的影响

Part Ⅱ　Reading Comprehension (Skimming and Scanning) (15 minutes)

Directions: *In this part, you will have 15 minutes to go over the passage quickly and answer the questions on* **Answer Sheet 1**. *For questions 1 – 7, choose the best answer from the four choices marked A), B), C) and D). For questions 8 – 10, complete the sentences with the information given in the passage.*

Seven Ways to Save the World

Forget the old idea that conserving energy is a form of self-denial — riding bicycles, dimming the lights, and taking fewer showers. These days conservation is all about efficiency: getting the same — or better — results from just a fraction of the energy. When a slump in business travel forced Ulrich Römer to cut costs at his family-owned hotel in Germany, he replaced hundreds of the hotel's wasteful light bulbs, getting the same light for 80 percent less power. He bought a new water boiler with a digitally controlled pump, and wrapped insulation around the pipes. Spending about 100,000 on these and other improvements, he slashed his 90,000 fuel and power bill by 60,000. As a bonus, the hotel's lower energy needs have reduced its annual carbon emissions by more than 200 metric tons. "For us, saving energy has been very, very profitable," he says. "And most importantly, we're not giving up a single comfort for our guests."

Efficiency is also a great way to lower carbon emissions and help slow global warming. But the best argument for efficiency is its cost — or, more precisely, its profitability. That's because quickly growing energy demand requires immense investment in new supply, not to mention the drain of rising energy prices.

No wonder efficiency has moved to the top of the political agenda. On Jan. 10, the European Union unveiled a plan to cut energy use across the continent by 20 percent by 2020. Last March, China imposed a 20 percent increase in energy efficiency by 2020. Even George W. Bush, the Texas oilman, is expected to talk about energy conservation in his State of the Union speech this week.

The good news is that the world is full of proven, cheap ways to save energy. Here are the seven that could have the biggest impact:

Insulate

Space heating and cooling eats up 36 percent of all the world's energy. There's virtually no limit to how much of that can be saved, as prototype "zero-energy homes" in Switzerland and Germany have shown. There's been a surge in new ways of keeping heat in and cold out (or vice versa). The most advanced insulation follows the law of increasing returns: if you add enough, you can scale down or even eliminate heating and air-conditioning equipment, lowering costs even before you start saving on utility bills. Studies have shown that green workplaces (ones that don't constantly need to have the heat or air-conditioner running) have higher worker productivity and lower sick rates.

Change Bulbs

Lighting eats up 20 percent of the world's electricity, or the equivalent of roughly 600,000 tons of coal a day. Forty percent of that powers old-fashioned incandescent light bulbs — a 19th-century technology that wastes most of the power it consumes on unwanted heat.

Compact fluorescent lamps, or CFLs, not only use 75 to 80 percent less electricity than incandescent bulbs to generate the same amount of light, but they also last 10 times longer. Phasing old bulbs out by 2030 would save the output of 650 power plants and avoid the release of 700 million tons of carbon into the atmosphere each year.

Comfort Zone

Water boilers, space heaters and air conditioners have been notoriously inefficient. The heat pump has altered that equation. It removes heat from the air outside or the ground below and uses it to supply heat to a building or its water supply. In the summer, the system can be reversed to cool buildings as well.

Most new residential buildings in Sweden are already heated with ground-source heat pumps. Such systems consume almost no conventional fuel at all. Several countries have used subsidies to jump-start the market, including Japan, where almost 1 million heat pumps have been installed in the past two years to heat water for showers and hot tubs.

Remake Factories

From steel mills to paper factories, industry eats up about a third of the world's energy. The opportunities to save are vast. In Ludwigshafen, German chemicals giant BASF runs an interconnected complex of more than 200 chemical factories, where heat produced by one chemical process is used to power the next. At the Ludwigshafen site alone, such recycling of heat and energy saves the company € 200 million a year and almost half its CO_2 emissions. Now BASF is doing the same for new plants in China. "Optimizing(优化) energy efficiency is a decisive competitive advantage," says BASF CEO Jürgen Hambrecht.

Green Driving

A quarter of the world's energy — including two thirds of the annual production of oil — is used for transportation. Some savings come free of charge: you can boost fuel efficiency by 6 percent simply by keeping your car's tires properly inflated(充气). Gasoline-electric hybrid(混合型的) models like the Toyota Prius improve mileage by a further 20 percent over conventional models.

A Better Fridge

More than half of all residential power goes into running household appliances, producing a fifth of the world's carbon emissions. And that's true even though manufacturers have already hiked the efficiency of refrigerators and other white goods by as much as 70 percent since the 1980s. According to an International Energy Agency study, if consumers chose those models that

would save them the most money over the life of the appliance, they'd cut global residential power consumption (and their utility bills) by 43 percent.

Flexible Payent

Who says you have to pay for all your conservation investments? "Energy service contractors" will pay for retrofitting（翻新改造）in return for a share of the client's annual utility-bill savings. In Beijing, Shenwu Thermal Energy Technology Co. specializes in retrofitting China's steel furnaces. Shenwu puts up the initial investment to install a heat exchanger that preheats the air going into the furnace, slashing the client's fuel costs. Shenwu pockets a cut of those savings, so both Shenwu and the client profit.

If saving energy is so easy and profitable, why isn't everyone doing it? It has to do with psychology and a lack of information. Most of us tend to look at today's price tag more than tomorrow's potential savings. That holds double for the landlord or developer, who won't actually see a penny of the savings his investment in better insulation or a better heating system might generate. In many people's minds, conservation is still associated with self-denial. Many environmentalists still push that view.

Smart governments can help push the market in the right direction. The EU's 1994 law on labeling was such a success that it extended the same idea to entire buildings last year. To boost the market value of efficiency, all new buildings are required to have an "energy pass" detailing power and heating consumption. Countries like Japan and Germany have successively tightened building codes, requiring an increase in insulation levels but leaving it up to builders to decide how to meet them.

The most powerful incentives, of course, will come from the market itself. Over the past year, sky-high fuel prices have focused minds on efficiency like never before. Ever-increasing pressure to cut costs has finally forced more companies to do some math on their energy use.

Will it be enough? With global demand and emissions rising so fast, we may not have any choice but to try. Efficient technology is here now, proven and cheap. Compared with all other options, it's the biggest, easiest and most profitable bang for the buck.

1. What is said to be the best way to conserve energy nowadays?
   A) Raising efficiency.   B) Cutting unnecessary costs.
   C) Finding alternative resources.   D) Sacrificing some personal comforts.
2. What does the European Union plan to do?
   A) Diversify energy supply.   B) Cut energy consumption.
   C) Reduce carbon emissions.   D) Raise production efficiency.
3. If you add enough insulation to your house, you may be able to _____.
   A) improve your work environment   B) cut your utility bills by half
   C) get rid of air-conditioners   D) enjoy much better health
4. How much of the power consumed by incandescent bulbs is converted into light?
   A) A small protion.   B) Some 40 percent.
   C) Almost half.   D) 75 to 80 percent.
5. Some countries have tried to jump-start the market of heat pumps by _____.
   A) upgrading the equipment   B) encouraging investments
   C) implementing high-tech   D) providing subsidies
6. German chemicals giant BASF saves 200 million a year by _____.

A) recycling heat and energy   B) setting up factories in China

C) using the newest technology   D) reducing the CO_2 emissions of its plants

7. Global residential power consumption can be cut by 43 percent if _____.

A) we increase the insulation of walls and water pipes

B) we choose simpler models of electrical appliances

C) we cut down on the use of refrigerators and other white goods

D) we choose the most efficient models of refrigerators and other white goods

8. Energy service contractors profit by taking a part of clients' _____.

9. Many environmentalists maintain the view that conservation has much to do with _____.

10. The strongest incentives for energy conservation will derive from _____.

Part Ⅲ   Listening Comprehension   (35 minutes)
Section A

Directions: *In this section, you will hear 8 short conversations and 2 long conversations. At the end of each conversation, one or more questions will be asked about what was said. Both the conversation and the questions will be spoken only once. After each question there will be a pause. During the pause, you must read the four choices marked A), B), C) and D), and decide which is the best answer. Then mark the corresponding letter on **Answer Sheet 2** with a single line through the centre.*

11. A) Proceed in his own way.   B) Stick to the original plan.

     C) Compromise with his colleague.   D) Try to change his colleague's mind.

12. A) Mary has a keen eye for style.

B) Nancy regrets buying the dress.

C) Nancy and Mary went shopping together in Rome.

D) Nancy and Mary like to follow the latest fashion.

13. A) Wash the dishes.   B) Go to the theatre.

     C) Pick up George and Martha.   D) Take her daughter to hospital.

14. A) She enjoys making up stories about other people.

B) She can never keep anything to herself for long.

C) She is eager to share news with the woman.

D) She is the best informed woman in town.

15. A) A car dealer.   B) A mechanic.

     C) A driving examiner.   D) A technical consultant.

16. A) The shopping mall has been deserted recently.

B) Shoppers can only find good stores in the mall.

C) Lots of people moved out of the downtown area.

D) There isn't much business downtown nowadays.

17. A) He will help the woman with her reading.

B) The lounge is not a place for him to study in.

C) He feels sleepy whenever he tries to study.

D) A cozy place is rather hard to find on campus.

18. A) To protect her from getting scratches.   B) To help relieve her of the pain.

     C) To prevent mosquito bites.   D) To avoid getting sunburnt.

Questions 19 to 22 are based on the conversation you have just heard.

19. A) In a studio.   B) In a clothing store.
    C) At a beach resort.   D) At a fashion show.
20. A) To live there permanently.   B) To stay there for half a year.
    C) To find a better job to support herself.   D) To sell leather goods for a British company.
21. A) Designing fashion items for several companies.
    B) Modeling for a world-famous Italian company.
    C) Working as an employee for Ferragamo.
    D) Serving as a sales agent for Burberrys.
22. A) It has seen a steady decline in its profits.
    B) It has become much more competitive.
    C) It has lost many customers to foreign companies.
    D) It has attracted a lot more designers from abroad.

Questions 23 to 25 are based on the conversation you have just heard.

23. A) It helps her to attract more public attention.
    B) It improves her chance of getting promoted.
    C) It strengthens her relationship with students.
    D) It enables her to understand people better.
24. A) Passively.   B) Positively.
    C) Skeptically.   D) Sensitively.
25. A) It keeps haunting her day and night.
    B) Her teaching was somewhat affected by it.
    C) It vanishes the moment she step into her role.
    D) Her mind goes blank once she gets on the stage.

Section B

Directions: *In this section, you will hear 3 short passages. At the end of each passage, you will hear some questions. Both the passage and the questions will be spoken only once. After you hear a question, you must choose the best answer from the four choices marked A), B), C) and D). Then mark the corresponding letter on **Answer Sheet 2** with a single line through the centre.*

Passage One
Questions 26 to 29 are based on the passage you have just heard.

26. A) To win over the majority of passengers from airlines in twenty years.
    B) To reform railroad management in western European countries.
    C) To electrify the railway lines between major European cities.
    D) To set up an express train network throughout Europe.
27. A) Major European airlines will go bankrupt.
    B) Europeans will pay much less for traveling.
    C) Traveling time by train between major European cities will be cut by half.
    D) Trains will become the safest and most efficient means of travel in Europe.
28. A) Train travel will prove much more comfortable than air travel.
    B) Passengers will feel much safer on board a train than on a plane.
    C) Rail transport will be environmentally friendlier than air transport.

D) Traveling by train may be as quick as, or even quicker than, by air.

29. A) In 1981.
    B) In 1989.
    C) In 1990.
    D) In 2000.

Passage Two

Questions 30 to 32 are based on the passage you have just heard.

30. A) There can be no speedy recovery for mental patients.
    B) Approaches to healing patients are essentially the same.
    C) The mind and body should be taken as an integral whole.
    D) There is no clear division of labor in the medical profession.

31. A) A doctor's fame strengthens the patients' faith in them.
    B) Abuse of medicines is widespread in any urban hospitals.
    C) One third of the patients depend on harmless substances for cure.
    D) A patient's expectations of a drug have an effect on their recovery.

32. A) Expensive drugs may not prove the most effective.
    B) The workings of the mind may help patients recover.
    C) Doctors often exaggerate the effect of their remedies.
    D) Most illnesses can be cured without medication.

Passage Three

Questions 33 to 35 are based on the passage you have just heard.

33. A) Enjoying strong feelings and emotions.
    B) Defying all dangers when they have to.
    C) Being fond of making sensational news.
    D) Dreaming of becoming famous one day.

34. A) Working in an emergency room.
    B) Watching horror movies.
    C) Listening to rock music.
    D) Doing daily routines.

35. A) A rock climber.
    B) A psychologist.
    C) A resident doctor.
    D) A career consultant.

Section C

Directions: *In this section, you will hear a passage three times. When the passage is read for the first time, you should listen carefully for its general idea. When the passage is read for the second time, you are required to fill in the blanks numbered from 36 to 43 with the exact words you have just heard. For blanks numbered from 44 to 46 you are required to fill in the missing information. For these blanks, you can either use the exact words you have just heard or write down the main points in your own words. Finally, when the passage is read for the third time, you should check what you have written.*

If you're like most people, you've indulged in fake listening many time. You go to history class, sit in the third row, and look (36)_____ at the instructor as she speaks. But your mind is far away, (37)_____ in the clouds of pleasant daydreams. (38)_____ you come back to earth: the instructor writes an important term on the chalkboard, and you (39)_____ copy it in your notebook. Every once in a while the instructor makes a (40)_____ remark, causing others in the class to laugh. You smile politely, pretending that you've heard the remark and found it mildly (41)_____. You have a vague sense of (42)_____ that you aren't paying

close attention, but you tell yourself that any (43)_____ you miss can be picked up from a friend's notes. Besides, (44)_____. So back you go into your private little world. Only later do you realize you've missed important information for a test.

Fake listening may be easily exposed, since many speakers are sensitive to facial cues and can tell if you're merely pretending to listen. (45)_____.

Even if you're not exposed, there's another reason to avoid fakery: it's easy for this behavior to become a habit. For some people, the habit is so deeply rooted that (46)_____. As a result, they miss lots of valuable information.

Part IV Reading Comprehension（Reading in Depth） (25 minutes)

Section A

Directions: *In this section, there is a short passage with 5 questions or incomplete statements. Read the passage carefully. Then answer the questions or complete the statements in the fewest possible words. Please write your answers on Answer Sheet 2.*

Questions 47 to 51 are based on the following passage.

Men, these days, are embracing fatherhood with the round-the-clock involvement their partners have always dreamed of — handling night feedings, packing lunches and bandaging knees. But unlike women, many find they're negotiating their new roles with little. "Men in my generation (aged 25 — 40) have a fear of becoming dads because we have no role models." says Jon Smith, a writer. They often find themselves excluded from mothers' support networks, and are eyed warily (警觉地) on the playground.

The challenge is particularly evident in the work-place. There, men are still expected to be breadwinners climbing the corporate ladder; traditionally-minded bosses are often unsympathetic to family needs. In Denmark most new fathers only take two weeks of paternity leave (父亲的陪产假) — even though they are allowed 34 days. As much as if not more so than women, fathers struggle to be taken seriously when they request flexible arrangements.

Though Wilfried-Fritz Maring, 54, a data-bank and Internet specialist with German firm FIZ Karlsruhe, feels that the time he spends with his daughter outweighs any disadvantages, he admits, "With my decision to work from home I dismissed any opportunity for promotion."

Mind-sets (思维定势)are changing gradually. When Maring had a daughter, the company equipped him with a home office and allowed him to choose a job that could be performed from there. Danish telecom company TDC initiated an internal campaign last year to encourage dads to take paternity leave: 97 percent now do. "When an employee goes on paternity leave and is with his kids, he gets a new kind of training: in how to keep cool under stress," says spokesperson Christine Elberg Holm. For a new generation of dads, kids may come before the company — but it's a shift that benefits both.

47. Unlike women, men often get little support or information from _____.

48. Besides supporting the family, men were also expected to _____.

49. Like women, men hope that their desire for a flexible schedule will be _____.

50. When Maring was on paternity leave, he was allowed by his company to work _____.
51. Christine Holm believes paternity leave provides a new kind of training for men in that it can help them cope with _____.

Section B

Directions: *There are 2 passages in this section. Each passage is followed by some questions or unfinished statements. For each of them there are four choices marked A), B), C) and D). You should decide on the best choice and mark the corresponding letter on **Answer Sheet 2** with a single line through the centre.*

Passage One

Questions 52 to 56 are based on the following passage.

Like most people, I've long understood that I will be judged by my occupation, that my profession is a gauge people use to see how smart or talented I am. Recently, however, I was disappointed to see that it also decides how I'm treated as a person.

Last year I left a professional position as a small-town reporter and took a job waiting tables. As someone paid to serve food to people, I had customers say and do things to me I suspect they'd never say or do to their most casual acquaintances. One night a man talking on his cell phone waved me away, then beckoned（示意）me back with his finger a minute later, complaining he was ready to order and asking where I'd been.

I had waited tables during summers in college and was treated like a peon（勤杂工）by plenty of people. But at 19 years old, I believed I deserved inferior treatment from professional adults. Besides, people responded to me differently after I told them I was in college. Customers would joke that one day I'd be sitting at their table, waiting to be served.

Once I graduated I took a job at a community newspaper. From my first day, I heard a respectful tone from everyone who called me. I assumed this was the way the professional world worked — cordially.

I soon found out differently. I sat several feet away from an advertising sales representative with a similar name. Our calls would often get mixed up and someone asking for Kristen would be transferred to Christie. The mistake was immediately evident. Perhaps it was because money was involved, but people used a tone with Kristen that they never used with me.

My job title made people treat me with courtesy. So it was a shock to return to the restaurant industry.

It's no secret that there's a lot to put up with when waiting tables, and fortunately, much of it can be easily forgotten when you pocket the tips. The service industry, by definition, exists to cater to other's needs. Still, it seemed that many of my customers didn't get the difference between server and servant.

I'm now applying to graduate school, which means someday I'll return to a profession where people need to be nice to me in order to get what they want. I think I'll take them to dinner first, and see how they treat someone whose only job is to serve them.

52. The author was disappointed to find that _____.
   A) one's position is used as a gauge to measure one's intelligence
   B) talented people like her should fail to get a respectable job
   C) one's occupation affects the way one is treated as a person
   D) professionals tend to look down upon manual workers

53. What does the author intend to say by the example in the second paragraph?
    A) Some customers simply show no respect to those who serve them.
    B) People absorbed in a phone conversation tend to be absent-minded.
    C) Waitresses are often treated by customers as casual acquaintances.
    D) Some customers like to make loud complaints for no reason at all.

54. How did the author feel when waiting tables at the age of 19?
    A) She felt it unfair to be treated as a mere servant by professionals.
    B) She felt badly hurt when her customers regarded her as a peon.
    C) She was embarrassed each time her customers joked with her.
    D) She found it natural for professionals to treat her as inferior.

55. What does the author imply by saying "... many of my customers didn't get the difference between server and servant" (Lines 3－4, Para. 7)?
    A) Those who cater to others' needs are destined to be looked down upon.
    B) Those working in the service industry shouldn't be treated as servants.
    C) Those serving others have to put up with rough treatment to earn a living.
    D) The majority of customers tend to look on a servant as a server nowadays.

56. The author says she'll one day take her clients to dinner in order to _____.
    A) see what kind of person they are
    B) experience the feeling of being served
    C) show her generosity towards people inferior to her
    D) arouse their a humble life

Passage Two
Questions 57 to 61 are based on the following passage.

What's hot for 2007 among the very rich? A $7.3 million diamond ring. A trip to Tanzania to hunt wild animals. Oh, and income inequality.

Sure, some leftish billionaires like George Soros have been railing against income inequality for years. But increasingly, centrist and right-wing billionaires are starting to worry about income inequality and the fate of the middle class.

In December. Mortimer Zuckerman wrote a column in *U. S. NEWS & World Report*, which he owns. "Our nation's core bargain with the middle class is disintegrating," lamented (哀叹) the 117th-richest man in America. "Most of our economic gains have gone to people at the very top of the income ladder. Average income for a household of people of working age, by contrast, has fallen five years in a row." He noted that "Tens of millions of Americans live in fear that a major health problem can reduce them to bankruptcy."

Wilbur Ross Jr. has echoed Zuckerman's anger over the bitter struggles faced by middle-class Americans. "It's an outrage that any American's life expectancy should be shortened simply because the company they worked for went bankrupt and ended health-care coverage." said the former chairman of the International Steel Group.

What's happening? The very rich are just as trendy as you and I, and can be so when it comes to politics and policy. Given the recent change of control in Congress, the popularity of measures like increasing the minimum wage, and efforts by California's governor to offer universal health care, these guys don't need their own personal weathermen to know which way the wind blows.

It's possible that plutocrats (有钱有势的人) are expressing solidarity with the struggling middle class as part of an effort to insulate themselves from confiscatory (没收性的) tax policies. But the prospect that income inequality will lead to higher taxes on the wealthy doesn't keep plutocrats up at night. They can live with that.

No, what they fear was that the political challenges of sustaining support for global economic integration will be more difficult in the United States because of what has happened to the distribution of income and economic insecurity.

In other words, if middle-class Americans continue to struggle financially as the ultrawealthy grow ever wealthier, it will be increasingly difficult to maintain political support for the free flow of goods, services, and capital across borders. And when the United States places obstacles in the way of foreign investors and foreign goods, it's likely to encourage reciprocal action abroad. For people who buy and sell companies, or who allocate capital to markets all around the world, that's the real nightmare.

57. What is the current topic of common interest among the very rich in America?
    A) The fate of the ultrawealthy people.
    B) The disintegration of the middle class.
    C) The inequality in the distribution of wealth.
    D) The conflict between the left and the right wing.
58. What do we learn from Mortimer Zuckerman's lamentation?
    A) Many middle-income families have failed to make a bargain for better welfare.
    B) The American economic system has caused many companies to go bankrupt.
    C) The American nation is becoming more and more divided despite its wealth.
    D) The majority of Americans benefit little from the nation's growing wealth.
59. From the fifth paragraph we can learn that _____.
    A) the very rich are fashion-conscious
    B) the very rich are politically sensitive
    C) universal health care is to be implemented throughout America
    D) Congress has gained popularity by increasing the minimum wage
60. What is the real reason for plutocrats to express solidarity with the middle class?
    A) They want to protect themselves from confiscatory taxation.
    B) They know that the middle class contributes most to society.
    C) They want to gain support for global economic integration.
    D) They feel increasingly threatened by economic insecurity.
61. What may happen if the United States places obstacles in the way of foreign investors and foreign goods?
    A) The prices of imported goods will inevitably soar beyond control.
    B) The investors will have to make great efforts to re-allocate capital.
    C) The wealthy will attempt to buy foreign companies across borders.
    D) Foreign countries will place the same economic barriers in return.

Part Ⅴ Cloze (15 minutes)

Directions: *There are 20 blanks in the following passage. For each blank there are four choices marked A), B), C) and D) on the right side of the paper. You should choose the ONE that best fits into the passage. Then mark the corresponding letter on **Answer Sheet 2** with a single line through the centre.*

In 1915 Einstein made a trip to Göttingen to give some lectures at the invitation of the mathematical physicist David Hilbert. He was particularly eager — too eager, it would turn __62__ — to explain all the intricacies of relativity to him. The visit was a triumph, and he said to a friend excitedly, "I was able to __63__ Hilbert of the general theory of relativity."

__64__ all of Einstein's personal turmoil (焦躁) at the time, a new scientific anxiety was about to __65__. He was struggling to find the right equations

that would __66__ his new concept of gravity,

__67__ that would define how objects move

__68__ space and how space is curved by objects. By

the end of the summer, he __69__ the mathematical

approach he had been __70__ for almost three years

was flawed. And now there was a __71__ pressure.

Einstein discovered to his __72__ that Hilbert had taken what he had learned from Einstein's lectures and was racing to come up __73__ the correct equations first.

It was an enormously complex task. Although Einstein was the better physicist, Hilbert was the better mathematician. So in October 1915 Einstein __74__

himself into a month-long frantic endeavor in __75__ he returned to an earlier mathematical strategy and wrestled with equations, proofs, correction and updates that he __76__ to give as lectures to Berlin's

Prussian Academy of Sciences on four __77__ Thursdays.

His first lecture was delivered on Nov. 4, 1915, and it explained his new approach, __78__ he admitted he did not yet have the precise mathematical formulation of it. Einstein also took time off from __79__ revising his equations to engage in an awkward

62. A) up B) over
    C) out D) off

63. A) convince B) counsel
    C) persuade D) preach

64. A) Above B) Around
    C) Amid D) Along

65. A) emit B) emerge
    C) submit D) submerge

66. A) imitate B) ignite
    C) describe D) ascribe

67. A) ones B) those
    C) all D) none

68. A) into B) beyond
    C) among D) through

69. A) resolved B) realized
    C) accepted D) assured

70. A) pursuing B) protecting
    C) contesting D) contending

71. A) complex B) compatible
    C) comparative D) competitive

72. A) humor B) horror
    C) excitement D) extinction

73. A) to B) for
    C) with D) against

74. A) threw B) thrust
    C) huddled D) hopped

75. A) how B) that
    C) what D) which

76. A) dashed B) darted
    C) rushed D) reeled

77. A) successive B) progressive
    C) extensive D) repetitive

78. A) so B) since
    C) though D) because

79. A) casually B) coarsely

fandango（方丹戈双人舞）with his competitor Hilbert.
Worried __80__ being scooped（抢先）, he sent Hilbert

a copy of his Nov. 4 lecture. "I am __81__ to know whether you will take kindly to this new solution," Einstein noted with a touch of defensiveness.

C) violently   D) furiously

80. A) after   B) about
    C) on   D) in
81. A) curious   B) conscious
    C) ambitious   D) ambiguous

Part Ⅵ   Translation   (5 minutes)

Directions: *Complete the sentences by translating into English the Chinese given in brackets. Please write your translation on Answer Sheet 2.*

82. But for mobile phones, _____（我们的通信就不可能如此迅速和方便）.

83. In handling an embarrassing situation, _____（没有什么比幽默感更有帮助的了）.

84. The Foreign Minister said he was resigning, _____（但他拒绝进一步解释这样做的原因）.

85. Human behavior is mostly a product of learning, _____（而动物的行为主要依靠本能）.

86. The witness was told that under no circumstances _____（他都不应该对法庭说谎）.

2007 年 12 月大学英语六级（新题型）试题答案与解析

Part Ⅰ
Sample Writing

The Digital Age

With the rapid advances in computer science and digital technology, a wide range of digital products, especially electronic gadgets, have made their way into our life, such as DVD, notebook computer, multi-function cell phone, MP4, digicam, and digital TV ect. We are entering a brand-new era — the Digital Age, also known as Information Age or Wireless Age.

All these digital products are coming together to shape the future in virtually every sphere of our lives. As a matter of fact, the way we work, communicate, shop and entertain ourselves is already undergoing some fundamental changes. The good news is that our life is getting increasingly convenient and colorful. For example, email, broadband and the Internet enable people to work at home, giving them flexible working hours; Digital TV and set-top boxes bring multi-channel programs into our home; With digital libraries, we have quick access to information in front of our PC; Instead of meeting face to face, young people enjoy developing virtual friendship with strangers in cyberspace; Lovers keep in touch through text-messages; And housewives can get their groceries through online shopping.

On the other hand, our digital age is still in its infancy, which means a number of critical issues that impact our lives negatively are yet to be solved. How to prevent teenagers getting addicted to online games? How to protect Internet users' privacy? How to control computer-assisted criminal activities such as identity theft? We believe that, with the maturation of information and communication technology, we will be able to make a wiser use of digital products and enjoy their enormous benefits.

Part Ⅱ

1. ［A］ 参见第一段第二句：These days conservation is all about efficiency: getting the same — or better — results from just a fraction of the energy.（现如今环保就是关于能源使用效率：从少量能源中获得同样或更多的东西。）故当今节能的最佳方式就是提高能源使用效率（raising efficiency）。

2. ［B］ 参见第三段第二句：...the European Union unveiled a plan to cut energy use across the continent by 20 percent by 2020.（欧盟推出计划拟在 2020 年前将欧洲大陆的能源使用削减 20%。）

3. ［C］ 参见"Insulate"部分第四句：The most advanced insulation follows the law of increasing returns（最先进的密封装置遵循收益递增法则）：if you add enough（insulation）, you can scale down（减少）or even eliminate heating and air-conditioning equipment.

4. ［B］ 参见"Change Bulbs"部分第一段：Lighting eats up to... Forty percent of that powers old-fashioned incandescent light bulbs... on unwanted heat.（照明消耗近 20% 的世界能源，大约相当于一天 600,000 吨煤。其中 40% 的能量用于老式白炽灯泡发光——这项 19 世纪的科技发明将大部分能源浪费在产生不必要的热量上。）故白炽灯所耗能源中只有 40% 转化为光能。

5. ［D］ 参见"Comfort Zone"部分第二段第三句：Several countries have used subsidies to jump-start the market...（使用政府津贴启动热泵市场……）

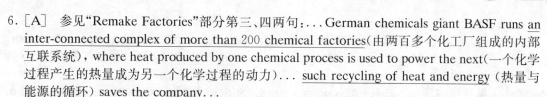

6. ［A］ 参见"Remake Factories"部分第三、四两句：...German chemicals giant BASF runs an inter-connected complex of more than 200 chemical factories（由两百多个化工厂组成的内部互联系统），where heat produced by one chemical process is used to power the next（一个化学过程产生的热量成为另一个化学过程的动力）...such recycling of heat and energy（热量与能源的循环）saves the company...

7. ［D］ 参见"A Better Fridge"部分第二、三句：...manufacturers have already hiked the efficiency of refrigerators and other white goods（提高了冰箱与其他大型家电的能量使用效率）...If consumers choose those models that would save them the most money（选择省钱型家电）...they'd cut global residential power consumption（削减全球民用能耗）by 43 percent.

8. annual utility-bill savings 参见"Flexible Payment"部分第二句："Energy service contractors" will pay for retrofitting in return for a share of the client's annual utility-bill savings.

9. self-denial 参见倒数第四段最后两句：In many people's minds, conservation is still associated with self-denial. Many environmentalists still push the idea（推广此想法）. self-denial,自我剥夺,即拒绝使用能耗设备。

10. the market itself 参见倒数第二段第一句：The most powerful incentives（节能激励措施），of course，will come from the market itself.

Part Ⅲ

11. C 12. B 13. A 14. C 15. B
16. D 17. B 18. C 19. A 20. B
21. A 22. B 23. D 24. B 25. C
26. D 27. C 28. D 29. A 30. C
31. D 32. B 33. A 34. D 35. B

36. squarely 37. floating 38. Occasionally 39. dutifully
40. witty 41. humorous 42. guilt 43. material

44. the instructor's talking about road construction in ancient Rome, and nothing could be more boring

45. Your blank expression, and the faraway look in your eyes are the cues that betray you inattentiveness

46. they automatically start daydreaming when a speaker begins talking on something complex or uninteresting

Part Ⅳ

47. mother's support network 参见第一段第二句和最后一句：But unlike women, many (men) find they're negotiating their new roles（适应他们的新角色）with little. They often find themselves excluded from mothers' support network（被排除在母亲互助网之外）...

48. climb the corporate ladder 参见第二段第一、二句：...men are still expected to be breadwinners climbing the corporate ladder（人们仍期望男人去挣钱养家,在职场上向上爬）...

49. taken seriously 参见第二段最后一句：As much as if not more so than women（如果待遇不能超过妇女,至少也要同女人们一样），fathers struggle to be taken seriously when they request flexible arrangements（父亲们希望拥有灵活的工作安排,并努力争取这一请求得到认真对待）.

50. in a home office 参见最后一段第二句：When Maring had a daughter, the company equipped him with a home office（为他配备了家庭办公室）and allowed him to choose a job that

could be performed from there.

51. stress 参见最后一段倒数第二句: When an employee goes on paternity leave and is with kids, he gets a new kind of training in how to keep cool under stress(得到一种如何在压力下保持镇定的新培训)...

52. [C] 参见第一段: ... my profession is a gauge(衡量标准)people use to see how smart or talented I am. Recently, however, I was disappointed to see it(my occupation)also decides how I'm treated as a person.故选 C(作者失望地发现你的职业会影响你作为一个人的待遇)。

53. [A] 第二段作者叙述自己做餐厅服务生时的"屈辱"待遇: I had customers say and do things to me I suspect they'd never say or do to their most casual acquaintances.(有些客人对我说的话和做的事十分过分,就是对待最普通的熟人他们也不至于那样。)可见,由于侍者职业地位卑微,客人对他们毫不尊重。故选 A。

54. [D] 参见第三段第一、二句: I had waited tables during summers in college and was treated like a peon(被当做勤杂工对待)... But at 19 years old, I believed I deserved inferior treatment from professional adults(但我才19岁,年少无知,觉得自己理应受到有事业的成年人的怠慢). 故选 D(作者19岁当侍者时,认为被专业人士当做下等人对待是很自然的事)。

55. [B] 根据倒数第二段第二、三句提到,服务性行业存在的目的是满足他人的需要。但是似乎许多客人并不清楚服务生与仆人之间的差异。由此可知,作者言外之意是就职于服务性行业的人不应被当做仆人对待。

56. [A] 最后一段提到,我正申请攻读研究生,这意味着将来的职业受人尊重,人们需要讨好我才能获得自己所需。这时我会先带那些有求于我的人去饭店用餐,根据他们对待服务生的态度再作决定。故选 A,作者带客户去饭店的目的是看对方是什么样的人(根据其对侍者的态度)。

57. [C] 参见第一段: What's hot for 2007 among the very rich? ... Oh, and income inequality. (2007年大富豪中间最热门的话题是什么? ……噢,还有收入的不平等。)故选 C(美国大富豪们共同的兴趣话题是财富分配的不平等)。

58. [C] 根据第三段可知,Moritimer Zuckerman 感叹道:"我们这个民族与中产阶级的核心协定(core bargain)正在瓦解。大部分经济收益都进了最富有阶层的腰包。普通家庭的平均收入已连续下降了五年。"由此可知,美国富人越来越富有,普通人收入越来越少,故选 C(根据 Moritimer Zuckerman 的感叹可知,美国尽管物质丰富,人们贫富差异却越来越大)。

59. [B] 第五段提到,富豪们像你我一样爱赶时髦,在政治与政策问题上也是如此。国会控制权近来发生变化、提高最低工资等措施开始普及、加州州长努力让人人享有医疗保健,在这些政策变化环境下,这些家伙(富豪们)无需私人气象员也能辨清风向。由此可知,富豪们对政治气候变化十分敏感。

60. [C] 参见第六、七、八段:富豪们表示与困境中的中产阶级加强团结,其部分目的可能是为了自我保护,将自己与无收益税收政策隔离开来(insulate themselves from confiscatory tax-policies)。但是收入不平等导致富人交纳更多的税,这样的前景他们也还可以容忍,并没使他们寝食难安。他们真正害怕的是:由于收入分配的不平等与缺乏经济安全感,维持对全球经济一体化的支持(sustaining support for global economic integration)在美国成为更加严峻的政治挑战。换言之,如果中产阶级继续挣扎于经济困境中而富豪们却越来越富,就更难从政治上继续支持不同国家间货物、服务与资本的自由流动。故选 C(富豪们要与中产阶层加强团结的真正原因是他们想赢得对全球经济一体化的支持)。

61. [D] 参见最后一段最后两句:如果美国对国外投资者及其产品设置障碍,必然导致外商以其人之道还治其人之身(reciprocal actions abroad)。故选 D(如果美国为其他国家的投资商或商品设置障碍,其他国家的也会同样设置经济障碍加以报复)。

Part V

62. [C] too eager, it would turn out — to explain... 结果看来实在是太迫切了——急于解释……turn up 出现；turn off 关闭；turn over 翻转。

63. [A] convince Hilbert of... 说服 Hilbert 相信……

64. [C] Amid all of Einstein's personal turmoil at the time 在爱因斯坦当时所处的各种焦躁之中。介词 amid 表示"在……之中"，后常接抽象名词。

65. [B] a new scientific anxiety was about to emerge 一场新的科学探讨上的焦虑即将产生。emerge vi. 出现；emit vt. 释放（烟雾气体等）；submit vt. 递交；submerge v. （使）浸没

66. [C] the right equations that would describe his new concept of gravity 可对他的重力新概念加以描述的正确等式。imitate 模仿；ignite 点燃，引燃；ascribe...to... 将……归因于……

67. [A] ones 替代前文的 equations，表泛指。

68. [D] how objects move through space 物体如何穿越太空。

69. [B] he realized 他意识到……

70. [A] the mathematical approach he had been pursuing for almost three years was flawed（意识到）自己三年以来一直努力尝试的数学研究方式存在缺陷。contend（for sth）vi. 奋争；contest n./vi. 争夺；比赛。

71. [D] there was a competitive pressure 存在竞争压力；compatible 相容的；complex 复杂的；comparative 相对的

72. [B] Einstein discovered to his horror that Hilbert had taken what he had learned from Einstein's lectures and 爱因斯坦发现 Hilbert 已汲取了自己讲座中的知识……（正努力赶超），这令他十分害怕。

73. [C] come up with the correct equations 提出正确的等式，固定搭配。

74. [A] threw himself into a month-long frantic endeavor 全身心投入了一个月之久的疯狂努力之中，固定搭配。hop v. 单脚跳；thrust v. 猛推，猛塞；huddle v. （使）挤作一团

75. [D] a month-long frantic endeavor in which he returned to...，定语从句关系代词。

76. [C] rushed to do sth = hurried to do sth 匆忙做某事。dart vi. 猛冲；dash vi. 冲刺；reel vi. 蹒跚，踉跄。

77. [A] four successive Thursdays 连续四个星期四。

78. [C] though he admitted 尽管他承认……，上下文逻辑关系。

79. [D] furiously revising his equations 奋力修正他的等式；furiously adv. 疯狂地；casually adv. 随便地；violently adv. 狂暴地；coarsely adv. 粗糙地

80. [B] worried about being scooped 担心被抢先

81. [A] I am curious to know... 很好奇地想知道……

Part VI

82. our communication would not have been so efficient and convenient

83. nothing is more helpful than humor/a sense of humor

84. but (he) refused to make further explanation/to further explain why

85. while animal behavior depends mainly upon/on their instinct(s)

86. should he lie to the court/is he allowed to lie to the court

2008 年 6 月大学英语六级(新题型)考试试题

Part Ⅰ　Writing　(30 minutes)

Directions：*For this part, you are allowed 30 minutes to write a short essay entitled **Will e-books replace traditional books**? You should write at least 150 words following the outline given below.*

Will e-books replace traditional books?

1. 随着信息技术的发展,电子图书越来越多
2. 有人认为电子图书将会取代传统图书,理由是……
3. 我的看法

Part Ⅱ　Reading Comprehension (Skimming and Scanning) (15 minutes)

Directions：*In this part, you will have 15 minutes to go over the passage quickly and answer the questions on **Answer Sheet 1**. For questions 1 - 7, choose the best answer from the four choices marked A), B), C) and D). For questions 8 - 10, complete the sentences with the information given in the passage.*

What will the world be like in fifty years?

This week some top scientists, including Nobel Prize winners, gave their vision of how the world will look in 2056, from gas-powered cars to extraordinary health advances, John Ingham reports on what the world's finest minds believe our futures will be.

For those of us lucky enough to live that long, 2056 will be a world of almost perpetual youth, where obesity is a remote memory and robots become our companions.

We will be rubbing shoulders with aliens and colonising outer space. Better still, our descendants might at last live in a world at peace with itself.

The prediction is that we will have found a source of inexhaustible, safe, green energy, and that science will have killed off religion. If they are right we will have removed two of the main causes of war — our dependence on oil and religious prejudice.

Will we really, as today's scientists claim, be able to live for ever or at least cheat the ageing process so that the average person lives to 150?

Of course, all these predictions come with a scientific health warning. Harvard professor Steven Pinker says："This is an invitation to look foolish, as with the predictions of domed cities and nuclear-powered vacuum cleaners that were made 50 year ago."

Living longer

Anthony Atala, director of the Wake Forest Institute in North Carolina, believes failing organs will be repaired by injecting cells into the body. They will naturally go straight to the injury and help heal it. A system of injections without needles could also slow the ageing process by using the same process to "tune" cells.

Bruce Lahn, professor of human genetics at the University of Chicago, anticipates the ability to produce "unlimited supplies" of transplantable human organs without the need for human donors. These organs would be grown in animals such as pigs. When a patient needed a new organ, such as a kidney, the surgeon would contact a commercial organ producer, give him the patient's immuno-logical profile and would then be sent a kidney with the correct tissue type.

These organs would be entirely composed of human cells, grown by introducing them into animal hosts, and allowing them to develop into an organ in place of the animal's own. But Prof. Lahn believes that farmed brains would be "off limits". He says: "Very few people would want to have their brains replaced by someone else's and we probably don't want to put a human brain in an animal body."

Richard Miller, a professor at the University of Michigan, thinks scientists could develop "an thentic anti-ageing drugs" by working out how cells in larger animals such as whales and humans resist many forms of injuries. He says: "It is now routine, in laboratory mammals, to extend lifespan by about 40%. Turning on the same protective systems in people should, by 2056, create the first class of 100-year-olds who are as vigorous and productive as today's people in their 60s."

Aliens

Colin Pillinger, professor of planetary sciences at the Open University, says: "I fancy that at least we will be able to show that life did start to evolve on Mars as well as Earth." Within 50 years he hopes scientists will prove that alien life came here in Martian meteorites(陨石).

Chris McKay, a planetary scientist at NASA's Ames Research Center, believes that in 50 years we may find evidence of alien life in the ancient permanent frost of Mars or on other planers.

He adds: "There is even a chance we will find alien life forms here on Earth. It might be as different as English is to Chinese."

Princeton professor Freeman Dyson thinks it "likely" that life from outer space will be discovered before 2056 because the tools for finding it, such as optical and radio detection and data processing, are improving.

He says: "As soon as the first evidence is found, we will know what to look for and additional discoveries are likely to follow quickly. Such discoveries are likely to have revolutionary consequences for biology, astronomy and philosophy. They may also change the way we look at ourselves and our place in the universe."

Colonies in space

Richard Gott, professor of astrophysics at Princeton, hopes man will set up a self-sufficient colony on Mars, which would be a "life insurance policy against whatever catastrophes, natural or otherwise, might occur on Earth.

"The real space race is whether we will colonise off Earth on to other worlds before money for the space programme runs out."

Spinal injuries

Ellen Heber-Katz, a professor at the Wistar Institute in Philadelphia, foresees cures for injuries causing paralysis such as the one that afflicted Superman star Christopher Reeve.

She says: "I believe that the day is not far off when we will be able to prescribe drugs that cause severed(断裂的) spinal cords to heal, hearts to regenerate and lost limbs to regrow.

"People will come to expect that injured or diseased organs are meant to be repaired from within, in much the same way that we fix an appliance or automobile: by replacing the damaged part with a manufacturer-certified new part." She predicts that within 5 to 10 years fingers and toes will be regrown and limbs will start to be regrown a few years later. Repairs to the nervous

system will start with optic nerves and, in time, the spinal cord. "Within 50 years whole body replacement will be routine," Prof. Heber-Katz adds.

Obesity

Sydney Brenner, senior distinguished fellow of the Crick-Jacobs Center in California, won the 2002 Nobel Prize for Medicine and says that if there is a global disaster some humans will survive — and evolution will favour small people with bodies large enough to support the required amount of brain power. "Obesity," he says. "will have been solved."

Robots

Rodney Brooks, professor of robotics at MIT, says the problems of developing artificial intelligence for robots will be at least partly overcome. As a result, "the possibilities for robots working with people will open up immensely".

Energy

Bill Joy, green technology expert in California, says: "The most significant breakthrough would be to have an inexhaustible source of safe, green energy that is substantially cheaper than any existing energy source."

Ideally, such a source would be safe in that it could not be made into weapons and would not make hazardous or toxic waste or carbon dioxide, the main greenhouse gas blamed for global warming.

Society

Geoffrey Miller, evolutionary psychologist at the University of New Mexico, says: "The US will follow the UK in realising that religion is not a prerequisite (前提) for ordinary human decency.

"Thus, science will kill religion — not by reason challenging faith but by offering a more practical, universal and rewarding moral framework for human interaction."

He also predicts that "absurdly wasteful" displays of wealth will become unfashionable while the importance of close-knit communities and families will become clearer.

These three changes, he says, will help make us all "brighter, wiser, happier and kinder".

1. What is John Ingham's report about?
   A) A solution to the global energy crisis.
   B) Extraordinary advances in technology.
   C) The latest developments of medical science.
   D) Scientists' vision of the world in half a century.
2. According to Harvard professor Steven Pinker, predictions about the future _____.
   A) may invite trouble   B) may not come true
   C) will fool the public   D) do more harm than good
3. Professor Bruce Lahn of the University of Chicago predicts that _____.
   A) humans won't have to donate organs for transplantation
   B) more people will donate their organs for transplantation
   C) animal organs could be transplanted into human bodies
   D) organ transplantation won't be as scary as it is today
4. According to professor Richard Miller of the University of Michigan, people will _____.

A) live for as long as they wish B) be relieved from all sufferings
C) live to 100 and more with vitality D) be able to live longer than whales

5. Priceton professor Freeman Dyson thinks that _____.
A) scientists will find alien life similar to ours
B) humans will be able to settle on Mars
C) alien life will likely be discovered
D) life will start to evolve on Mars

6. According to Princeton professor Richard Gott, by setting up a self-sufficient colony on Mars, humans _____.
A) might survive all catastrophes on earth
B) might acquire ample natural resources
C) will be able to travel to Mars freely
D) will move there to live a better life

7. Ellen Heber-Katz, professor at the Wistar Institute in Philadelphia, predicts that _____.
A) human organs can be manufactured like appliances
B) people will be as strong and dynamic as supermen
C) human nerves can be replaced by optic fibers
D) lost fingers and limbs will be able to regrow

8. Rodney Brooks says that it will be possible for robots to work with humans as a result of the development of _____.

9. The most significant breakthrough predicted by Bill Joy will be an inexhaustible green energy source that can't be used to make _____.

10. According to Geoffrey Miller, science will offer a more practical, universal and rewarding moral framework in place of _____.

Part III   Listening Comprehension   (35 minutes)
Section A
Directions: *In this section, you will hear 8 short conversations and 2 long conversations. At the end of each conversation, one or more questions will be asked about what was said. Both the conversation and the questions will be spoken only once. After each question there will be a pause. During the pause, you must read the four choices marked A), B), C) and D), and decide which is the best answer. Then mark the corresponding letter on Answer sheet 2 with a single line through the centre.*

11. A) The man might be able to play in the World Cup.
B) The man's football career seems to be at an end.
C) The man was operated on a few weeks ago.
D) The man is a fan of world-famous football players.

12. A) Work out a plan to tighten his budget.
B) Find out the opening hours of the cafeteria.
C) Apply for a senior position in the restaurant.
D) Solve his problem by doing a part-time job.

13. A) A financial burden. B) A good companion.
C) A real nuisance. D) A well-trained pet.

14. A) The errors will be corrected soon.
B) The woman was mistaken herself.

C) The computing system is too complex.

D) He has called the woman several times.

15. A) He needs help to retrieve his files.

B) He has to type his paper once more.

C) He needs some time to polish his paper.

D) He will be away for a two-week conference.

16. A) They might have to change their plan.

B) He has got everything set for their trip.

C) He has a heavier workload than the woman.

D) They could stay in the mountains until June 8.

17. A) They have to wait a month to apply for a student loan.

B) They can find the application forms in the brochure.

C) They are not eligible for a student loan.

D) They are not late for a loan application.

18. A) New laws are yet to be made to reduce pollutant release.

B) Pollution has attracted little attention from the public.

C) The quality of air will surely change for the better.

D) It'll take years to bring air pollution under control.

Questions 19 to 22 are based on the conversation you have just heard.

19. A) Enormous size of its stores.   B) Numberous varieties of food.

C) Its appealing surroundings.   D) Its rich and colorful history.

20. A) An ancient building.   B) A world of antiques.

C) An Egyptian museum.   D) An Egyptian memorial.

21. A) Its power bill reaches £9 million a year.

B) It sells thousands of light bulbs a day.

C) It supplies power to a nearby town.

D) It generates 70% of the electricity it uses.

22. A) 11,500.   B) 30,000.

C) 250,000.   D) 300,000.

Questions 23 to 25 are based on the conversation you have just heard.

23. A) Transferring to another department.

B) Studying accounting at a university.

C) Thinking about doing a different job.

D) Making preparations for her wedding.

24. A) She has finally got a promotion and a pay raise.

B) She has got a satisfactory job in another company.

C) She could at last leave the accounting department.

D) She managed to keep her position in the company.

25. A) He and Andrea have proved to be a perfect match.

B) He changed his mind about marriage unexpectedly.

C) He declared that he would remain single all his life.

D) He would marry Andrea even without meeting her.

Section B

Directions: *In this section, you will hear 3 short passages. At the end of each passage, you will hear some questions. Both the passage and the questions will be spoken only once. After you hear a question, you must choose the best answer from the four choices marked A), B), C) and D). Then mark the corresponding letter on* **Answer Sheet 2** *with a single line through the centre.*

Passage One

Questions 26 to 29 are based on the passage you have just heard.

26. A) They are motorcycles designated for water sports.
    B) They are speedy boats restricted in narrow waterways.
    C) They are becoming an efficient form of water transportation.
    D) They are getting more popular as a means of water recreation.

27. A) Waterscooter operators' lack of experience.
    B) Vacationers' disregard of water safety rules.
    C) Overloading of small boats and other craft.
    D) Carelessness of people boating along the shore.

28. A) They scare whales to death.   B) They produce too much noise.
    C) They discharge toxic emissions.   D) They endanger lots of water life.

29. A) Expand operating areas.   B) Restrict operating hours.
    C) Limit the use of waterscooters.   D) Enforce necessary regulations.

Passage Two

Questions 30 to 32 are based on the passage you have just heard.

30. A) They are stable.   B) They are close.
    C) They are strained.   D) They are changing.

31. A) They are fully occupied with their own business.
    B) Not many of them stay in the same place for long.
    C) Not many of them can win trust from their neighbors.
    D) They attach less importance to interpersonal relations.

32. A) Count on each other for help.   B) Give each other a cold shoulder.
    C) Keep a friendly distance.   D) Build a fence between them.

Passage Three

Questions 33 to 35 are based on the passage you have just heard.

33. A) It may produce an increasing number of idle youngsters.
    B) It may affect the quality of higher education in America.
    C) It may cause many schools to go out of operation.
    D) It may lead to a lack of properly educated workers.

34. A) It is less serious in cities than in rural areas.
    B) It affects both junior and senior high schools.
    C) It results from a worsening economic climate.
    D) It is a new challenge facing American educators.

35. A) Allowing them to choose their favorite teachers.
    B) Creating a more relaxed learning environment.
    C) Rewarding excellent academic performance.

2008 年 6 月大学英语六级（新题型）考试试题

D）Helping them to develop better study habits.

Section C

Directions： *In this section，you will hear a passage three times. When the passage is read for the first time，you should listen carefully for its general idea. When the passage is read for the second time，you are required to fill in the blanks numbered from 36 to 43 with the exact words you have just heard. For blanks numbered from 44 to 46 you are required to fill in the missing information. For these blanks，you can either use the exact words you have just heard or write down the main points in your own words. Finally，when the passage is read for the third time， you should check what you have written.*

I'm interested in the criminal justice system of our country. It seems to me that something has to be done，if we're to (36)＿＿＿＿ as a country. I certainly don't know what the answers to our problems are. Things certainly get (37)＿＿＿＿ in a hurry when you get into them，but I wonder if something couldn't be done to deal with some of these problems. One thing I'm concerned about is our practice of putting (38)＿＿＿＿ in jail who haven't harmed anyone. Why not work out some system (39)＿＿＿＿ they can pay back the debts they owe society instead of (40)＿＿＿＿ another debt by going to prison and，of course，coming under the (41)＿＿＿＿ of hardened criminals. I'm also concerned about the short prison sentences people are (42)＿＿＿＿ for serious crimes. Of course，one alternative to this is to (43)＿＿＿＿ capital punishment，but I'm not sure I would be for that. I'm not sure it's right to take an eye for eye. (44)＿＿＿＿＿＿＿＿＿＿＿＿ .

I also think we must do something about the insanity plea. In my opinion，anyone who takes another person's life intentionally is insane；however，(45)＿＿＿＿＿＿＿＿＿＿＿＿ . It's sad，of course，that a person may have to spend the rest of his life，or (46)＿＿＿＿＿＿＿＿＿＿

＿＿

Part Ⅳ   Reading Comprehension（Reading in Depth） （25 minutes）

Section A

Directions： *In this section，there is a short passage with 5 questions or incomplete statements. Read the passage carefully. Then answer the questions or complete the statements in the fewest possible words. Please write your answers on **Answer Sheet 2***

Questions 47 to 51 are based on the following passage.

If movie trailers（预告片）are supposed to cause a reaction，the preview for "United 93" more than succeeds. Featuring no famous actors，it begins with images of a beautiful morning and passengers boarding an airplane. It takes you a minute to realize what the movie's even about. That's when a plane hits the World Trade Center. The effect is visceral（震撼心灵的）. When the trailer played before "Inside Man" last week at a Hollywood theater，audience members began calling out，"Too soon！" In New York City，the response was even more dramatic. The Loews theater in Manhattan took the rare step of pulling the trailer from its screens after several complaints.

"United 93" is the first feature film to deal explicitly with the events of September 11， 2001，and is certain to ignite an emotional debate. Is it too soon？ Should the film have been made at all？ More to the point，will anyone want to see it？ Other 9/11 projects are on the way as the fifth anniversary of the attacks approaches，most notably Oliver Stone's "World Trade

Center." But as the forerunner, "United 93" will take most of the heat, whether it deserves it or not.

The real United 93 crashed in a Pennsylvania field after 40 passengers and crew fought back against the terrorists. Writer-director Paul Greengrass has gone to great lengths to be respectful in his depiction of what occurred, proceeding with the film only after securing the approval of every victim's family. "Was I surprised at the agreement? Yes. Very. Usually there're one or two families who're more reluctant," Greengrass writes in an e-mail. "I was surprised at the extraordinary way the United 93 families have welcomed us into their lives and shared their experiences with us." Carole O'Hare, a family member, says, "They were very open and honest with us, and they made us a part of this whole project." Universal, which is releasing the film, plans to donate 10% of its opening weekend gross to the Flight 93 National Memorial Fund. That hasn't stopped criticism that the studio is exploiting a national tragedy. O'Hare thinks that's unfair. "This story has to be told to honor the passengers and crew for what they did," she says. "But more than that, it raises awareness. Our ports aren't secure. Our borders aren't secure. Our airlines still aren't secure, and this is what happens when you're not secure. That's the message I want people to hear."

47. The trailer for "United 93" succeeded in _____ when it played in the theaters in Hollywood and New York City.
48. The movie "United 93" is sure to give rise to _____.
49. What did writer-director Paul Greengrass obtain before he proceeded with the movie?
   _____
50. Universal, which is releasing "United 93", has been criticized for _____.
51. Carole O'Hare thinks that besides honoring the passengers and crew for what they did, the purpose of telling the story is _____ about security.

Section B

Directions: *There are 2 passages in this section. Each passage is followed by some questions or unfinished statements. For each of them there are four choices marked A), B), C) and D). You should decide on the best choice and mark the corresponding letter on **Answer Sheet 2** with a single line thought the centre.*

Passage One

Questions 52 to 56 are based on the following passage.

Imagine waking up and finding the value of your assets has been halved. No, you're not an investor in one of those hedge funds that failed completely. With the dollar slumping to a 26-year low against the pound, already-expensive London has become quite unaffordable. A coffee at Starbucks, just as unavoidable in England as it is in the United States, runs about $8.

The once all-powerful dollar isn't doing a Titanic against just the pound. It is sitting at a record low against the euro and at a 30-year low against the Canadian dollar. Even the Argentine peso and Brazilian real are thriving against the dollar.

The weak dollar is a source of humiliation（屈辱）, for a nation's self-esteem rests in part on the strength of its currency. It's also a potential economic problem, since a declining dollar makes imported food more expensive and exerts upward pressure on interest rates. And yet there are substantial sectors of the vast U.S. economy — from giant companies like Coca-Cola to mom-and-pop restaurant operators in Miami — for which the weak dollar is most excellent

news.

Many Europeans may view the U. S. as an arrogant superpower that has become hostile to foreigners. But nothing makes people think more warmly of the U. S. than a weak dollar. Through April, the total number of visitors from abroad was up 6. 8 percent from last year. Should the trend continue, the number of tourists this year will finally top the 2000 peak. Many Europeans now apparently view the U. S. the way many Americans view Mexico — as a cheap place to vacation, shop and party, all while ignoring the fact that the poorer locals can't afford to join the merrymaking.

The money tourists spend helps decrease our chronic trade deficit. So do exports, which thanks in part to the weak dollar, soared 11 percent between May 2006 and May 2007. For the first five months of 2007, the trade deficit actually fell 7 percent from 2006.

If you own shares in large American corporations, you're a winner in the weak-dollar gamble. Last week Coca-Cola's stock bubbled to a five-year high after it reported a fantastic quarter. Foreign sales accounted for 65 percent of Coke's beverage(饮料) business. Other American companies profiting from this trend include McDonald's and IBM.

American tourists, however, shouldn't expect any relief soon. The dollar lost strength the way many marriages break up — slowly, and then all at once. And currencies don't turn on a dime. So if you want to avoid the pain inflicted by the increasingly pathetic dollar, cancel that summer vacation to England and look to New England. There, the dollar is still treated with a little respect.

52. Why do Americans feel humiliated?
    A) Their economy is plunging.   B) Their currency has slumped.
    C) They can't afford trips to Europe.   D) They have lost half of their assets.

53. How does the current dollar affect the life of ordinary Americans?
    A) They have to cancel their vacations in New England.
    B) They find it unaffordable to dine in mom-and-pop restaurants.
    C) They have to spend more money when buying imported goods.
    D) They might lose their jobs due to potential economic problems.

54. How do many Europeans feel about the U. S with the devalued dollar?
    A) They feel contemptuous of it.
    B) They are sympathetic with it.
    C) They regard it as a superpower on the decline.
    D) They think of it as a good tourist destination.

55. What is the author's advice to Americans?
    A) They treat the dollar with a little respect.
    B) They try to win in the weak-dollar gamble.
    C) They vacation at home rather than abroad.
    D) They treasure their marriages all the more.

56. What does the author imply by saying "currencies don't turn on a dime" (Line 2, Para 7)?
    A) The dollar's value will not increase in the short term.
    B) The value of a dollar will not be reduced to a dime.
    C) The dollar's value will drop, but within a small margin.
    D) Few Americans will change dollars into other currencies.

Passage Two

Questions 57 to 61 are based on the following passage.

In the college-admissions wars, we parents are the true fighters. We are pushing our kids to get good grades, take SAT preparatory courses and build résumés so they can get into the college of *our* first choice. I've twice been to the wars, and as I survey the battlefield, something different is happening. We see our kids' college background as a prize demonstrating how well we've raised them. But we can't acknowledge that our obsession(痴迷) is more about *us* than *them*. So we've contrived various justifications that turn out to be half-truths, prejudices or myths. It actually doesn't matter much whether Aaron and Nicole go to Stanford.

We have a full-blown prestige panic; we worry that there won't be enough prizes to go around. Fearful parents urge their children to apply to more schools than ever. Underlying the hysteria(歇斯底里) is the belief that scarce elite degrees must be highly valuable. Their graduates must enjoy more success because they get a better education and develop better contacts. All that is plausible — and mostly wrong. We haven't found any convincing evidence that selectivity or prestige matters. Selective schools don't systematically employ better instructional approaches than less selective schools. On two measures — professors' feedback and the number of essay exams — selective schools do slightly worse.

By some studies, selective schools do enhance their graduates' lifetime earnings. The gain is reckoned at 2—4% for every 100-point increase in a school's average SAT scores. But even this advantage is probably a statistical fluke(偶然). A well-known study examined students who got into highly selective schools and then went elsewhere. They earned just as much as graduates from higher-status schools.

Kids count more than their colleges. Getting into Yale may signify intelligence, talent and ambition. But it's not the only indicator and, paradoxically, its significance is declining. The reason: so many similar people go elsewhere. Getting into college isn't life's only competition. In the next competition — the job market and graduate school — the results may change. Old-boy networks are breaking down. Princeton economist Alan Krueger studied admissions to one top Ph.D. program. High scores on the GRE helped explain who got in; degrees of prestigious universities didn't.

So, parents, lighten up. The stakes have been vastly exaggerated. Up to a point, we can rationalize our pushiness. America is a competitive society; our kids need to adjust to that. But too much pushiness can be destructive. The very ambition we impose on our children may get some into Harvard but may also set them up for disappointment. One study found that, other things being equal, graduates of highly selective schools experienced more job dissatisfaction. They may have been so conditioned to being on top that anything less disappoints.

57. Why dose the author say that parents are the true fighters in the college-admissions wars?

A) They have the final say in which university their children are to attend.

B) They know best which universities are most suitable for their children.

C) They have to carry out intensive surveys of colleges before children make an application.

D) They care more about which college their children go to than the children themselves.

58. Why do parents urge their children to apply to more school than ever?

A) They want to increase their children's chances of entering a prestigious college.

B) They hope their children can enter a university that offers attractive scholarships.

C) Their children will have a wider choice of which college to go to.

D) Elite universities now enroll fewer student than they used to.

59. What does the author mean by saying "Kids count more than their college"(Line 1, Para. 4)?

A) Continuing education is more important to a person's success.

B) A person's happiness should be valued more than their education.

C) Kids' actual abilities are more important than their college backgrounds.

D) What kids learn at college cannot keep up with job market requirements.

60. What does Krueger's study tell us?

A) Getting into Ph. D. programs may be more competitive than getting into college.

B) Degrees of prestigious universities do not guarantee entry to graduate programs.

C) Graduates from prestigious universities do not care much about their GRE scores.

D) Connections built in prestigious universities may be sustained long after graduation.

61. One possible result of pushing children into elite universities is that _____.

A) they earn less than their peers from other institutions

B) they turn out to be less competitive in the job market

C) they experience more job dissatisfaction after graduation

D) they overemphasize their qualifications in job applications

Part Ⅴ   Cloze   (15 minutes)

Directions: *There are 20 blanks in the following passage. For each blank there are four choices marked A), B), C) and D) on the right side of the paper. You should choose the ONE that best fits into the passage. Then mark the corresponding letter on* **Answer Sheet 2** *with a single line through the centre.*

Seven years ago, when I was visiting Germany, I met with an official who explained to me that the country had a perfect solution to its economic problems. Watching the U.S. economy __62__ during the '90s, the Germans had decided that they, too, needed to go the high-technology __63__. But how? In the late '90s, the answer seemed obvious: Indians. __64__ all, Indian entrepreneurs accounted for one of every three Silicon Valley start-ups. So the German government decided that it would __65__ Indians to Germany just as America does: by __66__ green cards. Officials created something called the German Green Card and __67__ that they would issue 20,000 in the first year. __68__, the Germans expected that tens of thousands more Indians would soon be begging to come, and perhaps the __69__ would have to be increased. But the program was a failure. A year later __70__ half of the 20,000 cards had been issued.

After a few extensions, the program was __71__.

I told the German official at the time that I was

62. A) soar   B) hover
    C) amplify   D) intensify

63. A) circuit   B) strategy
    C) trait   D) route

64. A) Of   B) After
    C) In   D) At

65. A) import   B) kidnap
    C) convey   D) lure

66. A) offering   B) installing
    C) evacuating   D) formulating

67. A) conferred   B) inferred
    C) announced   D) verified

68. A) Specially   B) Naturally
    C) Particularly D) Consistently

69. A) quotas   B) digits
    C) measures   D) scales

70. A) invariably   B) literally
    C) barely   D) solely

71. A) repelled   B) deleted
    C) combated   D) abolished

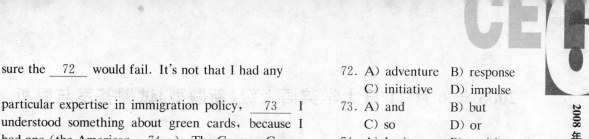

sure the ___72___ would fail. It's not that I had any

particular expertise in immigration policy, ___73___ I understood something about green cards, because I had one (the American ___74___). The German Green

Card was misnamed, I argued, ___75___ it never, under any circumstances, translated into German citizenship. The U. S. green card, by contrast, is an almost ___76___ path to becoming American (after five

years and a clean record). The official ___77___ my objection, saying that there was no way Germany was going to offer these people citizenship. "We need young tech workers," he said. "That's what this program is all ___78___ ."so Germany was asking bright

young ___79___ to leave their country, culture and families, move thousands of miles away, learn a new language and work in a strange land — but without any ___80___ of ever being part of their new home. Germany was sending a signal, one that was ___81___ received in India and other countries, and also by Germany's own immigrant community.

72. A) adventure   B) response
    C) initiative   D) impulse
73. A) and   B) but
    C) so   D) or
74. A) heritage   B) revision
    C) notion   D) version
75. A) because   B) unless
    C) if   D) while
76. A) aggressive   B) automatic
    C) vulnerable   D) voluntary
77. A) overtook   B) fascinated
    C) submitted   D) dismissed
78. A) towards   B) round
    C) about   D) over
79. A) dwellers   B) citizens
    C) professionals D) amateurs
80. A) prospect   B) suspicion
    C) outcome   D) destination
81. A) partially   B) clearly
    C) brightly   D) vividly

Part Ⅵ   Translation （5 minutes）
Directions: *Complete the sentences by translating into English the Chinese given in brackets.*
  Please write your translation on Answer Sheet 2.

82. We can say a lot of things about those _____（毕生致力于诗歌的人）: they are passionate, impulsive, and unique.
83. Mary couldn't have received my letter, _____（否则她上周就该回信了）.
84. Nancy is supposed to _____（做完化学实验）at least two weeks ago.
85. Never once _____（老两口互相争吵）since they were married 40 years ago.
86. _____（一个国家未来的繁荣在很大程度上有赖于）the quality of education of its people.

2008 年 6 月 21 日大学英语六级(新题型)试题答案与解析

Part I
Sample Writing

Will e-books replace traditional books?

Nowadays, information technology is developing by leaps and bounds. A good case in point is e-books which come flooding into our life. While many book lovers start to enjoy the wonder and ease of reading e-books, the prevalence of e-books has provoked a heated discussion in society.

As a relatively new invention in the recent decade, e-books are quite an attraction for some book-lovers. Some of them are convinced that e-books will replace traditional books someday. First and foremost, e-books enable people to access the information instantly and conveniently, getting information on almost everything without going out of home. What's more, e-books do take little place compared with traditional books. Finally, it has been argued that e-books will be a solution to today's environment problem, preventing more trees from being cut to make paper-books.

Admittedly, there is an element of truth in all these claims, but I would like to argue that e-books will unnecessarily replace traditional books in the future. Actually, reading e-books, to some extent, is harmful to people's health, with all its radiation from computers, mobile phones and other e-book devices. Therefore, the potential danger of e-books should not be neglected. Personally, I prefer traditional paper books for its elegance of design as well as its value for collection.

(华东理工大学国际经济与贸易中澳 052 张毅敏)

Part II

1. [D] 参见引言部分第一段最后一句:John Ingham reports on what the world's finest minds believe our futures will be. 其中"the world's finest minds"即指前文提到的"top scientists"。

2. [C] 参见引言部分最后一段最后一句:This is an invitation to look foolish, as with the predictions of domed cities and nuclear-powered vacuum cleaner that were made 50 years ago.(轻信这些预言会令你显得愚蠢,就像 50 年前关于圆顶城市与核动力吸尘器的预言一样愚蠢而不切实际。)

3. [A] 参见"Living Longer"部分第二段第一句:Bruce Lahn... anticipates the ability to produce "unlimited supplies" of transplantable human organs without the need for human donors.(无需捐献者就可"无限量生产供应"可移植的人体器官。)

4. [C] 参见"Living Longer"部分第四段第最后一句:... by 2056, create the first class of 100-year-olds who are as vigorous and productive as today's people in their 60s.(······到 2056 年,将创造出首批百岁老人,其活力与生产力相当于今天 60 岁的人。)

5. [C] 参见"Aliens"部分第四段:Princeton professor Freeman Dyson thinks it "likely" that life from outer space will be discovered(认为来自外太空的生命形式可能会被发现)before 2056...

6. [A] 参见"Colonies in space"部分第一段:Richard Gott... man will set up a self-sufficient colony on Mars(创建火星上自给自足的殖民区), which would be a "life insurance policy against catastrophes(防御地球灾难的终身保险), natural or otherwise, might occur on

Earth."

7. ［D］ 参见"Spinal injuries"部分第三段第二句：She predicts that within 5 to 10 years fingers and toes will be regrown（再生）and limbs（四肢）will start to be regrown a few years later.

8. artificial intelligence 参见"Robots"部分：... says that the problems of developing artificial intelligence（人工智能）for robots will be at least partly overcome. As a result，"the possibilities of robots working with people will open up immensely".

9. weapons 参见"Energy"部分第二段：... such a source（指前文提到的 inexhaustible green energy source）would be safe in that it could be made into weapons...

10. religion 参见"Society"部分第二段：Thus, science will kill religion — not by challenging faith but by offering a more practical, universal and rewarding moral framework for human interaction.（科学将消灭宗教，靠的不是挑战人们的信仰，而是为人类交往提供更实际、更普遍、更有回报意义的道德框架。）

Part III

11. D 12. D 13. C 14. A 15. B 16. A 17. D 18. C 19. B

20. B 21. D 22. B 23. C 24. A 25. B 26. D 27. A 28. B

29. D 30. D 31. B 32. C 33. D 34. B 35. C

36. survive 37. complicated 38. offenders 39. whereby

40. incurring 41. influence 42. serving 43. restore

44. The alternative to capital punishment is longer sentences. But they would certainly cost the tax payers much money

45. that does not mean that person isn't guilty of the crime, or that he shouldn't pay society the debt he owes

46. a large part of it in prison for acts that he committed while not in full control of his mind

Part IV

47. causing a reaction 参见第一段第一句：If movie trailer are supposed to cause a reaction, the preview for United 93 more than succeed.（如果电影预告片的目的是引起观众反响，"93 号联合航班"的预演可谓大获成功。）

48. an emotional debate 参见第二段第一句："United 93" is the first feature film（故事片）to deal explicitly with the events of September 11, 2001, and is certain to ignite an emotional debate. ignite ＝ give rise to 点燃，使……产生。

49. the approval of every victim's family 参见第三段第二句：Writer-director Paul Greengrass has gone to great lengths（费尽周折）to be respectful... proceeding with the film after securing（获得）the approval of every victim's family.

50. exploiting a national tragedy 参见第三段中间两句：Universal（环球电影公司），which is releasing the film，plans to donate 10%... That hasn't stopped criticism that the studio is exploiting a national strategy.（但这也无法阻挡关于公司利用国难发财的指责。）

51. raise awareness 参见第三段最后五句：But... it（指该影片）raises awareness（唤醒意识），our ports aren't safe. Our borders aren't safe...that's the message I want people to hear.

52. ［B］ 第一段提到，美元对英镑比率下跌到 26 年来最低点（slumping to a 26-year low against the pound），第二段继续提到曾经不可一世的强大的美元对欧元、加元、比索等多种货币的比率都大幅下跌。第三段第一句指出：The weak dollar is a source of humiliation...故选 B。

53. ［C］ 第三段第二句提到：It's also a potential economic problem, since a declining dollar makes imported food more expensive（下滑的美元使进口食品更加昂贵）...故选 C（当前美元状况对普通美国人的影响在于，他们不得不花更多的钱购买进口产品）。

54. [D] 第四段提到:...nothing makes people think more warmly of the US than a weak dollar(没有比美元贬值更让欧洲人对美国产生热情的东西了)...Many Europeans now apparently view the US the way many Americans view Mexico — as a cheap place to vacation(看成廉价的度假地)... 故选 D(由于美元的贬值,欧洲人将美国看成理想度假地)。

55. [C] 最后一段最后两句提到,如果你想避免美元贬值带来的痛苦,就取消英格兰的消夏之旅,改去新英格兰吧(新英格兰在美国),在那里,美元至少还得到一点尊重。故选 C。

56. [A] 最后一段前两句提到,美国游客无法指望(美元贬值状况)能很快缓解,如同许多婚姻的解体一样,美元正缓慢丧失实力,然后突然全面崩溃。根据"currencies don't turn on a dime"(货币一般不会在廉价的一角一分的基础上翻身反弹)前面两句内容推知,此句暗示:美元价值短期内不会反弹,故选 A。

57. [D] 推断题。第一段前两句提到,在大学入学战役中,我们做父母的才是真正的战士。我们逼迫自己的孩子争取更高的考分,修读 SAT 预备课程,丰富简历以便孩子们能进入我们替他们选出的理想高校。故选 D。

58. [A] 推断题。第二段前两句提到,父母关于名牌学校的恐慌已全面升级(a full-blown prestige panic),生怕没有足够的名校奖学金。忧心如焚的父母们敦促孩子申请更多的学校。故选 A(父母让孩子大量申请高校,想要增加孩子进入名校的几率)。

59. [C] 第四段提到,孩子自身情况比他们进哪所大学更重要。进入耶鲁名校可能表明了一个人的智商、天赋与抱负,但这不是唯一的衡量尺码,恰恰相反,大学教育的重要性正在下降。因为许多类似的人(考进名校的人)后来又转去了别的(普通)学校。进入大学也并非人生唯一的竞争。故选 C。

60. [B] 第四段提到 Krueger 关于某个一流博士录取项目的调查表明,决定谁能被录取的关键是 GRE 高分,而不是名牌大学学位。故选 B。

61. [C] 最后一段提到,父母强加给孩子的进入哈佛名校的远大抱负最终可能导致孩子将来的失望体验。调查表明,名校的毕业生更容易感受工作上的不满,因为他们长期以来习惯于高高在上,任何低一点的屈尊之位都会令他们失望。故选 C。

Part V

62. [A] Watching the US economy soar 看着美国经济腾飞。soar vi. 直线上升;amplify vi. (音量等)扩大;hover vi. 盘旋;intensify v. (程度)加强。

63. [D] go the high-technology route 走高科技路线。circuit n. 环形路线;trait n. 特征;strategy n. 策略;route n. 路线,道路。

64. [B] After all 毕竟。固定搭配。

65. [D] lure Indians to Germany 诱惑印度人来德国。lure vt. 引诱;import vt. 进口;kidnap vt. 绑架;convey vt. 传送。

66. [A] by offering green cards 靠提供绿卡。evacuate vt. 疏散;install vt. 安装;offer vt. 提供;formulate vt. 表达,确切阐述。

67. [C] announced that they would issue 20,000...宣布将发放两万张绿卡。confer vi. 磋商;infer vt. 推断;announce vt. 宣布;verify vt. 核实,验证。

68. [B] Naturally, the Germans expected...很自然,德国人以为大批印度人会趋之若鹜(这里反映了德国人的盲目自信)。specially adv. 特别地;particularly adv. 特别地;consistently adv. 前后一致地。

69. [A] the quotas would have to be increased 绿卡限额将不得不扩大。quota n. 配额;digit n. 数码;measure n. 措施;scale n. 范围。

70. [C] But the program was a failure. A year later barely half of the 20,000 cards had been issued. 但这项计划失败了。一年以后两万张绿卡发放量还不到一半。invariably adv. 总

是；literally *adv*.几乎；solely *adv*.唯一地，单独。

71.［D］ the program was <u>abolished</u> 计划被取消了。repel *vt*.排斥；combat *vi*.战斗；delete *vt*.(文字)删除；abolish *vt*.(计划、制度)取消，废除。

72.［C］ I was sure the <u>initiative</u> would fail 我坚信这项创举会失败。initiative *n*.主动行动；adventure *n*.冒险；response *n*.回复；impulse *n*.冲动。

73.［B］ It's <u>not</u> that…<u>but</u>…不是因为……而是……

74.［D］ the American <u>version</u> 美国版本的绿卡。version *n*.版本；heritage *n*.遗产；notion *n*.观念，概念；revision *n*.修改。

75.［A］ The German Green Card was misnamed, I argued, <u>because</u> it never, under any circumstance, translated into German citizenship. 我认为"德国绿卡"其实命名有误，因为该绿卡在任何情况下都不会转化为德国公民身份。

76.［B］ The US green card, by contrast, is an <u>automatic</u> path to becoming American. 而对比鲜明的是，有了美国绿卡，就自动踏上了成为美国公民之路。aggressive *adv*.侵犯的，进取的；vulnerable *adj*.易受伤害的；voluntary *adj*.自主自愿的。

77.［D］ The official <u>dismissed</u> my objection. 官方拒绝采纳我的反对意见。dismiss *vt*.拒绝考虑；submit *vt*.呈交；overtake *vt*.赶上；fascinate *vt*.使着迷。

78.［C］ That's what this program is <u>all about</u>. 这就是计划的主要内容。

79.［C］ bright, young <u>professionals</u> 聪明的年轻专业人士。professional *n*.专业人士；dweller *n*.居住者；citizen *n*.公民；amateur *n*.业余人士。

80.［A］ but without any <u>prospect</u> of ever becoming part of their new home 但毫无指望成为新家庭的一员。prospect *n*.期望；outcome *n*.结果；suspicion *n*.怀疑；destination *n*.目的地。

81.［B］ was clearly <u>received</u> 明白无误地得到理解。vividly *adv*.生动形象地；brightly *adv*.明亮地；partially *adv*.部分地。

Part VI

82. who devote their whole lives to poems

83. or she should have replied last week

84. have finished her chemistry experiment

85. has the old couple quarreled with each other

86. The future prosperity of a nation depends largely on